published work of, 9, 78, 89
Scarfe on, 243n11, 245n24
and self-realization, 48–50
suggestion for more study on,
  237
and Treece, 95, 244n17
view of selfhood, 109–10
Henein, George
  anarchism of, 101–02
  anti-Marxism of, 100, 101, 102
  and "Long Live Degenerate Art!,"
  97
  published in California, 98, 120,
  136
Heraldic Universe, 105, 110, 165, 181,
  248n16
Horizon (journal), 134
Howarth, Herbert
  in Bolero, 70, 72
  as "Deannarchist," 247n12
  in Egypt, 73, 74, 96, 99, 248n14
  and Personal Landscape, 74, 117
Howe, Graham, 76, 257n8
Hsaio Ch'ien, 145–46, 255n62
Hsaio Kung-Ch'uan, 144, 146
Hu Lin, 145
Hynes, Samuel, 3, 8–9, 10, 16–19,
  26–27, 29–30

Ibsen, Henrik, 145–46
Inside the Whale (Orwell), 26–27,
  30–31, 34, 35–36, 41, 58
Isherwood, Christopher, 51–52, 53,
  144

Jameson, Frederic, 154–60, 188–89
Johnson, Jack, 99, 253n47
Johnston, Denis, 241n10
Joyce, James, 34

Kahane, Jack, 61, 243n10
Kaiser, Ernst, 253n48
Keery, James, 85–86
Kerouac, Jack, 69, 134
Kingdom Come (journal), 9, 73–74, 77,
  89, 111, 116, 248n14
Kropotkin, Peter, 147

Lamantia, Philip, 134
Late Modernism, 1–2, 40–41, 41–43,
  125–26, 235–36
Late Modernism (Miller), 41–43
The Lathe of Heaven (Le Guin), 157–59
Laughlin, James, 100
Lawrence, D.H., 23, 109, 186–88
Le Guin, Ursula, 157–59
Leite, George, 97, 118, 119, 121–22, 127,
  252n47, 254n56
Levertoff, Denise, 134, 143, 248n19
Libertarian Circle, 133–34
Liddell, Robert, 25, 71, 96, 249n26
Lin Yutang, 144
London International Surrealist
  Exhibition
  activities at, 63–64
  critics' views of, 20, 37–38, 46,
  97
  and Gascoyne, 11, 12, 20, 30
  and Miller, xii, xv, 10–11, 77, 84,
  105, 164
  and Read, 105, 110, 133, 164
"Long Live Degenerate Art!," 97, 100,
  106
Lyra (anthology), 94–95

Mackenzie, Compton, 34
MacNeice, Louis, 65
MacSpaundays, xv, 36, 43. See also
  Auden group
Marcuse, Herbert, 181, 182

Marxism
    in *The Black Book*, 221–22
    criticism of in *New Roads*, 88
    Durrell's attitude towards, 164,
        165–66
    Egyptian Surrealists' critique of,
        100–02
    Gascoyne's views of, 20–21
    and individuality, 13–14
    Miller's rejection of, 11
    and misrepresentation of
        anarchism, 154–57
    Orwell and, 27
    and social being, 241n1
Mass-Observation, 9, 170
Mellor, Anthony, 19–24, 42, 45–46,
    244n17
Men God Forgot (Cossery), 98, 99–100,
    103, 120, 136
Miller, David, 150–51
Miller, Henry
    anarchistic view of, xiii, xv,
        10–11, 24–25, 31–32, 33, 34,
        35, 62–63, 91, 113, 208–10,
        245n20
    anti-authoritarian view of, 76,
        84–85, 167
    and Berdyaev, 142
    and *The Black Book*, 127, 128, 210,
        211, 213, 214, 217, 252n47
    and *Black Spring*, 9, 12, 33
    in California, 118, 128, 131, 139
    and *Circle*, 119–20, 127, 136
    and *The Colossus of Maroussi*, 206–10
    criticism of, 24–25, 27, 30, 34,
        41–42
    and Crowley, 257n8
    and desublimation of desire, 184
    friendship with Durrell, 66, 67,
        71, 79, 80–81, 113, 128, 138

    and Goldman, 62, 91, 249n24
    and *Hamlet*, 105, 110, 135, 200
    and Heraldic Universe, 105, 165
    impact of Lawrence on, 186,
        187–88
    and Leite, 127, 252n47, 254n56
    importance of death in work of,
        195–98
    influence of, 84–85, 140–43
    and London International
        Surrealist Exhibition, xii, xv,
        10–11, 77, 84, 105, 164
    Moore's book on, 75–76, 93,
        187
    moves during WWII, 71, 96
    and *Murder the Murderer*, 113–14,
        119, 135
    Orwell's view of, 31–36, 68, 141
    politics of, 11, 14, 31–36, 68
    praise for Cossery, 100, 120
    promoting Patchen, 129, 131
    published by journals, 31, 70, 73,
        75, 79, 85, 89, 90–91, 92, 93,
        127, 129, 135
    published by small presses,
        255n60
    and quietism, 32, 34, 68, 141, 179,
        209–10
    and Read, 13–14, 15, 77, 164
    rereading of *The Colossus of Maroussi*,
        206–10
    as sexual liberator, 91
    and *Sexus*, 10–11
    and Smart, 118, 126, 131, 224, 226,
        252n46
    stylistic connection to Kerouac,
        134
    as Surrealist, xii, 9, 12, 15, 63, 85
    and Thomas, 63, 79, 80–81, 140,
        253n47

Thompson's view of, 244n19
Treece on, 244n15
and *Tropic of Capricorn*, 81, 195–97
use of incoherence, 202, 203
use of womb analogy, 198–201, 222
Woodcock on, 91, 206
writing on selfhood, 110–11
See also "An Open Letter to Surrealists Everywhere"; *Tropic of Cancer*
Miller, Tyrus, 41–43
Moorcock, Michael, 161–63, 240n9
Moore, Nicholas
anarchism of, 244n17
book on Miller, 75–76, 93, 187
as journal editor, 89, 93
published in journals, 69–70, 73, 79, 128–29, 139
Moricand, Conrad, 257n8
Morris, Tom
anarchist personalist perspective, 2
author's use of work, 171–72
and distinction of power and authority, 173, 177, 178–79
and dual function of embodiment, 189–90, 191
on *Ego and its own*, 180, 182

Nazi Germany, 97
New Apocalypse movement
and anarchism, 87–88, 163, 168
and anti-futurism, 48
and Auden group, 27, 57–58, 87, 169–70
and *Calamiterror*, 46
and *By Grand Central Station*, 226–29
critics' view of, 22, 39–40, 47, 57, 85–88

defined as post-surrealist, xv–xvi, 239n4
forming of, 79–80
and Fraser, 6, 7, 15, 57, 58, 79, 81–84, 87, 95
Hendry on, 23–24, 79–80
and Howe, 76
importance of Berdyaev on, 142–43
journal support for, 70, 77, 89
members of, 239n2
Miller's influence on, 84–85, 245n20
and New Romantics, 92–95, 169
and pacifism, 111
popularity of, 57–58
and problem of aesthetic order, 83–84
and Surrealism, 21–22, 81–84
tenets of, 168–70
and Thomas, 10, 80
and Treece, 79, 168, 169–70, 250n29
Villa Seurat connection, 8
and vision of myth, 132
and vision of selfhood, 109–16
See also English Surrealists in Egypt; San Francisco Renaissance; Villa Seurat
The New British Poets (Rexroth), 119, 130, 140–43
Newman, Saul, 185, 186
New Road (journal), 76, 87–88, 88–89, 131
New Romanticism, 92–95
New Verse (journal), 92
Nietzsche, Friedrich, 107
Nin, Anaïs
and Barker, 253n50

and Duncan, 98, 129, 130, 252n47
and personal emphasis of writing, 252n43
published in California, 129, 135
published in journals, 69, 75, 85, 250n32
and Rank, 194
and war departure, 71
and *Winter of Artifice*, 9
Norman, Mrs., 128
NOW (magazine), 74, 89–91, 92, 139

Oasis (journal), 89
Obelisk Press, 9, 61, 75, 243n10
O'Connor, Phillip, 211, 256n2, 256n3
Orend, Karl, 91
Orientations (journal), 99
Orwell, George
    and *Down and Out in Paris and London*, 33–34
    and Durrell, 33, 68–69
    and *Inside the Whale*, 26–27, 30–31, 34, 35–36, 41, 58
    in *Late Modernism*, 41–42
    review of *The Booster*, 67–68
    view of Miller's politics, 31–36, 68, 141
Oxford Poetry (journal), 72

pacifism, 74–75, 90, 111, 207–10
Papadimitriou, Elie, 117
Patchen, Kenneth, 89, 128, 129, 131
Patmore, Derek, 250n29
Peake, Mervyn, 94, 162
Perlès, Alfred, 67, 69, 71, 75, 246n8
Personalism
    anarchism of, xii–xv, xvii, 132–33, 170–79
    attached to "quietist" label, 32

core tenets of, 132–33, 163–70
Durrell's ideas on, 165
excluded from *Late Modernism*, 41, 42
identifies as post-Surrealist, xii, xv–xvi
ignored by literary critics, ix–x, xvi–xvii, 38, 43, 52
members of, xi
and Miller, 35, 76
and open form/incoherence, 202–04
as part of *Personal Landscape* vision, 116, 117–18
published in *Transformation*, 78
Rexroth's view of, 142–43
role of embodiment in, 189–201
and self-realization, 48–50
and social realism, 47
and syntax problem, 108
viewed without political social context, 39–40
view of death in, 195–98
view of selfhood, 180–89
and womb analogy, 198–201
See also Egyptian anarcho-Surrealists; English post-Surrealists in Egypt; New Apocalypse movement; San Francisco Renaissance; Shanghai-based individualists; Villa Seurat
Personal Landscape (journal), 74, 103–04, 105, 116–18, 137, 239n3, 251n41
The Phoenix (journal), 35, 69, 73, 90, 127
Pierre, D.B.C., 213
Poems of this War by Younger Poets, 75
poetry, autocthonous, 132
Poetry Folios (journal), 89, 131, 135

and Circle, 118–20, 121, 122, 133–36,
138–39
and Circle Editions, 120–21
connections with England,
130–32, 143
critical attention to, 58–59
defined, 239n3
interactions among, 126–30
members of, 58
tie to Egypt, 97–98, 143
urban v. rural themes of, 46
Saroyan, William, 67, 69, 85
Savage, D.S., 73, 85, 90, 131, 250n33
Scarfe, Francis, 168–69, 242n8,
243n9, 243n11, 245n24
Schimanski, Stefan, 77
Schweitzer, Albert, 143
Seem, Mark, 184
Seferis, George, 67, 71, 75, 113
selfhood
author's self-identification,
171–73
Duncan on, 122–24, 231, 234,
256n4, 259n22
Durrell on, 110, 111, 181, 183
New Apocalypse and, 109–16
and Personalism, 180–89
See also Ego
self-identity, 51–57
self-realization, 48–50
Seven (journal)
and anarchism, 234
and "An Ark for Lawrence
Durrell," 234
and Asylum in the Snow, 28, 83, 107,
121, 127, 211, 232
and The Black Book, 215, 217
and post-Surrealism, 9–10, 15, 19
as publisher of New Apocalypse,
6, 69–70

publishing life of, 73–74, 75,
78–79, 80, 126
Shanghai-based individualists,
144–47
Shuang Shen, 144
Shukrallah, Ibrahim, 99, 117
Skelton, Robin, 39–40, 43
Smart, Elizabeth
and American avant-garde, 126
and Barker, 118, 126, 242n5
in Big Sur, 124, 131
and By Grand Central Station I Sat
Down and Wept, 94, 118, 126,
224–29, 252n46, 258n17
and Delta, 70, 118, 126, 254n53
and Durrell, 224, 225–26, 228,
242n5, 254n50, 258n16
and Miller, 118, 126, 131, 224, 226,
252n46
and Necessary Secrets, 258n16
social realism, 47
Součková, Milada, 67, 69
Spanish Civil War, 4, 20, 44–45,
67–68
Spark, Muriel, 170
Spencer, Bernard
and anarchism, 65–66
in critical reviews, 38
and Durrell, 65, 66, 74, 96
obituary, 120
other projects of, 249n27
and Personal Landscape, 103, 105, 116,
117
relocated after war, 118
shift away from Auden group,
65–66
Spender, Stephen, 3–6, 65
Spiers, Ruth, 103
Stanford, Derek
and The Black Book, 219

Other Titles from The University of Alberta Press

Landscapes of War and Memory
The Two World Wars in Canadian Literature and the Arts,
1977–2007
SHERRILL GRACE
600 pages | 30 B&W photographs, notes, bibliography, index
978–1–77212–000–4 | $49.95 (T) paper
War & Cultural Memory/Literature, Visual Arts & Film

From the Elephant's Back
Collected Essays & Travel Writings
LAWRENCE DURRELL
Edited and with an Introduction by JAMES GIFFORD
PETER BALDWIN, Foreword
300 pages | Preface, notes, bibliography, index
978–1–77212–051–6 | $39.95 (T) paper
978–1–77212–059–2 | $31.99 (T) EPUB
978–1–77212–060–8 | $31.99 (T) Amazon Kindle
978–1–77212–061–5 | $31.99 (T) PDF
Literary Essays/Cultural Studies/Travel Writing

"Collecting Stamps Would Have Been More Fun"
Canadian Publishing and the Correspondence of Sinclair Ross,
1933–1986
JORDAN STOUCK & DAVID STOUCK, Editors
344 pages | B&W photographs, appendix, biographical
chronology, index
978–0–88864–521–0 | $34.95 (T) paper
978–0–88864–755–9 | $27.99 (T) PDF
Letters/Canadian Literature

Chorus" is striking in its contradiction to Hynes's sense of Gascoyne's "unencumbered…future" in response to Auden:

> Let us fill
> One final fiery glass and quickly drink to the "Pre-War"
> Before we greet "the Forties," whose unseen sphinx-face
> Is staring fixedly upon us from behind its veil;
> Drink farewell quickly, ere the Future smash the glass.
> ("Farewell" 285)

The wartime future, already a lived future for Gascoyne since the fall of Paris, dually recalls the broken toasting wine glass of Bacchanalian pleasures from the 1930s as well as the Kristallnacht. It eerily foreshadows the closing lines of Keith Douglas's final completed poem as well, prior to his death in the war: "The next month, then, is a window / and with a crash I'll split the glass…// I fear what I shall find" ("On a Return" 130). Strikingly, Hynes's sense of "Gascoyne's assumption that since war had come in spite of the efforts of men of good will, those efforts must have been delusive and self-deceptive" is difficult to reconcile with the contents of the poem itself (Hynes 388–89). The "delusive peace" Gascoyne writes of is very clearly that of appeasement and the Franco-German declaration, and the "Steel-plated self-deception" is overtly held by a self-inclusive "we" in "Years through the rising storm of which somehow we grew / Struggling to keep an anchored heart and open mind, / Too often failing" ("Farewell" 285). These same years, which Hynes refutes while rightly noting their contrast to Auden, are also for Gascoyne "Years which bade / Less placid conscientious souls indignantly arise / Upon ten thousand platforms to proclaim the system mad" (285). However, Gascoyne's vision draws its difference by pointing to history, leaders, and Spengler with civil war (obviously Spain), orators, and flags leading men to their doom. For Gascoyne it is as if Hynes's "men of good will" are destructive by virtue of being persuasive leaders who entreat the world to follow. Coercion and following are at the heart of the crisis.

This then leads to the other possibility that is overshadowed by Hynes's Auden-centred interpretation, and it relates to Gascoyne's close affiliation with the Villa Seurat and Henry Miller's anarchist revision to Surrealism. By altering our angle, Gascoyne's shift after the 1936 London International Surrealist Exhibition becomes clear, such that, by late 1937, he could claim, "I tended to identify myself more and more with what Durrell had expressed" in the closing pages of his quietist-cum-individualist yet still surrealist novel *The Black Book* ("Fellow" 4). This was a major shift for Gascoyne, and it is apparent in these poems. His politics are no longer those of his 1935 manifesto, with clear names and enumeration. Instead, he embraces the vision of an individual existing in the social world who can be "transfigured by acceptance" such that "fear's armor falls away" ("Farewell" 287). This "fear's armor" is, however, both the closing and opening reference of the third section of the poem with fear having previously hidden the "dangerous truth" that was hidden already by the "self-deception" Hynes has noted. The striking issue for criticism is that the distinction could be buried under an alternate scheme for so long—fear coerces men to follow, but the quietist acceptance provides a release as "fear's armor falls away," which is precisely Miller's anarchist view.

And retracing that scheme now leads back to Orwell's myopia, which shaped Hynes's angle of vision. If we set aside Gascoyne and Auden, neither of whom figures in an important way in Orwell's *Inside the Whale*, we are left with Henry Miller, whom Hynes accepts as expounding an "extreme non-political, non-moral passivity" (386). This statement is the full extent of Hynes's attention to Orwell's primary topic in the book, even though Hynes's analysis covers four pages. This limited commentary returns attention to Hynes's comparison of Orwell to Thersites, the common man who as a soldier in the *Iliad* dared to critique Agamemnon and acknowledge the futility of war, despite the glorious propaganda that surrounds it, or what Gascoyne described as "macabre puppet orators" ("Farewell" 286). While Thersites is first known for his ugliness and low birth, subsequent commentators, in particular Marxists, attend to his capacity to speak truth to power. The genealogy for Hynes's sense of Miller's "extreme non-political, non-moral passivity" is thereby made curious; much as Thersites is not simply ugly and low class but is also a meaningful gadfly to political power, Miller too is more than simply "quietist" or "defeatist" (frequent euphemisms for "anarchist" and "pacifist").

Orwell initiated this vision of Miller when he described Miller's narrative voice as "from the third-class carriage, from the ordinary, non-political, non-moral, passive man" ("Inside" 108). In kindred terms, Orwell also notes "The *Booster*, a short-lived periodical of which he was part-editor, used to describe itself in its advertisements as 'non-political, non-educational, non-progressive, non-co-operative, non-ethical, non-literary, non-consistent, non-contemporary,' and Miller's own work could be described in nearly the same terms" (108). These are strong phrases, and they are difficult to reconcile with Miller's own statements about his anarchism. Miller organized for the Industrial Workers of the World, corresponded with Emma Goldman, read Benjamin Tucker and Peter Kropotkin, and regularly integrated the term "anarchic" into his discussions of anarchist writers and his own attitudes (at a time when he was keenly concerned with his own security). It is too easy to regard Miller's politics of the unpolitical as "non-political" or "non-progressive," but this is clearly a misinterpretation. Orwell hints at such a possibility when he describes "the novel [as] the most anarchical of all forms of literature" ("Inside" 125). He continues, "Good novels are written by people who are *not frightened*. This brings me back to Henry Miller" (125). This "anarchical" possibility, however, is buried for Orwell when "Miller replied in terms of extreme pacifism, an individual refusal to fight, with no apparent wish to convert others to the same opinion—practically, in fact, a declaration of irresponsibility" (126).

For Miller, "to convert others" is antithetical to his stated aims in "An Open Letter to Surrealists Everywhere," which Orwell read and reviewed on February 22, 1946, six years after *Inside the Whale* and nearly a decade after its publication, seven years after its anthologized form in *The Cosmological Eye*. Miller makes his sense of conversion and movements clear, as well as his anarchist politics, in two statements in his essay: "To get men to rally round a cause, a belief, an idea, is always easier than to persuade them to lead their own lives" (156) and

> I am fatuous enough to believe that in living my own life in
> my own way I am more apt to give life to others (though even
> that is not my chief concern) than I would if I simply followed
> somebody else's idea of how to live my life and thus become a

man among men. It seems to me that this struggle for liberty and justice is a confession or admission on the part of all those engaging in such a struggle that they have failed to live their own lives. (157)

To this he adds, if anyone could have missed the anarchist context of his comments, "I am against revolutions because they always involve a return to the status quo. I am against the status quo both before and after revolutions. I don't want to wear a black shirt or a red shirt. I want to wear the shirt that suits my taste" (160).[20] It is startling that Orwell could offer a remarkably similar assessment without recognizing Miller's intentions: "What he seems to be saying is that if one stiffens oneself by the contemplation of ugliness [corporeality in a godless world], one ends by finding life not less but more worth living" ("Review" 157).

In this context, Miller's "non-political" passivity takes on a far more specifically political and active position that is difficult to reconcile with Orwell's described "nihilistic quietism" ("Review" 135). The same "defeatism" ("Inside" 126), however, has staying power and reappears in Kathleen Raine's wording to describe the same group (15), though she admits to its anarchism and differences from the Auden group, both of which she explicitly binds to the post-surrealist interests. Even for Hendry, who advocated Personalism and was a "leader" of the New Apocalypse, "defeatism" took up the same meaning of quietist anarchism (Hendry, "Art" 141), though his disagreement was with the pacifism of the quietist component rather than the revolutionary elements of anarchism. By the time this misunderstanding's impact is felt in scholarship in the 1970s, the vision of quietism begun in *Inside the Whale* as Orwell's central metaphor for hiding from the world had become the normative interpretive "angle" for the entire personalist group of authors. Rather than Personalists with an anti-authoritarian politics, they were seen as quietists hiding from reality who could not understand their times.

Orwell's silence on Miller's anarchism is, however, very surprising. Not only did Orwell go to Spain to fight for POUM (Partido Obrero de Unificación Marxista) wearing Miller's overcoat (in the closing days of 1936) and thereby encounter Miller's explicit pacifism, but he corresponded with Miller beginning in 1935 (Miller, "Four" 3–8), reviewed *Tropic of Cancer* in 1936, and later reviewed the Villa Seurat's journal *The Booster* for *The New English Weekly* in November 1937 (Orwell, "Back" 30–31), thereby engaging in a print interaction with Durrell defending its position. In his review of *Black Spring*, Orwell returns to *Tropic of Cancer* with high praise and acknowledges its class-crossing ambitions "to get the thinking man down from this chilly perch of superiority and back into contact with the man-in-the-street" (230). The review draws on the phrases Miller specifically praised in Orwell's letters and goes so far as to adopt (as Orwell's own critique) Miller's explanations of his works in response to the correspondence (231). Miller's letters had a demonstrable impact on Orwell's thinking, and their contents make the unpolitical politics stand out in opposition to Orwell's. For Miller,

> the modesty and the naiveté combined give this chapter [22 in *Down and Out in Paris and London*] an eloquence and a poignancy far more effective than the dialectical tirades of the Marxists et alia. I don't think your argument holds water, but I like it enormously. I don't believe for a minute that we will ever get rid of the slave class, or rid of injustice. (Miller, "Four" 3)

Orwell's chapter was an interlocutory analysis of the plongeur's social position in Paris as a reflection of the exploitation of labour in a manner kindred to slavery insofar as false consciousness and the normalization of oppression make alternatives difficult for the exploited to conceive. In Orwell's conception,

> What makes the [plongeurs'] work in [hotels] is not the essentials; it is the shams that are supposed to represent luxury. Smartness, as it is called, means, in effect, merely that the staff work more and the customers pay more; no one benefits except the proprietor...Essentially, a "smart" hotel is a place where a hundred people toil like devils in order that two hundred may pay through the nose for things they do not really want. (Down 119)

For Orwell, ultimately, "A plongeur is a slave, and a wasted slave, doing stupid and largely unnecessary work. He is kept at work, ultimately, because of a vague feeling that he would be dangerous if he had leisure" (122). After a subsequent exchange, Miller adds to his approval of this chapter a note on the depth of his attachment to its critique, "It's a frightening condemnation of society, and it ought to have stirred England, and France, to the depths. To see it dismissed in a brief paragraph by a shit of a Compton Mackenzie makes my blood boil" ("Four" 5). In this more detailed context, which is what Orwell would have understood in their correspondence, Miller's "quietism" is certainly not a position that lacks care for the exploitation of mankind, but rather one that finds the revolutionary potential terribly limited.

Miller's reaction in the same letter also provides Orwell with his interpretation of quietism. Suggesting that Orwell have *Down and Out in Paris and London* appear in America, Miller states, "I should think now with the hue and cry for Communism there, that your book would be gobbled up....I have written several of my more radical friends over there about it. I don't take the least interests in politics myself" ("Four" 4). From this, Miller gives his rationale:

> I think we're in a mess that is bound to last a century or two....
> I think that human society is founded on injustice absolutely,
> and any attempts to alter that fundamental aspect must be
> tentative and transitory and doomed to failure. Everything we
> believe in has to go to the boards, lock, stock and barrel....
> I think we are in for an era of the bloodiest tyrants the world
> has ever seen. I think it will be a nightmare. (4)

This perspective is hardly the unconsciously apolitical man taken up by Hynes, and with these added materials, Orwell's Miller who hides from the world inside the whale, a surrogate womb to which he consciously retreats, makes more sense. It is also a result of Miller's anarcho-pacifism and previous experiences as an anarchist, labourer, and with organized labour (Orend 54). Finally, Orwell's comparison of Miller's works to James Joyce's "nightmare of history" ("Inside" 102–03, 105–06) is made sensible by Miller's closing sentence on the coming age.

The Personalism of Miller, even if Orwell did not recognize it as a form of anarchism (for Miller does not express it as such in his letters, though he made it explicit in several other places), comes through clearly in his advice of April 20, 1938 to Orwell after his wounded departure from Spain. It is advice perfectly consistent with the anarchist politics voiced in his contemporaneous "An Open Letter to Surrealists Everywhere" as a rebuttal to the Marxist position:

> Perhaps all you need is a rest—stop thinking and worrying about the external pattern. One can only do his best—you couldn't shoulder the responsibilities of the world. (That's for guys like Hitler and Mussolini—they thrive on it.) Do nothing! You'll find it's very difficult at first—then it becomes marvelous and you get to really know something about yourself—and yourself then the world. Everyone is a micro and macrocosm both, don't forget that. (7)

To this advice, Miller added bait, much like he baited Read before making his anarchism a bit clearer, though still implicit rather than explicit: "Presume you received a copy of 'The Phoenix?'" (7). The Phoenix was an openly radical anti-authoritarian, pacifist periodical produced from 1938 to 1940 by James Cooney in Woodstock, New York (with Robert Duncan). While expressly anti-fascist, the pacifism was not tolerated by Orwell, and he never took Miller's "bait" for a more complex discussion involving the politics of the unpolitical.

By the time Orwell came to revise his previous reviews and enlarge them as Inside the Whale, the misrecognition of Miller's unpolitical politics only makes sympathetic condemnation available to Orwell's pen, as was his approach to all his anarchist friends during the Second World War, such as Alex Comfort and George Woodcock (who wrote the first biography of Orwell, The Crystal Spirit):

> It was generally imagined that socialism could preserve and even enlarge the atmosphere of liberalism [which he binds tightly to the Auden group]. It is now beginning to be realized how false this idea was. Almost certainly we are moving into an age of totalitarian dictatorships—an age in which freedom of

thought will be at first a deadly sin and later on a meaningless abstraction. The autonomous individual is going to be stamped out of existence....Miller seems to me a man out of the common because he saw and proclaimed this fact a long while before most of his contemporaries." ("Inside" 131)

The recollection of Miller's summer 1936 letter quoted above is striking: "We are in for an era of the bloodiest tyrants the world has ever seen" ("Four" 4). The seeds for the dystopic 1984 are nearly impossible not to speculate over, and it is only in this more fully defined pacifism that Orwell finally explains his central cetacean metaphor: "what is happening is the destruction of liberalism....The passive attitude will come back, and it will be more consciously passive....Seemingly there is nothing left but quietism....Get inside the whale—or rather, admit you are inside the whale (for you *are*, of course)" ("Inside" 132).

Such a comparison of documents enriches the context of Orwell's seminal essay and illustrates the variety of revisions engendered by Hynes that lead to our present critical sense of the post-Auden group of writers. However, the problem remains in our critical inheritance of Hynes's "angle" and Orwell's very specific position of analysis, which was both based on personal interactions yet deprived of the radical political context from which Miller wrote. As Childs argues, "the association between the 1930s, as a decade of poetry, and four Oxford graduates, W.H. Auden, Stephen Spender, Cecil Day-Lewis, and Louis MacNeice, has become axiomatic and naturalised. Such assumed connections are in need of de-mythologising but not ignoring" (105). If we look to Elizabeth Smart, Lawrence Durrell, George Barker, David Gascoyne, and Dylan Thomas in the late 1930s and 1940s, the urgency to demythologize increases radically if we are to understand their literary production.

Skelton's anthologies for Penguin, Poetry of the Thirties (1964) and Poetry of the Forties (1968), both had a significant influence, and in many ways were the anthologies of record for each decade. They shaped the classroom as well as the tentative emergence of a canon of 1930s and 1940s literature, or at least normative works for inclusion and consideration as being representative of these two decades. Skelton expresses some of the same hesitations as Orwell, in particular hesitations over the easy didacticism and proletarian camaraderie professed by the bourgeoisie. For Skelton, in the first *Poetry of the Thirties* anthology and specifically in relation to the Auden group, "there is, in point of fact, something curiously adolescent in the use of phrases like 'The Enemy', 'The Struggle', and 'The Country', and in the deployment of such words as 'Leader', 'Conspiracy', 'Frontier', 'Maps', 'Guns', and 'Armies' in much the writing of the period" (18). He notes the common critique, the boyscouttish element Orwell identifies, which would be unremarkable were it not for the contrast this creates against other 1930s and 1940s poetry networks, which he largely depoliticizes and thereby decontextualizes:

> The didacticism is earnestly moral, thoroughly evangelical, and indisputably authoritative....[C. Day-Lewis] contributed a "Letter to a young Revolutionary" to *New Country*. In this letter he earnestly advised his undergraduate friend "to divide your outrageously long holidays between three activities." These he listed as,
>
> 1. Investigating the temper of the people...
> 2. Investigating the methods of capitalism...
> 3. Promoting the will to obey.
>
> This last injunction is carefully glossed; it means that the young man must learn to submit "to his natural leader." (22)

There is a startlingly clear difference between such a vision and that which was expressed from 1934 onward through the Villa Seurat, from 1937 onward in the English post-Surrealism linked to the Villa Seurat (Read, Gascoyne, Barker, and so forth), in the New Apocalypse in 1939, and in the emergence of the San Francisco Renaissance as well as Duncan's anarchist groups in New York and Woodstock. Yet, none of these merit inclusion in Skelton's vision (an influential vision) of the 1930s—despite his critique, in his editorial vision the 1930s are the MacSpaunday decade.

It is therefore unsurprising to discover that Skelton's views on the 1936 London International Surrealist Exhibition anticipate those of

Hynes's "telescoped" understanding. For Skelton, Surrealism "remained very much a continental affair....On the whole, it must be regarded as an influential idea rather than as another movement in the history of twentieth-century English poetry" (33). However, when Skelton turns to Breton's communist contention that "for us, Surrealists, the interests of thought cannot cease to go hand in hand with the interests of the working class and all armed attacks on it cannot fail to be considered by us as attacks on thought likewise" (33), he reveals the dominant worldview of the generation that made it seem that other forms of Surrealism had not existed in England and hence that Surrealism died before 1937 (conveniently, the year in which Read made his anarchism public and in which several of the English Surrealists read the proofs of Miller's "An Open Letter to Surrealists Everywhere" and Durrell's The Black Book). For Skelton, "the propagandist and the poet, the mass observer and the introvert, are all (apart from the word surrealist) in agreement; this is the central dogma of the thirties' generation" (33). Of course, this was the central dogma of the central years of the 1930s, but decidedly not of its dog days. Thereby, those who were not in agreement on this dogma were not intelligible in this reading paradigm.

This exclusion of the personalist groups from Skelton's study is made apparent in two ways. First, the regionalist vision of his collection excludes works written by Americans or foreigners in Europe or Britain, and it also generally excludes works published by British poets in venues outside of Britain. For this reason, as well as the deep focus of Poetry of the Thirties on works tied to the Audenesque ideology, he includes virtually no work by those tied to the Villa Seurat or the New Apocalypse and New Romanticism. George Barker appears only twice, Bernard Spencer appears only with his works most heavily influenced by Auden rather than poetry after his break from the Auden school of thought, and Dylan Thomas's works focus on his least surrealist and syntactically complex poetry. The only poet whose works would hint at this alternative view of the 1930s is David Gascoyne, whose selected poems for the volume are nearly all prior to 1936, with the exception of "Farewell Chorus," which closes the book and is contextualized via Auden's "September 1, 1939," which it follows after.

This exclusion from the *Poetry of the Thirties* is corrected in *Poetry of the Forties*, but the significant shift in this second volume is the same as the personalist poets felt in their own writing careers after the war; without the context of their 1930s work, their 1940s poetry appears apolitical, and from the backward retrospective perspective of the 1960s (when Skelton collected these anthologies), they made little sense. Although Skelton acknowledges that in addition to Barker, Gascoyne, and Thomas we also find Bernard Spencer and Lawrence Durrell, he is quick to note for all of them that, despite emerging in the 1930s, they "really came into their own" in the 1940s (*Forties* 16). Skelton also then collapses the opposition many 1940s poets felt toward Auden as a stylistic issue related to Romanticism and the function of the symbol rather than a political difference that drove the stylistic choices.

The political crux of these differences appears when Skelton notes that "though flag-waving patriotism did not appeal to the poets of the forties, and they were distrustful of authority, the threat of invasion caused them to look again at their national inheritance, and to attempt to grapple with that strange love of one's own place" (*Forties* 21). This attitude minimizes the political edge of their deliberate choice, and this approach seems natural to pursue since their 1930s context has been omitted. To make the matter more difficult, Skelton then separates these comments from the New Apocalypse by inserting between them his comments on military poetry, for which he trumpets the influence that *Personal Landscape* had under Durrell, Spencer, and Robin Fedden's editorship while removing it from any connection to those London-based poets who "were distrustful of authority" and likewise separate from the New Apocalypse, which he clearly disliked. The turn to the New Apocalypse names only Henry Treece and largely keeps him separate from J.F. Hendry. While it must be admitted that Treece's poetry is unlikely to be revived, he was nonetheless an astute critic and is an important poetic voice of the period. It is surprising then that Skelton chose to quote Treece's *How I See Apocalypse* using only its most obscure mystical comments rather than its clear politics. In doing so, Skelton selects from among Treece's most impoverished poems that show the same overemphasis on the symbol, but notably without any clear politics. By using Treece's

"Relics," only the poet's most tiresome weaknesses are clear. His more successful "XXXVI Confession in War-Time" or "XXX Pastoral 1941," both from his *Mystic Numbers* sequence, would give a far stronger sense of his uneven oeuvre.

This reconstructs the reader's understanding of the movement without its social or political context, and hence it simply does not make sense. The shocking contrast is with J.F. Hendry's selected inclusion, "London before Invasion, 1940" (93). The surrealist metaphor, "prophetic" incantation Treece discusses, and anti-authoritarian understanding of the city, state, and society would, if discussed in Skelton's introduction, make Hendry's poem quite alive. In a sea metaphor, "Walls and buildings stand here still, like shells" and "That tide is out" (93), but the metaphor continues across all four stanzas with the city "In the ebbing seas of heaven" that becomes the poet's and reader's "imagination floats, a weed, on water's vacancy" before in closing "Flood-tides returning may bring with them blood and fire" until "All time adrift in torrents of blind war" (93). This metaphor is enlivened substantially if the reader recognizes the bucolic anti-city in the New Apocalypse's sense of the organic, and hence the poet and reader are "a weed" that is not crushed by the sea nor the city. The prophetic also functions in the Apocalyptic vision of the sea's returning to wash out the city, which is like shells in the sand in the opening line of the poem. And finally, the poet's injunction to the reader is not to flee or protect the nation but rather to "Hold them to the ear" to hear the sound of the sea in the shells, which is timeless. As a simple poem about "London before Invasion, 1940," Hendry's work is clean but confused; as a New Apocalypse poem built from an anti-authoritarian vision that supports the organic and spontaneous, it is remarkably more engaging. Regardless, for Skelton, the work "approached the ludicrous" (*Forties* 29). He admits enough of a relation to note that "Dylan Thomas and George Barker could, from time to time, achieve tragic grandeur and prophetic intensity" (28), but this is ultimately with the aim of keeping these poets separate rather than acknowledging their commonalities.

Nevertheless, Skelton, Hynes, and Allen are of a past critical moment. Since the 1980s, Late Modernism has risen as a significant field, in many respects as a sharp contrast to the views built by Orwell,

Skelton, Allan, and their milieu. The development of new concepts of Late Modernism through the New Modernist Studies is in part through Tyrus Miller's work (as well as Jed Esty, Marina McKay, and Alan Wilde). In this more recent reconceptualization, the personalist authors were all outsiders to what Peter Nicholls has termed "hegemonic Modernism" (167), traditionally associated with Eliot, Joyce, Woolf, and Pound. However, Tyrus Miller opens his *Late Modernism* with his prime example of the titular notion of his influential book: Henry Miller via George Orwell's *Inside the Whale*. For Tyrus Miller, Orwell's treatment of Henry Miller is the defining moment of Late Modernism. Nonetheless, even though Hynes makes no appearance in Miller's book, the angle developed from Hynes persists and Miller can only be seen through the Audenesque political vision. As a consequence, despite being Tyrus Miller's opening salvo, Henry Miller vanishes, returning only at the conclusion of *Late Modernism* to again take up the mantle of the quintessential Late Modernist (7–8, 210). This "in-between" status for Miller reflects this entire network, existing in the space between Hegemonic Modernism and the few Late Modernist works that have successfully entered the critical mainstream, a mainstream that is sympathetic to Marxist analyses and deeply discomfited by anarchist histories. As occurred in Hynes's recasting of Orwell's work as principally a discussion of the Auden group, Tyrus Miller's analysis in *Late Modernism* again focuses on the Auden generation. For him,

> The historical panorama that Orwell sets out with such unforgiving concision serves to foreground the peculiar homelessness of Miller's work in this history. Miller, quite simply, doesn't fit in the big picture of his times. Out of frank disbelief, Miller avoids the progressive commitments of the Edwardians and the communist enthusiasms of the Auden generation; neither, however, does he exhibit, modernist-style, any faith in the power of carefully crafted, difficult art to redeem the squalid realities of his subproletarian existence. (8)

The rationale, of course, is Miller's anarchism, which Tyrus Miller refuses to recognize or in which he does not take an interest. This vision opens and closes *Late Modernism* as the quintessential instance of

Tyrus Miller's case, yet having re-examined Henry Miller and Orwell, the "historical panorama" of futility found in Orwell's analysis of Miller is quite obviously itself poached from his correspondence with Miller rather than a new critical vision engendered by reading the MacSpaundays. If "Miller, quite simply, doesn't fit in the big picture of his times," we must ask how this "big picture" could have been drawn from his nightmare vision of an "an era of the bloodiest tyrants the world has ever seen" (Miller, "Four" 4), which Orwell uses to develop his "pessimism" that Tyrus Miller finds it "hard not to concur with" (8). More to the point, how big can the "big picture" be if it excludes the widespread and internationally successful movement of writers of which Miller was a part—one that led to one of the most vibrant literary movements of the twentieth century in America and was tied to works of major influence and commercial success in Britain?[21]

My project here finds common ground with Tyrus Miller through his reconceptualizations of Late Modernism as a distinct entity from the hegemony of the Auden generation and its communism as well as High Modernism's elitism. Miller considers selective authors who rose to prominence after the *anna mirabilis* of 1922 yet were overshadowed by the Auden group during the 1930s, and this grants a broader frame of reference to the politics of modernist writers who were then active. Nonetheless, the persisting normative role of Auden and communism leads him to overlook the anarchist associations of several of his subjects, including his defining example of Late Modernism: Henry Miller in contrast to George Orwell. Even with Anthony Mellors's disputation of Tyrus Miller's periodization, in which "[Tyrus] Miller is right to see the emergence of a troubled, belated version of Anglo-American modernism, but wrong to confine it to the period before World War Two, and wrong to define it as essentially negative in character" (Mellors 22), the same binary emerges with the same elisions: communism vs. fascism without anti-authoritarian considerations and a cohesive vision of identity and myth in contrast to a fragmented construct of ideology.

The point in this re-examination is not to derogate Miller's excellent work that leads him to innovatively reconsider Samuel Beckett and Djuna Barnes, among others, in a Late Modernist paradigm. His project has been undeniably successful in this respect and reinvigorated such work. Rather, my aim is to return attention the received knowledge that guided Miller's perspective. As I have shown, that received knowledge has a long and stable foundation beginning with Orwell and moving forward. As Childs contends,

> The term "thirties writing" connotes a style as well as a period.…[A] pattern has been mapped on to the decade's literature, just as it has on to its history. Robin Skelton's 1930s anthology demonstrates this as well. His chosen poets are all male except for Anne Ridler and were all born between 1902 and 1916. The collection begins with four poems, one by each of Auden, Spender, MacNeice, and Day-Lewis: the "MacSpaunday" poets whose style and views have come to epitomise 1930s poetry. (114)

Disentangling this "pattern mapping" requires retracing it, and as the subject becomes less literary-historical and more a matter of stylistic concerns, the grip of the MacSpaunday paradigm remains tight although increasingly invisible. This is to say, the disruption that the personalist writers create in the stylistic paradigm makes them increasingly difficult to understand if the normativity of Auden, Spender, MacNeice, and Day-Lewis continues to operate unconsciously. As the MacSpaundays shaped the tastes and normative interpretations after the war, that which ran contrary became either "bad" writing or unintelligible.

Childs's book from the same year as Tyrus Miller's shows a more nuanced vision of the scope of authors active at the end of the 1930s and into the early 1940s, though it has enjoyed a far less spectacular influence on the discipline. However, the same critical resistance to recognizing an anti-authoritarian context for the literary works remains. This allows Childs to more seriously take up Orwell's unification of the Auden generation with liberalism in a way that carries forward Orwell's intended critique:

> The canonisation of Auden has been said by Adrian Caesar to have been because of his appeal to a "liberal middle-class

conscience" which has constructed the decade's value and
significance. Many of the most well-known writers of the 1940s,
several of whom began publishing in the 1930s, were socially
and politically different from the previous generation: two of
the leading poets, Dylan Thomas and George Barker, were from
lower middle-class backgrounds and entered neither public
school or Oxbridge. (Childs 120)

This "liberal middle-class conscience" seems undeniable in the
critical heritage, most of which was framed by the Auden generation
itself, and its liberalism is equally prominent as the major interpretive schema against which any other vision must seek to distinguish
itself. To look to Barker and Thomas, for Childs, is to look at authors
not very much concerned with the liberal values associated with the
Auden generation's communism or propagandist poetry, and it is also
a source of connection to Miller.

Neither Barker nor Thomas cared much for the easy accessibility
of their work to the class from which they arose; nor do they turn
to their art as a means of changing the world, as Auden had until the
war years. Both authors are also notable for their ties to post-Surrealism and their frequently overlooked surrealist works (for Thomas, his
creative prose in particular, which he'd had published by Miller and
Durrell in Paris). Moreover, while Thomas remained distant from any
serious political position, his focus on the individual and the individual's experience of war (often to the exclusion of the war itself) is
clear.

Barker, however, did write on Spain. While his May 1939 poem
"Elegy on Spain" is ambivalent in its affiliations,[22] it makes clear
his position on war (his self-description was as an "Augustinian
Anarchist"). With the photograph of the face of a child killed in
Barcelona pasted in to face the first stanza, the closing lines chill:
"O now, my minor moon, dead as meat / Slapped on a negative plate,
I hold / The crime of the bloody time in my hand" (98). As Cary
Nelson notes for Barker, "We are forced by this device to take the
description both literally and figuratively, for we hold the girl's image
in our hands as we read" (32). For Barker, however, there is no propa-
ganda to call one to participate in the war, and the ring is deeply akin

to Miller's pacifism (for Barker was reading Miller).[23] Barker closes the third section of the poem in its final stanza by returning the reader's gaze to the dead and disfigured face of the young girl whose image had been used for so much poster-propaganda in the war:

> So close a moment that long open eye,
> Fly the flag low, and fold over those hands
> Cramped to a gun: gather the child's remains
> Staining the wall and cluttering the drains;
> Troop down the red to the black and the brown;
> ....
> All this builds a bigger plinth for glory,
> Story on story. (103)

The effect is startling in that this previously postered image, a call to action, ends with the dropping of the national flag (and by proxy the nation) and a turn away from the red, black, and brown (the fascist military actors in the Civil War). As is noted later for Hendry, this group's sympathy for anarchism and the context of the poem ("red to the black *and* the brown"; emphasis mine) makes the reference more likely to the proxy actors: the red Russian communists, the brown German *Sturmabteilung* and the black Italian *camice nere*, even though from an Audenesque perspective this would be the fascists and anarchists alone. The concept of this turn away from the red, black, and brown is anathema to Auden's propagandistic "Spain" of the same moment. With the flags and accoutrements of authority and government shed, the only remaining action "on which triumph shall be found" is then the act of artistic creation through "Story on story" and the poetic telling.[24] This characteristic turn for the personalist poets directs ambivalence to the political conflict and empathy to the individuals caught up within it who can be redeemed in their suffering through art and *not* by sacrifice or victory. Again, the politics of this unpolitical turn matter deeply, even if their pacifism is difficult to understand from the liberal perspective.

Mellor makes a kindred comparison of Barker and Thomas, much like Childs's reading, although like Childs he avoids expanding the politics of his aesthetic observations as well as the scope of reference.

Mellor later describes the organic turn in the New Apocalypse and English Surrealism through attention to Barker's *Calamiterror*, which followed immediately after the 1936 London International Surrealist Exhibition, although this does not figure in his reading of "Elegy on Spain." With regard to Barker's *Calamiterror*, he notices,

> The sequence as a whole ends with an emergence from an investigation of the guts and sensations of selfhood—and, coupled with a heritage of radical romanticism, declares itself "for Spain." Connections between Barker's and Thomas' works and lives, were made by contemporary critics and have been repeated variously since. Just as in Barker's work, the human bodies in Thomas' late 1930s texts, in both poetry and prose, also exist in charged relationship with the organic world around them. This is partly a particularly Welsh preoccupation. (Mellor 91)

However, the Welshness of this trend in Barker and the Apocalyptics is not particularly Welsh. It is, instead, precisely the organic turn already seen in the Villa Seurat immediately following the growth of English post-surrealist preoccupation just after the exhibition of 1936. In this context, Barker's conclusion of *Calamiterror* fulfills a trend in which industry appears as "I see England / With the underground mines run bleeding along her like wounds" and warfare carries not glory nor Audenesque propaganda for "the struggle": "The dead is dead," "the large parasites that dilate like leech, / Torn, with war and agony," and "my mother world, with bomb holes in her bosom" (Barker, *Calamiterror* 52–53). These images of diseased industry and degenerate warfare add to the corruption of the urban locale for Barker where "London lies like a huge rot" and "Rome / Roars" (51). These images are all set in stark contrast against the rural organic imagery of the poem: "The centre of my heart like a red tree / Puts forth a hand and indicates the common red rose" (52). This combination of urban desolation and futile war set contrary to fecund organicism and rural locales would run across the Villa Seurat and New Apocalypse as well as the early San Francisco Renaissance as a shared preoccupation reflecting their common sympathies for pacifism, self-development, and anti-authoritarian quietism.[25]

When Childs moves on from his juxtaposition of Thomas and Barker against the Auden group (which differs profoundly), it is to take up the New Apocalypse (who are widely neglected in critical work, despite the demonstrable influence of the movement). However, the "angle" again neuters the political unpolitics:

> In the work of The New Apocalypse writers (including Henry Treece, J.F. Hendry, Dorian Cooke, and Norman MacCraig) Romantic poetry had a resurgence, as did the…experimental poetry of the surrealists. The Apocalypse poets rejected social realism and believed that society should adapt to the individual, who was determined by myth (which amounted to the individual's "aspirations and inspirations"). There is not space to dwell on their poetry here except to say that it aimed to be organic rather than mechanistic, personal rather than public, abstract rather than social. (Childs 120–21)

This moves further than we have seen in preceding critics (though Childs is not the first to take notice of the New Apocalypse), but the rejection of Social Realism is related only to a generalized individualism rather than a contradictory anarchist politics. In the context more fully established in the next chapter, the various personalist groups' move away from Social Realism (which seems for Childs to be akin to socialist realism) is for the New Apocalypse overtly anarchist and expressly based on Read's essay "The Politics of the Unpolitical." Moreover, the realist component that is abandoned in favour of an interior landscape and surrealist metaphor is far from politically neutral and shares with Social Realism a critique of injustice—it differs in that, unlike the Auden generation, those moving away from Social(ist) Realism were themselves often from the lower classes and without social privilege.

That for Childs "there is not space to dwell on their poetry" demonstrates the ongoing redirection of attention away from anything that would disturb the interpretive framework of a liberal–fascist dualism based on the context established already by previous scholarship and the Auden group itself. Even in one of the few moments in which he acknowledges a contrast between the new voices of the late 1930s and the Auden group, the contrast is quickly regressed to the terms and context of High Modernism and the Audenesque innovators:

> Rejecting the communal social perspective of the 1930s, Hendry declared in modernist style in his 1943 essay "The Art of History" that "There is no history—except the history of self-realisation" (Tolley 1985: 104). This contrasts sharply with Auden's personification of a portentous communal history "that never sleeps or dies, / And, held one moment, burns the hand" ("To a Writer on His Birthday")....But it was the intervention of the war in literary history which put a stamp on "thirties poetry," leaving it monolithically isolated and simplistically defined. The poetry of the decade had been engaged and committed, aware and prophetic, in complete contrast to the complacent conservative verse which preceded World War I. (Childs 120–21)

The difficulty Childs encounters here rests in his sources, which do not account for the continuation of authors like Hendry during and after the war. Hendry's "The Art of History" may stand out in sharp contrast to Auden, but it does not stand out in its own context.

Hendry's aims are overtly contrary to "in modernist style" and are (without attribution) taken from the first issue of the flagship periodical of the New Apocalypse, *Transformation* (in a technical sense a series of books rather than a periodical so as to satisfy paper rationing restrictions on new periodicals). Hendry's comments are printed in the shadow of Read's anarchist "The Politics of the Unpolitical" and Treece's "Towards a Personalist Attitude," which open the issue. Childs's quotation of Hendry is preceded in the essay by the anti-futurist sentiments that reflect the New Apocalypse's interest in the organic and the personal: "We do not, in spite of its sedulous manufacturers, the newsreels, 'live in the presence of history.' We are not mechanical slaves—yet" (Hendry, "Art" 140). The anti-futurist implications become overt for Hendry the page over. Moreover, if there could be no mistake over the allusion to Marx in the implicit phrase "[All history is] the history of self-realisation" (Childs 120; Hendry,

"Art" 140), it is made overt in the next paragraph when Hendry asserts, "Events are not dialectic or the U.S.S.R. would not have stood out of the war for so long" (140).

Inadvertently, Hendry introduces one of the crucial distinctions drawn by many of the personalist authors under discussion in this book, although they came to it in several different ways and often with different implications; the tenuous status granted to selfhood, autonomy, freedom, and character by virtue of "organic" or "unconscious" forces does not necessarily lead to the purely social vision based on material conditions that we find in vulgar Marxism nor to the bourgeois liberalism of the postwar Auden group (i.e., the "communal social perspective of the 1930s" [Childs 120]). Hendry is also overt in setting his vision against that of Auden, the French Surrealists, and anti-individualist notions of "the Classless Society" ("Art" 146). He gives an early articulation to something distinct:

> The era of ruthlessness begins, where the most ruthless are the greatest cowards: the men who run from History [i.e., self-realization], the men who close their eyes to Art....Auden was aware of the necessity for escape-art, not realizing that in a sense all art is escape-art, and all escape-art is myth-making.... Freedom is an illusion, yes; but not "the bourgeois" illusion. The bourgeois throughout Europe surrendered it because they did not believe in ideals or illusions. They did not know they affected the blood. It is precisely because Freedom is an illusion that it is necessary, that it is dynamic, that we can grow within it, that our real History [of self-realization] is still possible, and even our Art....Each man is his own Liberty. Each spirit must be defended—defended against nihilists, brown, black or non-descript...defended against the quislings of politics in the State. (146–47)

The notable feature of this impassioned exhortation is that the rise of subjectivity over selfhood and a Marxist critique of the false consciousness of industrial capitalism do not diminish the ideals of self-realization in a personalist-cum-anarchist sense of the individual. It also provides a middle ground between the brown or black shirts and the communists without becoming conservative or pro-capitalist. Moreover, as with Barker, the brown and black appear less a worry over the Nazi brown shirts and anarchists (as the Auden group would invariably recognize the latter colour as signifying) than the Nazi *Sturmabteilung* and the Italian *camicie nere*—Hendry's anarchism and anti-fascism are clear, even though an Auden-centred reading would paint this as anti-fascism and anti-anarchism by virtue of the altered lexicon of political signification.

Furthermore, Hendry's opening target is Christopher Caudwell's posthumous 1938 essay "Liberty: A Study in Bourgeois Illusion" from *Studies in a Dying Culture*, in which Caudwell identifies the only viable form of freedom as the transformation of materials conditions "when [the workers] will Communism and produce liberty" (228). All other forms of freedom are reduced to conservative, bourgeois attempts to maintain the status quo of exploitation and reciprocal restriction. For Hendry, the class struggle is a product rather than producer of power, and hence he vigorously resists Caudwell's anti-individualist (and thereby social authoritarian, vulgar Marxist) closing indictment: "bourgeoisdom…crucifies liberty upon a cross of gold, and if you ask in whose name it does this, it replies, 'In the name of personal freedom'" (Caudwell 228). For Hendry, in contrast, bourgeoisdom surrenders itself and the dream of freedom out of fear in the same sense that Enlightenment, instrumental "reason, if rooted in fear, has been a manifestation of the Power-complex" (Hendry, "Art" 149), which he analyzes through Read's anarchist framework. Hence, "Freedom is an illusion, yes; but *not 'the bourgeois'* illusion" (146). The false consciousness of both the bourgeoisie and the workers is, in this sense, produced by the exercise of power under the guise of authority that surrenders the illusion of freedom, and the economism of vulgar Marxism is reframed as a power relation predicated on fear, which can be avoided only by "overcoming our fear of living together" (150). Perhaps Hendry's most pointed reversal of the Marxist paradigm to an anarchist analysis is his sense that in fascist Italy, "instead of wealth concentrating power, power has concentrated wealth" (149).

While we may query the soundness of Hendry's justifications for his position, the crucial issue is the importance of contextualizing his comments as quoted by Childs and the new perspective that suddenly emerges when we do so. Again, my intention is not to critique Childs's cogent and useful work but rather to demonstrate the calcification of an interpretive paradigm begun in the 1940s by groups with which the Personalists were in conflict. The nuanced anti-authoritarian spirit shared among the Personalists, whether of an expressly anarchist or flirtatiously liberal variety, acts as a powerful acid on these calcified attitudes. Once Hendry's difference from Auden is explored in context, it reawakens the vitality of his generation's resistance to hegemonic literary forces and the commonalities of their various groups across continents during the war. It also makes sense of their aesthetics and makes their imagery intelligible and, in many instances, even compelling. In context, it is impossible to accept Childs's reading of Hendry in line with "the complacent conservative verse which preceded World War I" (121).

A further revision to the extant scholarship is also implicit in Hendry's discussion of self-realization and the symptomatic woes of selfhood it implies. The tension between the anti-authoritarian Personalism of the generation in question (very frequently self-identifying as an anarchist position) and the interpretive paradigms established in criticism develops in several stylistic and thematic directions, among them the nature of character in Late Modernism as identified by Alan Wilde. This constitutes another critical piece of the construction of Late Modernism and 1930s literature that— as with Tyrus Miller, Childs, Hynes, and Orwell—avoids the Personalists in favour of a binary opposition between traditionalist and progressive-cum-Marxist views. Wilde's distinction between the modernist and the postmodernist had its greatest impact prior to the New Modernist Studies and prior to Miller's redirection of attention in Late Modernism, but his approach has demonstrably shaped critical perspectives and continues to exert a significant influence.

Wilde offered a competing vision in 1981 of self-identity between Modernism and postmodernism with an intermediary Late Modernism, and this notion can be traced forward in the various disputations of definitional categories surrounding subjectivity in (post) modernist authors' works whereby the modernist is rekindled in the postmodernist's garb (e.g., Marlowe Miller 4, Harris 87–92, Raper 93–100, Sharratt 223–35). In Wilde's comparison of Christopher

Isherwood and E.M. Forster, the most notable contrast between High Modernism and the proto-postmodernist Late Modernism is

> the replacement of "well-made-characters who carry with
> them fixed identity, a stable set of social and psychological
> attributes—a name, a situation, a profession, a condition,
> etc." (characters like Forster's, presumably) by what Raymond
> Federman, speaking for one group of postmodern writers, calls
> "word-beings," fictional creatures who "will be as changeable, as
> unstable, as illusory, as nameless, as unnamable, as fraudulent,
> as unpredictable as the discourse that makes them." (Wilde 106)

Wilde's interpretation is based on Forster's well-known reaction to and hesitations over Isherwood's *Mr Norris Changes Trains* (*The Last of Mr. Norris* in American publications). As a comparison between the High Modernists and the Auden generation, it is apt and attracts attention to the conflict between the bourgeois individualism of the Georgians (one might even say the Fabians) and the economism of the socially minded Auden group and other 1930s Marxist writers (appearing in the structuralist frame of discourse here). Nevertheless, the "self-realization" of Hendry, the individualism of any of the anarchist authors, and the Personalism of the later 1930s writers does not comfortably function within the "early"/"late" dualism that Wilde constructs. The stability of the former in either social or psychological terms is immediately open to critique through the Personalists' use of Marxist criticism to disrupt socially imposed identities; yet the illusory nature of identity implicit in "word-beings" that casts selfhood as "fraudulent" or a bourgeois illusion is likewise rejected as socially authoritarian and vulgar Marxism. Anarchist philosophy offers a third position. The particular problem has concerned anarchist critics for more than a century, and it is unlikely a single resolution is viable; yet the existence of this third perspective denies the restriction of the analysis to a false binary.

Wilde expands the importance of this distinction between the two generations based on

> what Forster sees as the major consolation of fiction, its ability
> to provide us with "a reality of a kind we can never get in daily

life" (p. 44). The contrast between the unsatisfactoriness of life, in which "we never understand each other" (p. 32), and the power of art to create a structured space of belief, or desire, and thus to "solace us" (p. 44) runs throughout *Aspects* (and through most of modernism). (107)

This is certainly a point that has aroused debate since Wilde raised it, but his concern over art's consolation (whether it meshes with reality or not) stands, and it is a genuine conflict between Forster and Isherwood. The stability and growth of Forster's "flat" and "round" characters no longer functions in the materialist world that by and large considers character a function of conditions, or by proxy superstructure a function of the base. Caudwell's critique would surely place Forster's *Aspects of the Novel* and its discussion of character (and by extension, human selfhood) as a function of cultural hegemony, a form of false consciousness that makes the pursuit of freedom that is implicit in modeling ourselves after the forms of identity built up in such characters become a means of enshrining the class position of the bourgeoisie.

Wilde's argument, however, merits further nuance, which he provides. The product continues to emphasize the modern/postmodern distinction that became fashionable in the following decades as a stable/unstable sense of identity politics. For Wilde, Forster's traditional and stable (and realistic) characters remain the norm through the High Moderns with the only proviso being that

> speculative and inferential knowledge has become, the center—Jacob [in Woolf's *Jacob's Room*], "a young man alone in his room" (p. 94)—holds; and we are enjoined "to penetrate" (p. 92) the reality behind phenomena: "the skeleton [that] is wrapped in flesh" (p. 162). Character has not been dissolved, nor has the self been lost; though both have become manifestly more problematic. (Wilde 107)

This precise argument sits behind the list of (post)modernist readings that followed on Wilde's work, whereby the modernist author could be found anticipating the destabilized identity politics of the postmodern in any instance in which identity proved capable of transformation or purely superficial functioning. This holds unless the social constructivism implicit in 1930s Marxism is made more prominent. To this, Wilde offers a particularly tempting refinement:

> Indeed, the faith in some central core of being not only persists, as in Forster's theory, it is deepened by the mystery of that core's recessive presence; and the passion of the quest for dozens of Jacobs in the early decades of the century, translated into an almost obsessive concern with depth, is validated by just that underlying belief that, at some level, character remains intact. (108)

This tempts the critic to align Wilde's sense of the essential stability of modernist notions of identity (if we continue to accept this analysis) with the anarchist vision of selfhood seen above in Hendry as well as across his generation. The two visions of selfhood, however, cannot be conflated, even if both conflict with the social constructivists to a degree, and it also disputes Wilde's immediately subsequent claim that "With the thirties...there is a noticeable, if somewhat ambiguous, shift to surface and along with it, inevitably perhaps, a change in attitudes toward character and characterization" (278) and thereby, or therefrom, notions of identity.

The conflict over the Ego, between Forster and Hendry, is not based on shared notions of stability or of a persisting core. The sense of identity most prevalent in anarchist theory as well as across the later 1930s writers I have identified as personalist is not necessarily immutable despite being individual, and it need not be stable nor essential. It need only be *one's own*. This is to say, the self may not be fully known even to the individual living it or who brings the self into being by living it; yet its necessary dream is of an existence beyond the determinism of its material conditions. The Ego is its own.

As a good example of the anarchist approach to such problems of identity, I take Jesse Cohn's reworking of attitudes to critical theory, mainly the Frankfurt School, in his fine study *Anarchism and the Crisis of Representation*. Cohn argues that the subject is seen as a false image or a reified structure imposing itself on the unnamable. If the self is actually a creative nothingness, "a fluctuating element," as Herbert Read writes, then it cannot be fixed through mimetic "mirror knowledge" or "representation," and "we...cannot know a self; we can only betray our self....All art is in this sense an unconscious self-betrayal." Accordingly, for Read, the lesson of Stirner's *Ego and His Own* was its warning against "surrendering one's self to an abstraction, to an illusion of any kind," including the illusion of an ideal, unified self: "the Self (with a capital S) is not an essence to which the self (with a small s) must pay homage." (126)

This position leads Cohn to return to artistic practices and those that were a particular influence on the Villa Seurat's creative work and thereby the English Personalists:

> Thus, for the Dadaists, the fluctuating self could be recognized in "a fluctuating style," an anarchist aesthetic in which "the separate parts of the sentence, even the individual vocables and sounds, regain their autonomy." Seen in this light, the decadent art that has most frequently been depicted as a mere aesthetic reflection or symptom of modern urban anomie can be reinterpreted as a deliberate "expression of anarchist politics" in the form of "aesthetic individualism." (Cohn 126)

This vision of identity and individuality as well as the movement toward freedom can still admit of the critique of cultural hegemony without finding the self as a social construct. Instead, the self is the possession of the individual in Max Stirner's sense, and in its being possessed, it exists. The faith in a persistent core need not coincide with this proximate, embodied human possession of the self, a possession without transferability, exchange value, or continuously stable features. The self may be the illusion of the subject, yet for Hendry's generation,

> It is precisely because Freedom is an illusion that it is necessary, that it is dynamic, that we can grow within it, that our real

History [of self-realization] is still possible, and even our Art.... Each man is his own Liberty. Each spirit must be defended... against the quislings of politics in the State. (Hendry, "Art" 146–47)

Likewise, even in "overcoming our fear of living together" (150), such individuals do not find what Childs calls the "communal social perspective of the 1930s"; nor do they become Wilde's "fictional creatures who 'will be as changeable, as unstable, as illusory, as nameless, as unnamable, as fraudulent, as unpredictable as the discourse [and thereby material conditions] that makes them'" (277).

One articulation, offered by Morris, is that "Without significant qualification, one argues from Marx that 'social being...determines consciousness.'...[And] the body seems to have become...endlessly pliable, docile, radically without its own claims, a vehicle of either domination or despair" (52). Thereby, the organic, the embodied, the limited become the basis for resistance in which our history is the "History of self-realization" and each "man is his own Liberty." The embodied and limited individual becomes the basis for overcoming fear and resisting cultural hegemony rather than a bourgeois system of control. Alternatively, "the enclosed, defensive 'I' becomes the 'me' of self-concern. The object 'me' becomes the denied subject 'I.' Resistance privatizes" (Morris 81). In other words, the defensive "I feel" becomes the "what does that mean to me?" in the object form of the subject's self-contemplation, which then becomes the realized "object" in self-reflection that craves to become the denied contents of the "I." I finds the Ego as its personal possession via its self-contemplation as the object me. We retreat from the subject position as a defense (Hendry's "fear"), but in doing so while invoking the object "me" of the thinking "I," we again return attention to what the "I" desires in its needful embodiment, and hence the turn to resistance. always is private and personal. For Wilde's vision of the tension between depth and surface of the self in Modernism and Late Modernism, this is already a contested topic, and as will be discussed more fully in the "Authority's Apocalypse" chapter, even the High Modernist notions of selfhood are subject to review, such as through D.H. Lawrence's notion of the allotropic self, in particular how

Lawrence was adopted and adapted by Miller, Durrell, and Nin and subsequently by the New Apocalypse.

The only text that meaningfully takes up this broader consideration in criticism is Arthur Edward Salmon's historically oriented *Poets of the Apocalypse* from 1983. Salmon's interests were most likely piqued by his earlier critical study of Alex Comfort in 1978. In both instances, his focus is on elucidating the literary products of the figure or figures in tandem with a historical contextualization. *Poets of the Apocalypse* is the first and still most thorough history of the post-1936 English post-surrealist group through the war years. He acknowledges but does not emphasize their anarchism, and by and large both works avoid engaging with conflicting trends in critical theory, so Salmon's excellent historical introductions required expansion in order to productively force a reconsideration of the New Apocalypse in the context of Late Modernism. My work here enacts such an expansion and places the New Apocalypse poets in relation to the larger international network of which they were a part and through which the theoretical underpinnings of their anti-authoritarian philosophy developed.

The critical trend uncovered to this point is variable and complex, but its repeated focus in mainstream scholarship is a dualist vision of the conflicts in Modernism that occlude the anti-authoritarian spirit of the later 1930s, in large part due to the early contextualizing influence of the Auden group's own writings, Stephen Spender most particularly. This is not, however, something unanticipated at the time by the personalist poets themselves. As G.S. Fraser commented in the first major essay on the New Apocalypse, in their second anthology, "The poets represented in this volume are, perhaps, not likely to have the same immediate popularity as the generation that immediately preceded them, the generation of Auden, Spender, and MacNeice" ("Apocalypse" 25). The contrast between themselves and the Auden group was prominent from the outset, but they had not anticipated the degree of disregard and misrepresentation they would encounter, despite their significant readership and influence at the time. For Fraser, the distinction was primarily one of style and situation, such that "This is partly true due, of course, to the rather unpropitious circumstances of the moment, but it is also due to a genuine contrast in attitude. The Auden group were in what, in a rather special sense, one might call a classical tradition, and the Apocalypse are what, again in a rather special sense, one may call romantics" (25). The past tense is perhaps more telling than the particulars of the distinction, as is Fraser's sense of the term "attitude," which avoids the startling refusal for reciprocal acknowledgement. Apart from the Apocalyptic writers specifically, the same division holds true for the international groups with which they were intimately connected—the Personal Landscape poets, the San Francisco Renaissance, the Villa Seurat group, etc.—who have likewise failed to appear in the histories of the period, even when otherwise highly successful. As I have already noted, the ubiquity of Orwell's Inside the Whale to discussions of 1930s writing is obvious, but the fact that the essay is primarily concerned with Henry Miller and his group, what Orwell calls the Villa Seurat School ("Inside" 133), is ignored in an equally ubiquitous fashion. The influence of the San Francisco Renaissance is undeniable, but its own early and formative contact with the Villa Seurat group and the Personal Landscape poets has remained largely unnoticed. When Durrell, Comfort, and Thomas rose to fame and bestseller status, as perhaps the three most prominent British writers in this group, their context was decidedly postwar, as if their decade of early writing had not been noted. When Fraser, Hendry, Derek Stanford, and Herbert Howarth ascended to academic positions, they were cast into a literary context in which their ties to the High Modernists were in far greater demand than their knowledge of their contemporaries, and all were turned to this fact in their monographs. In short, when a member of the Auden group, such as C. Day-Lewis, could ask, "Where are the war poets?," he could do so precisely for the reason that he was not in the war with them, and as a consequence, those war poets who did not subscribe to his school had "unpropitious circumstances" under which to protest their exclusion from his histories. Those circumstances have continued to cast a shadow over the New Modernist Studies from seventy years past. The Personalists offer a corrective.

The situation with the San Francisco Renaissance is far more straightforward. Criticism has by and large recognized its politics and Romanticism, even if it does not always attend to it. Rather than fundamentally misunderstanding them, critics have simply overlooked the extent of its European influences and ties to the Villa Seurat generation, even while exploring its influence on others abroad. Citing an absence is pedantic, so in a far more direct way, this study simply adds to and expands the discussion of American 1930s and 1940s poetry groups. The task of the remaining chapters, then, is to return attention to the narrative history of this generation in America and Britain after Auden in order to recontextualize its impact on the period and its role in literary criticism. This is followed by a formulation of their anti-authoritarian and anarchist positions, varied as they are, under the general rubric of Personalism: a fourth option among the already-established conservatism-cum-fascism, Marxism, and neoliberalism of the period (or the plural forms of each). Finally, with a recontextualization of the critical literature, a new narrative history, and a theory of anarcho-anti-authoritarian politics in place, this book will conclude by offering selected rereadings of seminal texts by the authors of this generation through this new critical lens. These "rereading vignettes" focus on Henry Miller, Lawrence Durrell, Elizabeth Smart, and Robert Duncan. They take the lead in Chapter 4 because they were able to break through to "major-minor" status despite the established critical decontextualization of their works. As I noted at the outset of this chapter, it is not possible to read alphabet-ically from A to B: Auden to the Beats. Whether it is decontextualized major authors or overlooked minor poets, the intermediary in this literary history hinges on the deep influence of these later personalist writers of the 1930s whose careers were frozen during the war years and then, by virtue of being the avant-garde, were denied ascendancy after the war to positions of editorial and academic authority, the very positions from which their existence was then ignored by their predecessors and successors.

2

Narrative Itinerary
From the Villa Seurat
to English Post-Surrealists

With the exception of Isherwood at Cambridge, the Auden group all shared Oxford as a home. The High Modernist poets, though not forming a "school" per se, generally all shared wartime London. The Imagists famously shared the British Museum tearoom. For Henry Miller, 1930s Paris was a locus of activity that eventually centred on the Villa Seurat after he took over Antonin Artaud's rooms in 18 Villa Seurat, 14th arrondissement, Paris, on September 1, 1934. The contrast is notable, although Miller had already slept on the floor of the building and had integrated this into his novel *Tropic of Cancer*, published by Jack Kahane's Obelisk Press earlier in the same year. The building had long been a home to artists, including the pointillist painter Georges Seurat, as well as Marc Chagall, Salvador Dalí, André Derain, and Chaïm Soutine (Bloshteyn 67–69). When Miller arrived, the same trend persisted, and he was to share the space over time with the writers Alfred Perlès, Anaïs Nin, and Michael Fraenkel, as well as the painter Henri Michaux, among others. Into this locale various other artists and authors inserted themselves as residents or visitors, ranging from Brassaï (in the later 1930s) to Lawrence Durrell and David Gascoyne. As a result of the fame Miller enjoyed following the publication of *Tropic of Cancer*, his correspondence networks broadened rapidly, looking back to the High Modernists who read it, such as Eliot, Pound, and Read, as well as forward to the rising generation, including Durrell, Orwell, Dylan Thomas, Robert Duncan, and Elizabeth Smart. Notably, no response to the novel is to be found among the Auden group.

Miller's literary cache has fallen, and though he is still a popular author among readers, scholarly studies of his work only occasionally reach the academic mainstream. None of the major studies of Late Modernism have made more than cursory reference to Miller despite his ubiquity in literary discussions after the mid-point of the 1930s. Nonetheless, the rapid growth of his fame following on *Tropic of Cancer*'s publication in 1934 is difficult to adequately express. Within a year, the book was eliciting responses from America, Greece, Shanghai, and Britain from the unlikely admirers Ezra Pound, T.S. Eliot, George Orwell, Edmund Wilson, and Herbert Read, all of whom publicly supported Miller's prohibited work. This overnight fame made Miller a desirable contact for correspondents, as did his stylistic innovations, and his letters are prolific. A difficulty in charting distribution of his works lies in their banned status and the frequently covert methods of distribution, but the readily available nature of the book reported by Miller's correspondents demonstrates its widespread notoriety.[1]

Miller's background, moreover, has not garnered the same critical attention in much of the extant scholarship, mainstream or otherwise. His ties to the International Workers of the World, his connection with Emma Goldman, and his repeatedly expressed anarchism are not taken up as one would expect. Nor has *Tropic of Cancer* been read through such a perspective in the mainstream of literary criticism. In contrast, Miller is largely regarded as apolitical and out of touch with his contemporary circumstances. Apart from Miller's own repeated statements of preference for the "anarchic," his correspondent Wallace Fowlie notes,

> He has always been the pure singer of individual freedom who was a-political because he believed that to give up a capitalistic regime for a socialistic regime was simply to change masters. His personal creed may be attached in part to the European utopia of the noble savage, and in part to the American tradition of return to nature we read in Thoreau and Whitman. His sense of anarchy is partly that of Thoreau and partly that of the Beat Generation. (Fowlie 16)

To this a great number of additions could be made, ranging from Miller himself to his milieu and his activities.

Nevertheless, when the combination of Miller's Paris home and his quasi-surrealist passages in the novel are considered, it is little surprise that he would be an early contact for the English authors involved with the 1936 London International Surrealist Exhibition. Miller was already in correspondence with Herbert Read, who had been given *Tropic of Cancer* by T.S. Eliot, and he was joined in Paris in 1937 by the very young David Gascoyne, whose *A Short Survey of Surrealism* had drawn much English attention in 1935. According to Gascoyne,

> Connolly told Miller I was a young English Surrealist; Miller sent me a proof copy of "Open Letter to Surrealists Everywhere"; and when in the late summer of 1937, having settled into a Paris garret, I went to see Miller in his Villa Seurat atelier, he at once introduced me to the twenty-five-year-old Durrell, just back from Corfu....Within a month, Durrell had allowed me to read a typed copy of *The Black Book*....I tried to tell him how much... [he] had helped me realize that it was exactly from what in his book he termed the English Death that I was then struggling to free myself. ("Fellow" 4)

The impact on Gascoyne of this meeting, after the 1936 Surrealist exhibition and outside of England, is clear just as much as it has been invisible to regionalist criticism focused on London events and developments. Miller had also been in correspondence with Dylan Thomas and was publishing Thomas's surrealist works.

The London International Surrealist Exhibition of 1936 garnered much attention, but it had as much humour and silliness as it had serious intentions. Herbert Read was the critical voice of the moment, giving the primary lecture on "Art and the Unconscious" as well as other ancillary talks and creating a print afterlife for the event through his volume *Surrealism*. In contrast, Dylan Thomas famously offered visitors boiled string and Gascoyne had to rescue Salvador Dalí from suffocating inside a copper-hat diving helmet during his lecture, which were less influential contributions. While English Surrealists continued to be active, the critical consensus was that it died as

a movement very shortly after the 1936 exhibition when it failed
to integrate into the political climate, as Hynes (219) has argued.
Nonetheless, the coterie of writings continued to be active and continued to integrate surrealist metaphor and concepts into their writing, even as they increasingly abandoned the communist affiliations
of the French Surrealists. Most indicative of this general trend was
Herbert Read, whose "The Necessity of Anarchism" appeared across
three issues of the *Adelphi* in the very next year, which put to rest his
short-lived conciliatory tone toward the Communist Party.

In any case, this surrealist impulse across the channel increased
Miller's cache as a correspondent and garnered increasing interest
from those who had participated, eventually leading to an egoic form
of post-Surrealism that displaced pure psychic automatism with
conscious shaping. Gascoyne's timeline for revised attitudes is typical
and worth outlining as an example. As has already been noted briefly,
in 1935, his surrealist manifesto was predicated on a series of enum-
erated communist principles entailing "complete agreement[,]...
complete adherence...[and] complete and unrelenting opposition"
in line with the communist views on the Spanish Civil War and
Surrealism's communist stance (Ray 87). The complete and unrelenting opposition most specifically includes "anarchic individualism"
and "religious fidelism [fideism]" (Ray 87), both of which Gascoyne
subsequently endorsed emphatically after this contact with Miller and
Durrell.

By September 19, 1936, when he reviewed *Tropic of Cancer*, he was
hesitating by expressing deep admiration for Miller mixed with his
reproach: "Miller's chief weakness is perhaps his complete indiffer-
ence to politics, to anything resembling an objective view of society"
(Gascoyne, "Henry" 288). To expand on this previously noted stance,
by September 1937, his journal records "Ambivalence of my attitude
towards Breton" (*Paris* 20), and by November 1937, his "Blind Man's
Buff" in Miller's journal *The Booster* could start to satirically question
communist affiliations openly, in exact coincidence with Read's anarchist *Adelphi* articles:

> What sort of consolation for the horror of existence could there
> be in *any* form of society?

> The Communist (no doubt)—"Your argument is that of a
> neurasthenic bourgeois."...
>
> With happily smiling faces the Communist League of Youth
> marches past in the Red Square, the People's Leader smilingly
> returns their gay salute. Everything is for the best in the best of
> all possible worlds. (Gascoyne, "Blind" 36)

The echo of Voltaire's *Candide* makes clear his satire of communism
just after his time in Spain while reading the works of and interacting
with the Villa Seurat writers. Shortly thereafter, Gascoyne was living
in Paris, interacting with Durrell and Miller, frequently visiting Villa
Seurat, and, by the end of the year, he was deeply affected by reading
Durrell's *The Black Book* in typescript as well as Miller's anarchist "An
Open Letter to Surrealists Everywhere," after which he "tended to
identify [him]self more and more with what Durrell had expressed"
("Fellow" 4). This was Gascoyne's moment of transformation after
his disillusioned departure from Spain, and it occurred in the Villa
Seurat context.[2] Derek Stanford, who did not know Gascoyne until 1938, assumes this transformation in his discussions of the poet,
writing, "Gascoyne has both a communal and individual meaning;
a double value, which makes it an exception" (*Freedom* 40). Stanford
becomes even more direct in refuting Gascoyne's earlier communist
views (and actions), which leads him to contend, "While many of
the older poets of the 'thirties were busy squaring their imaginative
sense with the partisan tenets of Lenin and Marx, Gascoyne succeed-
ed in keeping both his poetry and politics free....His affinities were
probably more with *The Soul of Man under Socialism* than the party-man's
Bible *Das Kapital*" (*Freedom* 42–43). As Stanford sums up in the closing
comment, the anarchist background of Oscar Wilde's essay implies a
definite politics for Gascoyne: "Gascoyne has maintained his non-
party approach" (68).[3]

Although less is known of Bernard Spencer's political conversion,
he was among the closest to the Auden group, having co-edited
Oxford Poetry with Stephen Spender after knowing Louis MacNeice at
Marlborough College. However, this was before his turn away from
the group during his growing friendship with Lawrence Durrell in
Greece and then Egypt during the war, all following the 1936 London

International Surrealist Exhibition. As Mark Ford notes, Spencer's poetry in

> Oxford Poetry in 1931…reveals…how very quickly Auden, whose first commercial book, Poems, appeared only the year before, had transformed the concept and language of poetry for his contemporaries. Spencer's early efforts are mainly in this mode. A short but telling note that he wrote for the November 1937 Auden special issue of New Verse (where he was working as an editorial assistant to Geoffrey Grigson, and where most of his own early work appeared) implies that as the 1930s progressed Spencer slowly came to realise that Auden was not the charismatic leader whose example he should follow, but his poetic antithesis: "He succeeds," the note concludes, "in brutalising his thought and language to the level from which important poetry proceeds." (23)

The rationale for Spencer's transformation is not known, but in less than two years he would be in Athens working beside Durrell and then co-founding a poetry journal with him in Egypt that espoused a distinctly anti-authoritarian vision of poetry, poets, and the function of literature in society. In all three aspects, it would be the antithesis of the Auden generation, and especially so in its ties to Egyptian anarchists and distribution to wartime anarchist poetry groups in England and America.

During this same time in the middle of the 1930s, the greatest impact on Miller through a correspondent came from Lawrence Durrell, who wrote to Miller after reading Tropic of Cancer in 1935. Their letters continued for another forty-five years, and Durrell made two trips to Paris from his home in Greece to visit Miller before the Second World War. Durrell had begun to experiment with surrealist prose, and his "Asylum in the Snow" and The Black Book (both shaped by his contact with Miller) can be seen as among the most successful post-surrealist prose works in English at the time. During Durrell's residencies in Paris, he and Gascoyne became fast friends, and Gascoyne frequently caged meals from the Durrells while reconsidering his previous communist sensibilities. Durrell, at this moment, was openly mocking

communist sensibilities in English letters while idealizing the cultivation of the individual—all while his contemporaries flocked to Spain
with Durrell watching from Corfu. The Spanish scenario and revolutionary activity are mocked in the opening of his pseudonymously
published 1937 novel *Panic Spring*, despite the book's anti-capitalist
and anti-classist argument for social- and self-transformation, which
marks his quietism and pacifism. When Miller came to Greece to visit
Durrell, these surrealist connections broadened further through contact with George Seferis and the historical roots of Greek Modernism
in ties to Paris, including Surrealism (Kayalis 97).

By September 1937, Miller, Durrell, and Alfred Perlès had begun
the periodical *The Booster*, which was actually Perlès's takeover of the
journal of the American Country Club of France (beginning as *The
Booster* for vol. 3, no. 7). While retaining the advertising contents
and revenues of the American Country Club of France—for golf
balls, Imperial Airways, United States Lines, and a variety of alcohols,
candies, and local Parisian shops—the Villa Seurat group quickly set
up a literary journal with high aspirations. In the first four months,
before the American Country Club of France threatened various
actions if the group did not disband, they had already published
excerpts from Durrell's third novel *The Black Book*, Miller's *Tropic of
Capricorn*, and various works by Perlès, Anaïs Nin, Mulk Raj Anand (in
Urdu), Milada Součková (translated into French from Czech), William
Saroyan, and David Gascoyne's first dissent from communism in
excerpts from his notebooks. As Perlès notes, the club thought "it
was highly immoral and dangerously anarchic" (*My Friend* 139), and he
repeats the "anarchic" description of Miller and the Villa Seurat's activities.[4] All this with the advertising adjacent to each piece could not
last, and after four issues, *The Booster* rolled over to Durrell's editorship
and became *Delta* (from London, Paris, and Corfu).

Under the *Booster* heading, the journal also attracted the attention
of George Orwell, despite its only four-month run. In *The New English
Weekly* on October 21, 1937, Orwell condemned the politics of *The
Booster* as a return to the 1920s and as "supreme futility…unutterably
meaningless and stupid…a safe and feeble way of hitting back at
Hitler, Stalin, Lord Rothermere [Harold Harmsworth], etc" ("Back"
30). Barely ten month previous, Orwell had travelled to Spain wearing

Henry Miller's overcoat while volunteering to fight in the Spanish Civil War. Miller had told Orwell that to volunteer for a war was "stupid," and to go without a coat could not have helped. As Miller would comment years later in an interview for the *Paris Review*, while discussing Orwell and political idealism, when asked, "You don't have much use for politics?" he answered, "None whatever. I regard politics as a thoroughly foul, rotten world. We get nowhere through politics. It debases everything" (Miller, *Conversations* 56). This comment, in tandem with Orwell's unintended combination of Stalin and Hitler, shows Miller's true intention, which was the undermining of political authority in general, not only of a fascist or communist variety. The precise objection Orwell makes, although not as overtly as elsewhere, is the same he raised repeatedly during the war with those later influenced by Miller, the anarchists George Woodcock and Alex Comfort. That is, during a time of war with Nazi Germany, anarchism was not a viable option for Orwell. It was "unutterably meaningless and stupid" ("Back" 20). Orwell inadvertently touches on the real matter when he notes, "The only definitely comic feature in the magazine is the advertisements....The entire tribe of Paris-American snob-shops...seem to have been caught hopping" (30), and three weeks later, sensing his unsympathetic stance, he recommended that Hugh Gordon Porteus review the second issue of *The Booster*. Porteus had greater sympathy for and ties to the English Surrealists, as seen in his positive reviews of Miller's *Tropic of Cancer* (from 1934) and Durrell's *The Black Book* (from 1938).[5] In any case, Orwell softened in time to allot praise to the same works in his seminal essay *Inside the Whale*, but even in this instance he applies the term "defeatist" to Miller's quietism (126), which he still regarded as the same "gesture of supreme futility."[6] Durrell's lengthy discussion of quietism in his second novel *Panic Spring* (from 1937) is also tied to pacifism and to his rebuttal of Orwell's borrowings from his own 1935 novel *Pied Piper of Lovers* for Orwell's 1936 novel *Keep the Aspidistra Flying* (Gifford, Preface ix).[7] While that particular debate could be extended, the essential matter is that Orwell had understood the position taken by Miller and by the periodical, even if he unfairly mocks it without acknowledging it openly. Most readers, however, did not understand the politics of the unpolitical, which prevented them from engaging with it or disagreeing with it, as Orwell did.

This disputation by Orwell, which received a spirited response from Durrell and yet another from Orwell (Durrell and Orwell having swapped materials in their early novels as well) makes one return attention to the contents of those first four months of The Booster and the authors involved. Saroyan (who along with Miller later had a profound influence on the young Jack Kerouac) is famous for writing, "The writer is a spiritual anarchist, as in the depth of his soul every man is" (145); Anand has significant anarchist sympathies and published in the anarchist press, despite his wife's deep Marxist ties; Součková expresses sympathies for anarchism and is associated with it repeatedly; Perlès is most assuredly oriented to self-preservation but is tied to anarchist ideals by several critics and identifies as an anarchist in his own works[8] (Perlès, Round 115–19), and Miller is a self-described anarchist. Of the other major contributors, Durrell was notoriously obscure in his politics,[9] and Gascoyne was in the midst of radical change. If reread from this perspective, The Booster may be disagreeable to Orwell, but the reasons for disagreement radically alter our interpretation of its contents and function as well as the influence it bore on the participants in its endeavours.

In this immediate context, and five months after having rebutted Orwell in print, Durrell relaunched the endeavour as Delta with the stated editorial proviso, "The change [in title] merely marks a voluntary break with an ambience which never was ours. It neither means a change of heart nor even one of attitude" (n. pag.). The restrictive "which" is characteristically Durrell's rather than Miller's or Perlès's, as is "attitude." The issue also opens with a full-page advertisement (unpaid) for the American anarchist, pacifist journal Phoenix published by James Cooney with help from Robert Duncan, with both of whom Miller was in correspondence. Delta immediately became more aligned toward poetry and began to draw on the English post-Surrealists to a much higher degree, in particular those with whom Durrell had closer contact such as Antonia White (the close friend to Djuna Barnes), Gascoyne, Dylan Thomas, and Nicholas Moore. Moore then began to publish Durrell, Miller, and Nin the following summer in his first issue of the Cambridge-based post-surrealist journal *Seven*. Other contributions were dominated by Durrell's close colleagues in Greece and London: John Gawsworth, Theodore Stephanides, and Patrick Evans.

Delta went on to cement a relationship between the fragmented English Surrealists, the Villa Seurat group, and Durrell's circle of Greek modernists as well as those who would become the primary publishers and editors of the resurgence of English post-Surrealism: the New Apocalypse. By the time *Delta* saw its final issue for Easter 1939, co-edited between Durrell and Gascoyne and published by John Goodland in Cambridge, it featured an advertised list of authors who would become the energetic promoters of the personalist groups described in the rest of this chapter: Tambimuttu's first poetry appearance prior to his *Poetry London*; Howarth, whose "Deannarchist" appeared at the same time in John Waller's Oxford journal *Bolero*; Gascoyne himself; Dylan Thomas whose influence over the anti- and post-Auden generation of English writers was deep, and in America as well; Dorian Cooke,[10] with whom Durrell would become acquainted more closely through the *Personal Landscape* group in Egypt; Elizabeth Smart, who would bridge Canadian, British, and American avant-gardes during the war years, and so forth. At the same time across 1938 and 1939, *Delta* advertised the burgeoning New Apocalypse group prior to its public launch by promoting the various involved authors' contributions to *Seven*. This was no great surprise since the third and final issue of *Delta* revised its mailing address at the Villa Seurat in Paris to the same London address used by John Goodland for *Seven*, and Goodland became the publisher for the single issue. Moreover, as Dylan Thomas casually notes, he, Durrell, Miller, and Goodland enjoyed lunch together in London, which cements their contact with each other (Thomas, *Collected Letters* 350).

In miniature, we find *The Booster* and *Delta* (as a single journal) prefiguring the post-Auden literary movements that would prove to be among the most dynamic literary coteries during the war years. Perhaps most importantly, their close relations and interconnected natures are also laid bare in the Villa Seurat periodicals and correspondences in a way that does not otherwise become visible.

Prior to the war's arrival in France, Miller left for Greece to visit Durrell, from whence he fled at the end of 1939 to return to America. Durrell was ultimately relocated from Corfu to Athens where he assisted in the production and dissemination of anti-fascist materials until replaced by the formal British representatives, including Robert Liddell, with whom he would share a long friendship and love for the Greek poet C.P. Cavafy. As Athens fell to the Nazis, Durrell fled from his new base in Kalamata where he represented the British Council. He left as a refugee by caïque to Crete and from thence to Alexandria and Cairo, as did the contributors to the Villa Seurat, Theodore Stephanides and George Seferis. Stephanides recounts his military service at this moment in his memoir *Climax in Crete*.[11]

Looking back across *The Booster* and *Delta* as well as the correspondence networks that made them possible, the revisions to received literary histories that stand out most prominently are the political revisions to English Surrealism and central meeting point these periodical provided to American, British, and European-cum-North African anti-authoritarian literary groups. The English post-surrealist movement, which is typically seen as abandoned, was continuing to be published in Paris until mid-1939 in a manner that aligned with Henry Miller's critique of Surrealism's communist politics as authoritarian: a new egoic post-Surrealism. This group, however, could not continue to maintain a centre in Paris beyond late 1938, and most certainly not through 1939. Miller had left for Greece under the fear of war, Perlès and Nin were preparing their departures, and travel for Durrell was becoming increasingly limited as was his continued residence on Corfu near to Albania and the pending invasions. Nevertheless, the web of interactions initially strung through the Villa Seurat continued in a decentralized anarchist fashion with no definite centre yet maintaining robust engagements and mutual aid. By the time the New Apocalypse rose in London, the various participants in the Villa Seurat publishing ventures had been spread to South Africa, Egypt, Japan, London, New York, and San Francisco. That various new movements should emerge is to be expected—that they would maintain a dense interaction for more than a decade via the channels built in the Villa Seurat is remarkable.

From Old Surrealism to the New Oxbridge: Apocalypse and Romantics

After the London International Surrealist Exhibition, the communist group of English Surrealists proceeded to collapse in the manner outlined by Samuel Hynes (219) with regard to Grigson's *Contemporary Poetry and Prose* periodical, which did not survive beyond 1937. This gives no particular surprise, except that the previous section of this chapter shows that the same network of authors continued with much activity in Paris through the Villa Seurat's *The Booster* and *Delta* throughout the same period immediate following the collapse of *Contemporary Poetry and Prose*. However, after the two years of Surrealism's demise in England, the Auden generation's flagship journal, *Oxford Poetry*, collapsed as well and was replaced by John Waller's *Bolero*. The journal opens with a modest manifesto-cum-editorial from Waller. After his opening dismissal of Grigson, Waller contends,

> The poet of to-day, if he is to be of any future significance, must come down to earth. Present day scenery is made up of factory chimneys, slums, cinema houses, advertisement hoardings, and dance halls. It is a world in which people work in mines, are a cog in the machinery of mass-production, take a holiday to watch football, go to the seaside for a week-end, and snatch the greater part of their education from the news-papers. (Waller, "Editorial" n. pag.)

Furthermore, the post-surrealist component of the journal might go unnoticed were it not for Herbert Howarth's article "Deannarchist" (n. pag.), which appears in the early pages of the first issue and humorously emphasizes the same anarcho-anti-authoritarian impulse noted in the above discussion of the Villa Seurat, through which he published poetry at the same time.[12] Howarth would then appear in all issues of *Bolero*, and subsequently go on to serve in Egypt with Durrell and Spencer, contribute to the kindred periodicals there as well, and translate Arabic poetry before becoming a quiet professor and writing the scholarly book for which he is now best known, *Notes on Some Figures Behind T.S. Eliot*, in 1964.[13]

Bolero began in the summer of 1938 to replace *Oxford Poetry*, and it lasted until the spring of 1939, at which point it was replaced on November 17, 1939 by *Kingdom Come: The Magazine of War-time Oxford*, again under Waller's editorship until his own relocation to Egypt where he too began to interact with Durrell (and brought copies of *Kingdom Come* with him) through their mutual friend Howarth, who had relocated to Cairo for a teaching position at King Fuad University.[14] When Nicholas Moore, Kay Boyle, and Howarth appear in the journal, it is in parallel to their ties to the Villa Seurat and previous publications in the associated periodicals. At the same time, Moore and John Goodland, with much material sent from the Villa Seurat, were beginning in the same summer of 1938 the journal *Seven* at the University of Cambridge, where Moore's father G.E. Moore taught philosophy. The first authors of the first issue were D.S. Savage and Henry Miller, both anarchists and both pacifists (as was Moore). Although it was little known until the discovery of Goodland's papers, Goodland was far more than a financial backer and had a significant role in the conceptual structure of *Seven*, and his interests in both Miller and anarchism at this period were sizeable, as demonstrated in his personal journals and his financial and administrative backing of *Delta*. Dylan Thomas also establishes the direct link between Goodland, Durrell, and Miller (Thomas, *Collected Letters* 350), and Moore was deeply interested in Miller's works and published a book on Miller during the war through the pacifist Denys Val Baker, though Moore's contact was initially through Durrell (*Durrell–Miller* 106, 161). Miller had also already discussed publishing his book on D.H. Lawrence with Baker, and this same interest fostered Miller's first contacts with James Cooney and Robert Duncan in Woodstock, who were producing the D.H. Lawrence-oriented anarchist journal *Phoenix*. Of the two British periodicals, *Kingdom Come* had the greatest longevity and *Seven* the greatest daring. Both supported the work begun in the Villa Seurat and its egoic form of Surrealism: *Kingdom Come* more indirectly and *Seven* quite overtly. Both are also clearly inheritors of the surrealist impulse begun in *Contemporary Poetry and Prose*, though it underwent a significant transformation via the Villa Seurat's anarchist influence. The remarkable transformation, however, is that the central poets of *Kingdom Come* were relocated by the war to Cairo and Alexandria, where they worked with

Durrell directly and the periodicals with which he was involved. In this manner, Seven most overtly showed influence while Kingdom Come perpetuated the directional flow of talent prior to the war. The journal's editor John Waller, the prolific contributors G.S. Fraser and Keith Douglas,[15] and the first contributor to refer to anarchism, Herbert Howarth (in Bolero), were all sent to North Africa, and all became involved in Lawrence Durrell's Personal Landscape journal, which he edited in tandem with the pacifist Robin Fedden and the previous editor of Oxford Poetry and Auden group defector, Bernard Spencer.

Seven and Kingdom Come present a legitimate avant-garde in English society after Auden, yet they receive virtually no attention in the critical literature. In many respects, this is startling. Kingdom Come takes on the most overt anarchist affiliations through Savage, Woodcock, and Read while advertising (without fee) other anarchist poetry magazines such as Woodcock's NOW. As the war years begin, Kingdom Come increasingly includes Gascoyne, Anne Ridler, and Henry Treece, the authors previously tied to the Villa Seurat and to Cambridge's Seven, the more overtly post-surrealist journal. As Seven folded, its authors immediately began to appear in Kingdom Come, just as the remaining materials from Delta had been folded into Seven earlier, almost certainly based on the friendship among the editors and their shared work producing the issues. Perhaps symptomatically, Waller begins the winter 1940–1941 issue of Kingdom Come by arguing, "For the individual as distinct from the mass, to take part in warfare is both tedious and embarrassing" (Waller, "Hell" 35). Yet, Waller's concern is primarily that of the autonomous self, and by the end of his winter 1940–41 issue, his editorial could close with the deeply anarchic (though again not self-implicating) statement, "the real start comes with a knowledge of the world and of the self....Hell is·where one starts from; selfhood is eventually achieved" (36). This vision of the self should bring no surprises; nor should it seem remarkable in association with the Villa Seurat. Its genealogy is also unmistakable.

At the same time, in another Oxford publication, we find the culmination of Gascoyne's move away from his support of communism, which had led him to travel to the Spanish Civil War, followed by his disillusioned departure. Contrary to his past critiques of Henry Miller for failing to support communist aims (during his period of closest contact with the French Surrealists), Gascoyne aligned himself with the Villa Seurat in 1937 through 1939, and by 1942 his "The Uncertain Battle" takes on a decidedly pacifist vision. After the militaristic imagery of "steel-blue lightning" and "the startled sound / Of trumpets," Gascoyne moves to "that pit / Of silence which lies waiting to consume / Even the braggart World itself" and leaving only a lonely (and neutral) hermit to report, "No-one ever came / Back down the hill, to say which side had lost" (Gascoyne, "Uncertain" 18). For Gascoyne to aim this work to *Poems of this War by Younger Poets* is notable, particularly given his work's refusal to take side or glorify the battle.

Of these new periodicals to appear in England under the Villa Seurat's influence, *Seven* was the first and was released in 1938, shortly after *Delta* had taken over from *The Booster*. Moreover, the interactions between *Seven* and *Delta* went significantly beyond mutual advertising. *Seven* was distributed through Jack Kahane's Obelisk Press in Paris, Durrell, Miller, and Nin's publisher at the time, and all three were included in the first issue of the journal. The same issue includes an excerpt, "Ego" (22–25), from Durrell's Obelisk Press novel, *The Black Book*, which was in the midst of being released at the time. Perlès, Nin, and Kay Boyle then appear in the second issue, and Durrell and Miller again (more than once) in the third. When it ceased production in the spring of 1940 with its eighth issue, not one issue had failed to include authors previously published in *The Booster* and *Delta* with at least one of the Villa Seurat writers themselves appearing in all but two issues, both of which contained authors only accessible via the Villa Seurat. Gerald Durrell, Lawrence Durrell's precocious younger brother, contributed a poem to the fifth issue (mistakenly numbered "4" on its contents page), and Durrell's friend in Athens, George Seferis, contributed poetry to the seventh issue. Gascoyne also published several poems from Paris across *Seven*'s print run, all after his post-Spain transformation and disillusionment with communism following his interactions with Durrell and Miller in Paris in 1937 through 1939. This influence reappears four years later in Nicholas Moore's slim book on Henry Miller through Opus Press, which dedicates an entire chapter to *The Booster* and *Delta* (21–28), both of which he had clearly read very closely. His opening quotation from Nin is taken from *The Booster* (6), he emphasizes "Lawrence Durrell's great novel, THE BLACK BOOK" (23) as found in *The Booster*, and takes up Miller's use of Graham Howe's notion of the "Whole Man" (Moore 25). Howe was already tied to the New Apocalypse group, which had invited him to discuss their anarchist vision in relation to his own ideas of psychotherapy. More to the point, Moore's vision of Miller and the Villa Seurat as a whole is specifically oriented toward its anti-authoritarian quietist vision, which marks how the English would have read these works. Moore's quotations from Miller include, "man has got to learn the doctrine of acceptance, that is, unconditional surrender, which is love" and "It is not only the 'dictators' who are *possessed*, but the whole world of men everywhere; we are in the grip of demonic forces....To act intuitively one must obey the deeper law of love, which is based on tolerance, the law which suffers or permits things to be as they are" (Moore 25). Moore's presentation of Miller critiques Agamemnon's warlike drive against peace in *The Colossus of Maroussi* (Moore 14–15) and extols pacifism in *Murder the Murder* in unequivocal terms that set the individual against the state. Miller repeats these ideas in the interview that Moore includes in the book:

> I refuse to go to war, whether for a just or an unjust cause. If that means being killed by the government advocating war, then I am willing to be killed. It is possible that I might murder a man in anger; that would be an individual act for which I would assume full responsibility. Governments may go to war; individuals are not obliged to unless they choose....To kill or not to kill, to defend oneself or not to defend oneself, are questions which each individual has to answer for himself. (Moore 32)

Moore's Miller, then, is very much a model for the personalist movement of which he was a part, and Moore's publications in *The Booster* and *Delta*, as well as his publication of the Villa Seurat authors in *Seven* and later as printer to *New Roads*, marks the bond he saw between the groups: a shared anti-authoritarian vision and manner of understanding the literary works of the Villa Seurat authors.

These Oxbridge journals, however, do not simply situate themselves in a position of influence from Paris, through which they received a revised notion of English post-Surrealism preserved from the London of a few years earlier. They also became an influence themselves, repeating this revised vision of an anti-authoritarian post-Surrealism back to London culture and to literary figures of their generation across the United Kingdom. Those who would become involved in the subsequent New Apocalypse movement (and its later New Romanticism and personalist revisions) began to publish in *Bolero*'s revivification as *Kingdom Come*. In the spring of 1939, *Bolero* closed with a review of the Marxist Christopher Caudwell's *Studies in a Dying Culture*, to which J.F. Hendry would respond four years later. Alec Darbyshire's review, which professes his own Marxism, takes up the same problem of Freedom and the bourgeois false consciousness of Liberty from Caudwell to which Hendry would later return. Hence, when Hendry turns his pen on Caudwell's chapter "Liberty: A Study in Bourgeois Illusion" to argue, "Freedom is an illusion, yes; but not 'the bourgeois' illusion" ("Art" 146), he is doing so in the shadow of Darbyshire's comments on the same chapter. Hendry had already contributed to *Kingdom Come* by November 1941 when its editorship was passed from Waller to Alan Rook, Stefan Schimanski, and Henry Treece, the latter two of whom would return the editorial focus to materials from Anand, Read, and Miller in the final three issues. When *Kingdom Come* was ended in autumn 1943, it was immediately re-placed by Schimanski and Treece's new periodical (published in book form to circumvent paper shortage restrictions), *Transformation*, which continued to draw on the same authors and cement the group's anar-chist affiliations.

The first volume of *Transformation* was printed by Victor Gollancz in 1943. Treece had already been recruited to the Royal Air Force by this time but he and Schimanski still list their editorship of *Kingdom Come*, even though it would not produce another issue. However, this first issue also closes a narrative loop. When Henry Miller first chided Herbert Read in October/November 1935 over sympathies with the Surrealists' communism and then rebutted Read's communist lectures at the 1936 London International Surrealist Exhibition in an October 16, 1936 letter, it began the chain of influences that led to Durrell's *The Black Book*, Miller's "An Open Letter to Surrealists Everywhere" that asserted an anarcho-Surrealist vision, and to *The Booster* and *Delta*.

From these journals, other writers developed interests that shaped
Seven, *Bolero*, and *Kingdom Come*, which directly spawned *Transformation*.
Transformation begins its editorial, "Towards a Personalist Attitude:
Introduction," by stating, "we here wish to assert our belief in the
individual man." It then reconstructs Caudwell in line with Hendry's
vision in order to state Treece and Schimanksi's anarchist vision:

> Because we conceive a new type of being emerging with
> new values and acts out of a dying culture, our Personalist
> belief rejects all politics which do not grow, organically, from
> living...; where lust for power and security have separated
> man from man, have disembodied the spirit, have disrupted
> the community and have made freedom the perquisite of the
> leisured few.
>
> Similarly, it rejects those fascist systems which control the
> defects of society by curtailing the liberty of the individual,
> which subordinate the destinies of men to the whims of a
> Leader..., which denies them from their Selves....Personalism
> rejects all forms of government which ignore spiritual values,
> which do not see in man an autonomously creative unit whose
> supreme vocation is the understanding and healing of the Self.
> (Treece and Schimanski, "Towards" 13)

If there could be any doubt as to the anti-authoritarian, anarchist
philosophy espoused by Schimanski and Treece as the heritage of
these various journals that led to *Transformation*, it is swept away by
the first text included in the issue: Herbert Read's classic anarchist
essay "The Politics of the Unpolitical," which appeared as the titular
essay in his book of the same year. Six years after his first public
declaration for anarchism, there was no mistaking Read's stance nor
that of *Transformation* and the group it represented as "personalist" for
the first time. Nor can one mistake its line of descent from Miller
and Read's correspondence across the 1930s.

Treece and Hendry had both begun to appear in *Seven* in the third
issue, during the winter of 1938. Hendry's "The Eye in the Triangle" is
a socially minded critique of war set in Ljubljana, and Treece's "Dylan
Thomas and the Surrealists" begins through reference to Gascoyne's

A Short Survey of Surrealism and Read's *Art Now*. Treece's essay follows after two poems by Thomas and Henry Miller's "Peace! It's Wonderful!" The challenge for Treece would have been that Thomas's more overtly surrealist work "Prologue to an Adventure" was appearing at the same time, in the same winter, in the second issue of *Delta* in Paris through the Villa Seurat, with its shifting notions of post-Surrealism, and Gascoyne, whom he was quoting, was doing the same. Nicholas Moore, who published *Seven*, was also appearing in *Delta* at the same time, and the back cover of the issue bespoke the connection between the two journals with the otherwise unexplained exhortation, "Peace! It's Wonderful!" in reference to Miller's article in the other journal.

By 1938, Treece, Fraser, and Hendry had formed the New Apocalypse, which blended anarchism and Surrealism through Herbert Read's influence and their adoption of the surrealist literary experiments developed by Dylan Thomas and the other continuingly active English-language Surrealists like David Gascoyne, Lawrence Durrell, and Henry Miller, all of whom were in close contact with each other. In addition to Fraser's close contact with Durrell after being moved to Egypt during the war and Treece's frequent references to Miller, Stanford demonstrates the deep reading that continued in London from the Villa Seurat through to the *Personal Landscape* journal being produced in Egypt in the 1940s.[16] Thomas was the most apart from the New Apocalypse and was also the most overt influence on Treece and Hendry, but he was reading and meeting with Durrell, Miller, and Gascoyne more than is acknowledged in his biographies.[17] Treece and Hendry, at the same time, were reading Miller and Durrell while forming their movement with other poets who were doing the same.

By 1939, Cooke edited the first Apocalypse anthology, *The New Apocalypse: An Anthology of Criticism, Poems and Stories*. Cooke had already appeared in *Delta*, *Seven*, and *Kingdom Come*, and he would go on to appear in virtually all of the other periodicals listed in this chapter. The second anthology in 1941, *The White Horseman*, was edited by Hendry and Treece themselves, but opened with a manifesto essay written by G.S. Fraser, who, like Cooke, had and would appear in virtually all of these publications. Fraser's essay, "Apocalypse in Poetry," clearly sets out the movement's influences and revisions, both of which align with those already initiated by the Villa Seurat and brought back to England by the journals from which the New Apocalypse formed itself.

Such derivations from the Villa Seurat are a trend. Thomas contributed the short story "The Burning Baby" and a poem to Cooke's *The New Apocalypse* in 1939, a prose text he had initially intended for publication through the Villa Seurat in Paris. Just as Villa Seurat authors appeared in the rising English publications, the materials Paris could not publish under its various constraints were refunded back into print through *Seven*, *Kingdom Come*, and the Apocalypse anthologies, even from the Apocalypse's great influence, Thomas.

Thomas's letter of June 16, 1938 to George Reavey points to his connections with Durrell and Miller, whom he met in person in December 1937 in London:

> The only story I can think of which might cause a few people a small and really unnecessary alarm is "The Prologue to an Adventure." This I could cut from the book [*The Burning Baby: 16 Stories*]....Publication first in Paris seems very sensible...I am pretty confidant that, through Durrell and Miller, [the Obelisk Press] would publish the book. (Fitzgibbon, *Life of Dylan* 237)

The book never came to fruition in this form, but "Prologue to an Adventure" was republished in Paris six months later in *Delta*, under Durrell's editorship. I have elsewhere discussed the textual variant of Thomas's surrealist story "Prologue to an Adventure," which Thomas corrected and amended for the *Delta* publication, though only the earlier variant from *Wales* is included in Thomas's collected works (Gifford, "Durrell's *Delta*" 19–23). Based on the revisions made by Thomas, it is safe to argue the significance of the friendship between Thomas, Durrell, and Miller had solidified. Thomas wrote to Durrell in 1937 that he had already given Henry Miller "two prose pieces" ("Letters" 3) for *The Booster*, which later became the *Delta*. Significantly, the date of Thomas's statement is misconstrued by at least a year in Constantine Fitzgibbon's *Selected Letters of Dylan Thomas* (210), but a comparison between Durrell's statement that the letter "followed upon our first meeting" (Thomas, "Letters" 1) and his contention that this was concomitant with his appointment with Anne Wickham in 1937

("Shades" 56) places the date securely in December 1937. Moreover, this places Thomas's submission of two stories ("Prologue to an Adventure" and "The Burning Baby") to some time prior to his meeting both Durrell and Miller in London in December of the same year. This is further supported by Miller's direct comparison of Durrell's "Asylum in the Snow" to Thomas's prose work (MacNiven, *Lawrence Durrell* 39), which suggests Miller had read Thomas's submissions at some point prior to January 3, 1937, likely much earlier.

Furthermore, Durrell writes on November 5, 1938, "A letter from Dylan Thomas—I like him more and more" (MacNiven, *Lawrence Durrell* 107), which decisively precludes the possibility of their first exchange occurring a month later in December of the same year, as Fitzgibbon dates it. This also troubles the implication in Paul Ferris's work that this first meeting occurred in January 1939 (*Dylan* 167), when he is most likely referring to the later meeting described by Durrell in "Shades of Dylan Thomas." A basis for this connection develops—Thomas refers to Durrell's *The Black Book* repeatedly as a shocking influence in his letters, much like Gascoyne. Fitzgibbon remarks, "Dylan at this time admired Durrell's writing" (Fitzgibbon, *Life of Dylan* 210), while Durrell gives heavy praise to Thomas. Thomas also read Miller's *Tropic of Cancer* shortly after its publication and continued to acquire Miller's works in England, despite the risks of confiscation and prosecution. Jonanthan Fryer describes Ivy and Ebie Williams, proprietors of the Brown Hotel in Laugharne: "Dylan kept Ivy amused with his wicked imagination and he shared with her some of the juicier products of contemporary Anglo-American literature, such as Henry Miller's *Tropic of Capricorn*, which was published in Paris that year [1938]. Ivy kept that book hidden in the oven so her husband Ebie wouldn't find it" (107). In any case, the attachment between Thomas and the Villa Seurat is overlooked in the critical literature, and Thomas's recycling of influential materials from the Villa Seurat publications to the New Apocalypse gives evidence for the ongoing stream of influence and his sense of their connection.

To continue the derivations I must turn to G.S. Fraser's introductory essay for the second anthology, *The White Horseman*. Fraser makes the case, "The New Apocalypse, in a sense, derives from Surrealism....It denies what is negative—Surrealism's own denial of man's right to exercise conscious control, either of his political and social destinies, or of the material offered to him, as an artist, by his subconscious mind" ("Apocalypse" 3). This ordering of the surrealist impulse became a characteristic trait of the New Apocalypse, New Romantic, and personalist authors in England, and it is a revision to Surrealism deriving from the Villa Seurat group as well as Dylan Thomas's extensive rewriting process as a poet: rewriting and rethinking the surrealist metaphors he brought to his works and thereby bringing them under conscious control. The combination suggested by Miller was his recrafting of the products of "pure psychic automatism" according to conscious will. This was very much, as Fraser notes above, in tandem with his political vision in his letters to Read:

> I'd like to add another thing, about the business of war and revolutions. The courage to die for an ideal leaves me quite cold. We have been watching people die for ideals all throughout history. When will the poor bastards live for their ideals? Or live their ideals—which is still better, closer to what I mean. (Miller and Read 63–64; Miller, "Henry Miller's" 22)

The combination of consciously crafting surrealist metaphor, practising organicism, and refusing authority are a continual refrain. In this vein, Fraser notes "man's right to exercise conscious control, either of his political and social destinies, or of the material offered to him, as an artist, by his subconscious mind" (3). This leads him to cast the Apocalypse and its anarchist post-surrealist impulse as "a flexible philosophy; a philosophy which hardly dictates to anyone how he is to write or feel" (6).

Like Miller, Fraser extols both egoic Surrealism and pacifism. Although Fraser's own politics remain largely unstated, though he would much later simply call himself a liberal, he did align himself from 1937 until some time after World War II with the New Apocalypse and Villa Seurat. He would write for the New Apocalypse from Egypt,

> The Army is one of these things which Nicholas Moore, Henry Treece, and the New Apocalypse School generally, call with fear and hatred an *object-machine*.

Only, the army is not an *object-machine* in quite the same sense...: it is a machine made up of human beings...: the only defence against it which an organic human personality has, probably is to sham dead. And it is possible that it is this, quite against my conscious will and my conscious moral political beliefs, that my personality has been doing....We all want to live in freedom, because without freedom we can know no completeness. (Fraser, "Inside" 195–96)

The relations are complex among "freedom," "completeness," and living versus dying for one's beliefs, and the repudiation of French Surrealism's "denial of man's right to exercise conscious control, either of his political and social destinies" (Fraser, "Apocalypse" 3). However, the relations clearly exist for him and mean much for those involved.

In this frame of reference, Fraser looks back to the shaping influences these concepts bore on the New Apocalypse anthology *The White Horseman*, and he finds the same author whose works transformed Gascoyne's surrealist concepts. In his autobiography, *A Stranger and Afraid*, Fraser notes that the only materials he had read by Durrell at this point in time were his pieces in *Seven* and *The Black Book* (Fraser, *Stranger* 123), which directs attention to the post-surrealist short story "Asylum in the Snow" in *Seven* as the inspiration for his description of the Apocalypse's "flexible philosophy": "Durrell, more pessimistically, seems to say 'Look what sheer chaos I get when I give rein to all my impulses. I must find order, I must select, even though this leads neither to a coherent philosophy nor a real religion'" (Fraser, "Apocalypse" 7).[18] This is how Durrell's story, first published in the same issue of *Seven* as Treece's first essay on Thomas and Surrealism, is structured—the mad surrealist improvisations of the text finally resolve into the source of order, "the annihilating ego" (Durrell, "Asylum" 54), which becomes the author himself, consciously creating the surrealist text: an egoic post-Surrealism.

This problem of aesthetic order as the artistic practice worked upon the products of the unconscious is then a direct parallel to the problem of order in the world. For Fraser,

This problem of life and order suggests the more immediate theme of the relation of the movement to politics....The group exhibits, generally speaking, a rather ruthless scepticism about political thought. Thus J.F. Hendry has spoken of the possibility of members of the group taking part actively in politics, helping to found newer and smaller governing groups, with decentralized control, so as to permit "the greatest personal freedom and responsibility." ("Apocalypse" 7–8)

In this short span, Fraser has drawn from the Villa Seurat's contributions to English periodicals in order to return to the anarcho-surrealist vision debated between Read and Miller, Read having gone on to foster the New Apocalypse and publish through Routledge the volume in which Fraser's essay appears. Miller's response to the London International Surrealist Exhibition in 1936 led to his "An Open Letter to Surrealists Everywhere," which was in many respects a model for the Apocalyptic manifesto. It is far more difficult to chart the development of a series of influences and revisions cast among collaborators who freely come and go out of each other's lives than it is to detail a school with precepts, members, and even ostracized members. And Miller outlines precisely such a vision of artistic give and take in his anarchist revision to Surrealism:

> I am fatuous enough to believe that in living my own life in my own way I am more apt to give life to others (though even that is not my chief concern) than I would if I simply followed somebody else's idea of how to live my life and thus become a man among men. It seems to me that this struggle for liberty and justice is a confession or admission on the part of all those engaging in such a struggle that they have failed to live their own lives. Let us not deceive ourselves about "humanitarian impulses" on the part of the great brotherhood. The fight is for life, to have it more abundantly, and the fact that millions are now ready to fight [in World War II] for something they have ignominiously surrendered for the greater part of their lives does not make it more humanitarian. (Miller, "Open" 157)

To this charge, Miller bluntly adds a direct contradiction to the Parisian Surrealists, to which I have already drawn attention though it merits emphasis: "I am against revolutions because they always involve a return to the status quo. I am against the status quo both before and after revolutions. I don't want to wear a black shirt or a red shirt. I want to wear the shirt that suits my taste" (160). In accepting Surrealism as a technique and influence while rejecting it as a movement, Miller fuelled similar disenchantments among those who admired surrealist works but could not accommodate its orthodoxy. He also opened it to conscious direction by the Ego. By feeding this egoic form of Surrealism back to the English poets through those who took part in the Villa Seurat, Miller's revised post-Surrealism fulfills his belief "that in living my own life in my own way I am more apt to give life to others." He did, and the New Apocalypse was one such gift.

After the Apocalyptic anthologies, Treece and Schimanski's *Transformation* ran for four issues until just after the end of the Second World War. By the final issue, the editors had turned back to their origins by including works from Henry Miller, Anaïs Nin, Wallace Fowlie (Miller's good friend at this time), and William Saroyan. In some respects, it was a homecoming to *The Booster's* stable of authors. James Keery has given the most innovative study to date of this moment in the New Apocalypse and its genealogy. Keery never describes them as anarchist and avoids politics, despite the scope of his ten-part, multi-sectional recuperation of the New Apocalypse in PN *Review*, but he comes closest when noting,

> Like the Apocalypse itself, Goodland's philosophy emerges out of a matrix of sophisticated, highly topical debate, in which communism, "religious anarchism," pacifism and fascism are amongst the identifiable vectors. The other product of the same matrix is *Seven*. (Keery, "Burning [4]" 29)

The most obvious source of "religious anarchism" is D.S. Savage, though self-describing anarchist authors appear across his series of articles repeatedly. In this sense, even in a brilliantly recuperative project such as Keery's, one which is highly successful, the political context and origins of the New Apocalypse remain easily overlooked.

Keery's lengthy article series is the most thorough reconsideration of the New Apocalypse extant, and his tone is largely critical of the literary authorities who have dismissed the New Apocalypse out of hand or with prejudice and significant misunderstanding. It is difficult not to agree with his assessment of bias at several points, though as the Introduction here suggests, the myopia of an interpretive schema that renders these several related movements unintelligible due to their politics and aesthetics can go further than personal animosities among a handful of critics. Initial reviews of the New Apocalypse acknowledge their position as a group, and they appear to do so without prejudice yet carry significant misunderstandings. The *Times Literary Supplement* review of June 7, 1941 of *The White Horseman* acknowledges the group and its principle authors by name, giving it a place beside the Hogarth Press' announcement for Virginia Woolf's forthcoming *Between the Acts*. The pith of the review, which is scrupulously neutral, is the note regarding Fraser's introductory essay and the makeup of the group itself: "the new school was a development, in some respects, of pre-war surrealism: 'the next stage forward'; but denying what was inactive in that movement. All the poets and prose-writers represented are under thirty years of age" (Tomlinson 269). The difficulty here is not a biased tone or off-handed dismissal but rather a minimization of the New Apocalypse's context and the close relationship between its aesthetics and politics, which are frank in the essay under discussion but elided in the review.

Routledge repeats the same in its advertisement in the *Times Literary Supplement* the next week, saying "this volume represents the work of a group of poets and critics all under 30 years of age, who have in common a certain attitude to the technique of writing, and a certain philosophy of life to which they have given the name *The New Apocalypse*" ("The White" 346). As with a first-year composition essay, the vagueness of the repeated term "certain" draws attention more for what it covers than what it explains—and this hiding of the group's "attitude" to technique and "philosophy" is precisely what left them incomprehensible to the casual critic, just as Fraser had anticipated when writing of the contrasts between the New Apocalypse and its immediate predecessors in the Auden group (Fraser, "Apocalypse" 25, 27, 29). A direct statement of "anarchist affiliations" may have deterred some potential readers, but it would have the merits of clarity to critics. For Fraser, the combination of "unpropitious circumstances of the moment…[and] a genuine contrast in attitude" (25) made the New Apocalypse "not likely to have the same immediate popularity as the generation that preceded them" (25). When Hugh Fausset turns to a more formal review, the same recurs with his clear sympathy for the group and interest in its poetics becoming little more than a return to Surrealism and a turn away from politics, which again decon-textualizes the group and the provenance of Apocalypticism. When Fausset returns to the New Apocalypse in direct contrast to the Auden group in "Where Poetry Stands" at the end of the same summer, it is to apply the Auden group's social perspective on the Apocalypse's anarchist post-surrealist impulse, and the results are unsurprisingly critical of the latter and laudatory for the former. Fausset grants that

> The interest of the movement for which Mr. Fraser speaks and the group who contribute to this anthology is that they are seeking beneath the social and political surface, with which their predecessors were often arbitrarily concerned, for the perennial roots of poetry in imagination itself. (450)

However, in acknowledging this distinction, he immediately shifts to casting personal faults for poetic failings and turns attention back to the Auden group's "political surface" for the remainder of the review.

The contextualizing descriptions of the group continue to be accessible only within their own writings rather than in critical responses, even when these responses are generally favourable. Of the various contemporary reviews of the products of this personal-ist group in the loose affiliation I am sketching from 1938 onward, only those published in their own periodicals or volumes mention anarchism, but for one. R.D. Charques goes as far as recognizing Stanford's introduction to the first issue of Alex Comfort's *New Road* as describing

> "A Forward Movement—a group of 'revolutionary pacifists,' the Anarchist and the Apocalyptic Movements" [(Stanford, "New" 5)]….But what can be gathered from the opening article, by

Derek Stanford, is for the most part of a negative and too youthful character. The forward movement is apparently in protest against the materialism or Marxism of the poets of the twenties and the thirties, and seeks instead "to humanize Socialism, to establish a society with a less impersonal shape, and to reassert the importance of individual effort and the individual as final criterion of society" [(Stanford, "Now" 5)].... Apocalyptic movements and manifestos, revolutionary pacifism and the rest do not seem to touch at all closely the good poetry in this volume. (Charques 381)

The most overt critique is that Stanford and his editor Alex Comfort were both self-identifying anarchists, pacifists, and legally conscientious objectors during the war, and the "Forward Movement" is clearly a singular avant-garde that Stanford expressly traces back to Herbert Read's "The Philosophy of Anarchism," the pamphlet begun with his first public statement of his anarchism in the Adelphi in 1937 (Stanford, "New" 5). The critique of "materialism or Marxism" that Charques finds "too youthful" (381) is the same critique with which Read opens his 1937 "The Necessity of Anarchism," which became the pamphlet from which Stanford quotes. Moreover, their politics are quite clearly in their poetry in the volume, in the same tradition that had been running for five years in England and for seven years in English letters. In response to the continuation of authoritarian socialism under Stalin, Read argues, "There is nothing to be gained by disguising the fact that the post-revolutionary history of Russia has created among socialists, if not a state of open disillusionment, at any rate some degree of secret embarrassment" (89). Charques, obviously, disagrees and finds such secret embodiment "too youthful" (381).

Comfort's New Road carried on in 1943 and continued to prioritize anarchist perspectives. Comfort is now best known as the author of The Joy of Sex rather than an anarchist theorist, though his lifelong dedication to anarchism is remarkable across such a varied career, as is the extent of his writings on the topic in tandem with his novels and poetry (especially since he was primarily a medical researcher). New Road expressly broadened its perspective to include European authors, including German authors, during its run, and the works from the Apocalyptic poets brought forward their politics, such as Treece's overt "The only way left, as I see it, is that of anarchism" ("Considerations" 147). The journal was also published by Nicholas Moore and Wrey Gardiner in Grey Walls Press, which had done so much New Apocalypse work and was closely linked with the Villa Seurat.[19] The acknowledgements in the first issue turn to the now familiar names of Herbert Read, Nicholas Moore, Stefan Schimanski, and *Kingdom Come*, as well as the perhaps surprising *Arson* and *Oasis*, the former being Tony del Renzio's New York anarchist periodical and the latter a product in Egypt of G.S. Fraser while in service.[20] *Oasis* then became a bridge between the London poets and the Cairo poets, although once again the pre-war history of the Villa Seurat reappears and stakes its claim.[21] The war poets included in *New Road* invariably came from the servicemen among the New Apocalypse as well as those who had been sent to Egypt, most notably Cooke and Fraser who had both worked with the New Apocalypse and fostered contact with Durrell, who was in Cairo and then Alexandria. Just over a year after its publication in wartime Cairo, Durrell's "For a Nursery Mirror" appeared again in *New Road* after Comfort's solicitation of (unpaid) work from Durrell.[22]

Comfort pursued the same breadth of poetic offerings in *Poetry Folios*, which began with his fellow anarchist poets Treece, Moore, and Hendry but grew to repeatedly include Kenneth Patchen and Kenneth Rexroth while acknowledging Henry Miller as important American figures. Comfort specifically includes Patchen's anarchist criticism of Ezra Pound's fascism in "Ezra Pound's Guilt" in 1946 (n. pag.). *Poetry Folios* was produced by Comfort and Peter Wells from an anarchist commune at Havengore. Patchen, Rexroth, and Miller were all anarchist writers, and the journal began to include another young figure who had already made appearances in *New Road* and *Kingdom Come*: George Woodcock. Woodcock appeared in the winter 1942 issue of *Poetry Folios* after a 1940 appearance in the summer issue of *Kingdom Come*, both of which led to inclusion in the debut 1943 issue of *New Road*. Woodcock had also begun, in Easter 1940, his own expressly anarchist periodical *NOW* through Freedom Press.

NOW began with a statement against bias in selection apart from a criteria of high quality, or in other words a resistance to measuring work against any particular political school—this notion dominates the critical commentary on the first series of the journal from 1940 to the fall of 1941, at which point it became overtly run through Freedom Press, which had already been involved in printing and distribution.[23] However, this apolitical stance is demonstrably not the case even in the first issue's statement, which equally exhorts a pacifist and anti-authoritarian position: "Art is antithetical to evil and violence. And evil and violence have their supreme avatar in war.... It is no particular violence, e.g., Nazi violence, that we must oppose, but all violence, no matter what the cause that uses it" (Woodcock, "Introduction" 1). The same first issue includes D.S. Savage's anarchist essay "The Poet and War," which culminates in "the centrality of persons" (9). Little mistake can be made about the journal's position, in particular after its two advertisements for the American anarcho-pacifist journal *Phoenix* published by James Cooney with help from Robert Duncan (for which Woodcock notes contributions by Miller, Kay Boyle, and Savage).

When *NOW* was restarted in 1943 after its seventh issue, it became directly published through Freedom Press (not just distributed) with a stated social vision: "the volumes of NOW will be edited from an anarchist point of view" (Woodcock, "Note" 2). This did not mean, however, that one could very easily equate inclusion in *NOW* with anarchism. The social commentary was more or less exclusively anar-chist, but literary contributions were exempted by Woodcock, though authors clearly knew they were publishing in the anarchist press and did so without remuneration of any kind: "In fairness to these writers we must point out that their appearance in *NOW* does not mean necessarily that they subscribe to anarchist doctrines" (2). This being said, nearly all contributors aligned themselves with anarchism of one form or another, and virtually all are reasonably described as anti-authoritarian.

When Henry Miller appeared in 1943, in the second issue, it was boxed between works by Woodcock and Herbert Read immediately following on the "Note": "[*NOW*'s] outlook, as readers will realize, is anarchist, and, in general, those writers whose contributions touch on social matters adhere to the broad fundamental doctrines of an-archism" (Woodcock, "Note" 4). In the issue, all works are anarchist in nature, and Miller's is clearly no exception—his "Dream of Mobile" having been excerpted from his *Air-Conditioned Nightmare*, which only appeared in book form in 1945 (the work appeared in Charles Henri Ford's surrealist magazine *View* in New York at the same time). Although twenty-five years later, Woodcock would associate Miller and Durrell with the non-anarchist contributors to NOW by identifying them as libertarian rather than anarchist (*Anarchism* 384), Miller's own stated anarchism shows this is not the case. Woodcock also shows that his views changed from during and after the war, since he argued in the journal itself (rather than decades later) that "the real grudge [the censors] have against Miller is that he is a dynamic social critic, and that he uses his obscenity as a means of jerking people into consciousness of the corruption in the world where they live. Miller is being persecuted not because his books are obscene, but because they are subversive" (Woodcock, "Editorial" 5–6). Karl Orend has written the only thorough discussion of Miller's anarchism, and in doing so he also corrects previous errors in the biographies. According to Orend,

> Miller's meeting with Goldman was something he would often refer to over the years. At the end of her speech, he introduced himself to Goldman and Reitman. From the latter, he purchased two books that were to alter his life: Nietzsche's *The Anti-Christ* and Max Stirner's *The Ego and his Own*....Stirner would, as I have shown in the book *Brotherhood of Fools and Simpletons*, have a major impact on his worldview. Under the influence of Goldman, Miller became an anarchist. He remained one all his life. (54)[24]

To this, Orend adds a major revision to Miller's reputation as a sexual liberator: "One of the most important and surprising facts about Henry Miller, at the time he met Goldman, was that at the age of 21 he was a puritan who felt guilty about sex. Goldman contributed to Miller's liberation from puritan beliefs by her essays on sexuality, the literature she exposed him to and by her own example" (55). As Orend also points out, from his biographer's perspective, "Miller had a distrust of all authority. He did not even have a bank account until he was over sixty years old" (70).

Miller's reasons for feeling kinship with Woodcock are clear, and his level of support for a magazine across the Atlantic, NOW, is reinforced in the subsequent issue when he submitted two works, one again from *The Air-Conditioned Nightmare* and a second very long (not fully printed) excerpt from *The Rosy Crucifixion*. Although the post-Surrealists would not play a significant role in NOW's poetic interests, both Durrell and Miller were significant literary contributors and the only two not otherwise expressly affiliated with the journal's political interests. (Kathleen Raine may be a third, although she held anti-authoritarian views and was closely affiliated with English Surrealism through her first and second husbands, Hugh Sykes Davies and Charles Madge.) Miller and his "group" are, however, identified as anarchist by several of the poetic contributors to NOW, such as Woodcock and Stanford.

Woodcock's own political orientation was and is clear, having already published several anarchist works prior to NOW and subsequently writing *Anarchism*, the most widespread history of the movement. Tambimuttu's *Poetry London* become another and longstanding vehicle for authors in these groups, but more as a part of the network and without any clear political orientation, although A. Trevor Tolley does identify if as firmly a part of the New Romanticism that carried on the New Apocalypse (Tolley, *Poetry* 126–27). Tolley took pains to divide these movements, the New Apocalypse and the New Romantics, but the fact remains they had the same views and participants.[25]

Despite the mockeries of Tambimuttu's *Poetry London* being "Tuttifrutti" and "loony and eccentric" in *New Verse*, it became a major force by bringing exciting poetic voices to the British public at a time when they were being excluded from the likes of *New Verse*. As Tolley notices,

> The principal contributors of poems during Tambimuttu's editorship were: Dylan Thomas, Lawrence Durrell, Henry Treece, G.S. Fraser, Laurence Clark, Kathleen Raine, David Gascoyne, Nicholas Moore, Anne Ridler, J.C. Hall, Stephen Spender, Louis MacNeice, George Barker, Dorian Cooke, J.F. Hendry, Alun Lewis, Vernon Watkins, Stephen Coates, Norman Nicholson, Keith Douglas, Sidney Keyes, Terence Tiller, Bernard Spencer, and Iain Fletcher. (120)

The large number of Apocalyptic-cum-New Romantic poets and the *Personal Landscape* poets does not stand out for Tolley, nor does their continued distribution through contacts made via the Villa Seurat, which had itself published Tambimuttu in *Delta* prior to the beginning of *Poetry London*. This exclusion of the Villa Seurat network and its influence leads Tolley to further speculation that constructs an unlikely reason for the presence of Villa Seurat authors when he briefly notes Poetry London Imprints as publishing the first of Henry Miller's books to appear in England, "probably at the prompting of Nicholas Moore, who joined the *Poetry London* editorial staff in 1944" (121). While Moore, along with Wrey Gardiner from Grey Walls Press, was devoted to Miller's works, the reason for their inclusion was almost certainly Tambimuttu's own already existing contact with Miller and ongoing contact with Miller's very close associate, Durrell. While Moore would certainly have enthusiastically supported Miller's inclusion, especially given the associative boost this would give to his own monograph on Miller at exactly the same time, it is also highly unlikely that Moore was the origin for the impulse to print Miller's works. Tambimuttu was already in contact with Miller and was well aware of his program for an anarchist revision to English Surrealism and had been published by Miller and Durrell in Paris. It is convenient though that Moore, Miller, and Gardiner were all anarchists.

While it may be unkind to chastise a critic directly, Tolley's work gives a very poor impression of the networks behind these journals, and it must be corrected, especially since his *The Poetry of the Forties in Britain* purports to be the work of record on the subject and is constructed almost as a reference text (and it is used as such by Childs and other critics). From Tolley's perspective,

> The New Romanticism has loomed large in memories of British poetry of the nineteen-forties. Its rejection has sometimes been seen as implying a rejection of the whole renewal in Romanticism during that period. It is certainly true that, partly because the paper shortage made publishing a seller's market, the poets of the Apocalypse and the New Romanticism got themselves into print very frequently. In fact their work is in no way central to the poetic achievement of the decade. An

admiration of Romantic poetry is certainly explicit on the
part of George Barker, Vernon Watkins and Kathleen Raine;
and it is hard to imagine Tambimuttu without his advocacy
of Romanticism. Nevertheless, none of these showed a strong
support for the majority of writers discussed in this chapter,
and Tambimuttu's perceptive championing of Keith Douglas
as well as Kathleen Raine and David Gascoyne shows a feeling
more for quality than for doctrine. A renewed availability of
Romantic poetry as a model was not crucial to the poetry of
the decade, where continuities with the thirties remained
important. (*Poetry* 126–27)

The contention that these writers did not support each other is false,
as has already been demonstrated. Moreover, the influence lived on
fairly clearly and for an extended period, but often in prose and often
in America in the Beats, as will appear toward the end of this chapter.
Nevertheless, while Britain may have turned to the Movement, these
poets all remained active in Britain to varying degrees, though often
turning to other genres, such as Treece's turn to fantastic fiction
(which makes us rethink the Romanticism of his contemporary and
fellow Romantic Mervyn Peake as well as Treece's support from the
fantastic writers of Cambridge). Tolley's view also overlooks the
ongoing stream of works like Smart's *By Grand Central Station I Sat Down
and Wept* and perhaps most obviously, the wildly successful *Alexandria
Quartet* by Durrell in the late 1950s and across the 1960s, all of which
show a Romantic streak and were penned by authors tied to the
1940s New Romantic movement. The movement was itself simply a
continuation of the New Apocalypse, inspired by the Villa Seurat's
anarcho-Surrealism.

Tolley goes on to reconfigure the New Romanticist poets substantially, apparently with a view to divide up these groups into unrelated
and distinct movements:

The anthology that signalled the new grouping of "Romantic"
writers was *Lyra*, edited by Alex Comfort and Robert Greacan,
and published in 1942 by Wrey Gardiner at Grey Walls.
Although the editors claimed that "like all anthologies" theirs

was "a completely arbitrary parade of the editors' taste in contemporary writing," they conceded "that the book becomes, of itself, a contribution to a new romanticism...We feel that the over-thirty classicism which still insists on calling itself 'younger' has ceased to represent the growing edge of poetry" [i.e., the Auden generation]. Herbert Read begins his preface: "This anthology appears in the third year of a war which every day reveals more clearly its apocalyptic character"; but it is clear that this is not a reference to the Apocalypse movement and that the contributors do not consider themselves as part of that movement. (*Poetry* 107)

Tolley then goes on to list several of the contributors, presumably to demonstrate that they are not Apocalyptics, yet he includes some of the principle figures in the New Apocalypse, including G.S. Fraser whose essay on the topic had defined the movement and opened its second anthology the previous year. That the book both includes and was printed by Wrey Gardiner and Nicholas Moore, both of whom were deeply influenced by Henry Miller and Herbert Read, further unifies this group. That they also all identified as anarchists draws further attention. It is also easy to point out Treece's own ongoing use of the Apocalyptic notion of myth from Hendry in his own later poetry (increasingly medieval in tone and mythic, as Tolley even notes [108]) as well as in his postwar historical fantasy novels, which profoundly rely on Hendry's notion of myth. However, in an even more rudimentary way, simply noting that the introduction by Read identifies it as Apocalyptic and that the contributors were all aligned with the New Apocalypse, and as well that it was published by two poets closely allied with the New Apocalypse, one of whom co-founded the journal that first supported the New Apocalypse, would adequately dispel Tolley's fallacious contention that "it is clear that this is not a reference to the Apocalypse movement and that the contributors do not consider themselves as part of that movement" (107). Such clarity is opaque and obfuscates. They are demonstrably the same movements in both spirit and person.

From the Villa Seurat and Apocalypse to Egypt's *Personal Landscape*

While the movement from Miller and Read's disagreement in correspondence to the radical transformation they prompted of English Surrealism into the anarchist post-surrealist "Personalism" is remarkable, it is not the full scope of this literary network. Not half even. The most stunning branches of this network move far beyond a Paris–London dialogue.

When Miller left Paris to visit Durrell in Greece, it coincided with the ending of *Delta* but began a network of Greek connections that drew on another vision of Surrealism via Greek Modernism. Miller recounts this nearly half-a-year period in Greece in *The Colossus of Maroussi*, but the war he endeavoured to keep from the travelogue forced him to flee back to America while Durrell remained in Athens producing anti-fascist materials while awaiting representatives of the British Council. Robert Liddell was among them when they arrived,[26] and Durrell was brought into their employ, moving to Kalamata. Bernard Spencer and Durrell met under the same circumstances.[27] As the Nazis invaded, this group of English writers in Greece as well as many Greek poets (in the Government in Exile[28]) fled to Egypt. For Durrell this was a dramatic escape from Kalamata in a small fishing caïque to Crete with his wife and infant daughter and a subsequent escape from Crete to Alexandria. Portentously, his first border crossing in the Alexandria harbour as a refugee involved being asked by the British soldier on port duty about Henry Miller, the Villa Seurat, and *The Booster* while his documents were checked (Hodgkin 269). The soldier, John Braun, "had read and admired *The Black Book*" (269), which foreshadowed the literary community Egypt had in store. The literary connections in Egypt, in Cairo in particular, were surprisingly rich. Durrell, Spencer, and Liddell were suddenly in the company of Herbert Howarth, an instructor at King Fuad University with whom Durrell had already published and interacted through *The Booster* and *Delta*. John Waller, from Oxford (editor of *Bolero* then *Kingdom Come*),[29] was sent to Egypt, as was Durrell's eccentric friend from London, John Gawsworth. G.S. Fraser, who wrote the critical outline "Apocalypse in Poetry" of the post-surrealist New Apocalypse movement for its second anthology, *The White Horseman*, was also sent to serve in Egypt after having written about Durrell and Miller prior to his departure. Dorian Cooke was also frequently in Cairo, and as Keery has emphatically demonstrated, Cooke was the driving force behind the New Apocalypse movement in England (Keery, "Burning [8]" 60).

This much is known even if overlooked, but criticism has so far failed to recognize the unexpected relationship between Egyptian radical literature of the 1930s to 1940s and what *Harper's Magazine* called in 1947 "The New Cult of Sex and Anarchy" in Big Sur and Berkeley, California. Both literary groups share surprising affinities to the anti-authoritarian developments of English Surrealism after the 1936 London International Surrealist Exhibition, after which many of the younger generation fell under the sway of the anarchists Herbert Read and Henry Miller. The link between these groups effects a change in how we conceive the internationalism of Late Modernism and its influence on the postwar literary world. Specifically, George Henein and Albert Cossery, two Egyptian authors writing primarily (but not only) in French,[30] were involved in the anti-fascist, anarchist Egyptian surrealist movement described in their 1938 manifesto "Long Live Degenerate Art!," which rejected Adolf Hitler's racist and propagandist attack on modern art during the 1937 "Entartete Kunst" exhibition in Munich. The Nazi exhibition featured works by Pablo Picasso, Henri Matisse, Max Ernst, and Vincent Van Gogh, whose works were all mocked as degenerate art and the product of Jewish Bolsheviks (despite most artists being neither Jewish nor communist). Over four thousand of the artworks were eventually burned in anti-Semitic and anti-communist campaigns. The next year, Henein released the anarchist "Long Live Degenerate Art!" manifesto in Cairo signed by several other Egyptian authors, including Cossery, who used a variant spelling of his name, Koseiry, in the Latin alphabet. This manifesto was translated and published in periodicals across Europe, including England. Later, in 1944 and half a world away, George Leite created the magazine *Circle* in Berkeley, California, again an anarchist, anti-fascist project,[31] which he co-edited with Bern Porter, a physicist who had been involved in the Manhattan Project but who became a publisher of West Coast poetry. Leite also opened daliel's bookstore in San Francisco, which prefigured City Lights Books and gave an early venue for the authors of the San Francisco Renaissance.[32] Virtually all of the Circle Editions series of books were later republished by City Lights Publishing. The remarkable surprise, however, is to find Leite in California publishing Henein's anarcho-surrealist poetry and the first English translation of Cossery's novel *Men God Forgot*. Behind this literary migration stands the dense network of authors from Cairo and Alexandria who brought their work through Athens, London, and New York to finally reach the Pacific coast. The bridge between these two worlds, it turns out, was comprised of the English post-Surrealists who were scattered by the war after formulating a distinctly anti-authoritarian vision of Surrealism focused on the individual, which marks their difference from (and rejection of) the politics of the then dominant Auden generation of authors, perhaps best seen in relation to the Marxist critic Christopher Caudwell. The relations among these nations and generations of writing and their shared concerns propels this chapter by calling for an analysis of the history, poetics, and politics that were common to their works. Unpacking these relations then makes visible the vital importance of the anti-authoritarian steam of anarchism to Late Modernism's poetics and aesthetics.

To this end, the task is to reconstruct poetry networks in the 1930s and 1940s in relation to the anarchist revisions to Surrealism begun by American, British, and international writers in Paris who were centred around the Villa Seurat and the aftermath of the 1936 London International Surrealist Exhibition.

These writers linked to and published by the Villa Seurat were already international in perspective, residing in Britain, France, Czechoslovakia, and Greece, publishing in Urdu, German, Czech, French, Greek, Armenian, and English, and originating from as many different countries. However, 1939 saw them further dispersed by war across North America and North Africa where they met kindred groups. Miller left Paris to visit Durrell, but the war forced him to flee to America while Durrell remained in Athens producing anti-fascist materials and awaiting representatives of the British Council, all of whom later fled to Egypt. A similar series of connections began in North America when Anaïs Nin, Miller's lover and collaborator during his Paris years, relocated to New York in August 1939 and then began a love affair with the young Robert Duncan, who was already in contact with the Villa Seurat through the journal *The Phoenix*, which he helped to produce with James Cooney in Woodstock.[33] Duncan would publish Nin, Miller, and Durrell in his own *Experimental Review*, and the journals of his lover Jack Johnson record their dreams in New York City in March 1941 about Durrell's surrealist short story pair "Zero" and "Asylum in the Snow" at this time (Johnson 112–14). Concurrently, Duncan was trying to publish Durrell's stories and novel with illustrations by Virginia Admiral, who was also in the same intimate relationship with Johnson, Duncan, and Nin (Admiral is now most famous as Robert De Niro's mother).

When Durrell, Spencer, and Liddell fled to Crete and thence to Egypt, the literary networks they joined in Cairo were a reunion of sorts. As has already been mentioned, the three philhellenic authors collaborated with Howarth at King Fuad University. Waller was also in Egypt, as were Fraser and Dorian Cooke. The result of these migrations is striking: the editors and contributors to some of the most prominent anti-authoritarian English post-surrealist periodicals reassembled in Egypt and worked with their Arab ideological counterparts while their colleagues continued on in London publishing them as well as their new friends abroad.

Although much of this literary Cairo was only inconsistently recounted years later,[34] the degree of interaction was significant. Howarth taught in the same English department from 1939 to 1941 at King Fuad University in which subsequent Egyptian literary figures studied (though Naguib Mahfouz finished his studies two years prior). This put Howarth in contact with the local Egyptian anarcho-surrealist group that included Cossery. It also led Howarth to complete a co-translation of Arabic poetry with Ibrahim Shukrallah entitled *Images from the Arab World: Fragments of Arab Literature*, which was published in 1944. Harold Edwards, Howarth's colleague, translated Cossery into English, and Fraser published selections of the short-story-collection-cum-novel in his wartime periodical *Orientations*, most prominently "The Human Sound of the Street" in 1943 (6–10; Bowen 214). Cossery's "The Postman Gets His Own Back" from *The House of Certain Death* then later appeared in John Waller's postwar *Middle East Anthology* in 1946, this time in Erik de Mauny's translation. In the same year, Cossery's full *Men God Forgot* was published in Berkeley by

the anarchist Circle Editions, run by Leite in affiliation with Rexroth
and Duncan, and later reprinted in 1955 by City Lights Books with a
new introduction provided by Miller. Miller's introduction, however,
uses the present tense to describe the first appearance of the novel
in English and was intended for the 1945 first printing, about which
he had also written for *Circle*. Miller's strong influence over James
Laughlin also influenced New Directions' reprinting of Cossery's
second novel, *The House of Certain Death*, in English translation, again by
de Mauny.

Clearly, the scope of this anarchist distribution network is broad,
but their politics are also more nuanced than has been recognized.
The manifesto of the Egyptian anarcho-surrealist group appeared
in various translations and publications, but it is best known in
English from its 1938 translation from Arabic and French to English,
published in all three languages in the *London Bulletin*: "LONG LIVE
DEGENERATE ART!" (Henein, "LONG" 16–17).[35] It begins by resisting the Nazi rejection of "Degenerate Art" and by refuting the vulgar
Marxist notion "that modern society looks with aversion on any
innovative creation in art and literature which threatens the cultural
system on which that society is based, whether it be from the point
of view of thought or of meaning" (148). This is to say, it rejects a
deterministic Marxism or economism, which was emphasized for
British readers of this period in Caudwell's works, in particular his
Studies in a Dying Culture and *Illusion and Reality: A Study of the Sources of Poetry*,
which discusses the Auden group. Notably, the English periodicals
I have already mentioned—*Seven*, *Bolero*, and *Kingdom Come*—contain
socially progressive yet anti-authoritarian viewpoints that critique
Caudwell on this point. This is part of the unique situation developing in Egypt just prior to the arrival of the English post-Surrealists.
Despite being tied to the Parisian Surrealists and their communist
views, the Egyptians repeatedly emphasize the *individual*, as did the
Villa Seurat writers, and as the English post-Surrealists whom they
influenced *were* doing at the same time as the Egyptians. Henein
and Cossery also overtly flouted socialism despite maintaining an
anti-capitalist critique: "Works by great German artists...have been
confiscated and replaced by worthless Socialist art" (Henein, "LONG"
148) though "Socialist" is replaced by "Nazi" in other versions of the

manifesto. The term, however, does not appear to be a translator's slip for *Nationalsozialist*. The name taken by the group, "Art and Freedom," highlights the tension in 1930s Marxist movements over bourgeois freedom, again in Caudwell's formulation (*Studies* 193). For Caudwell, who died fighting in the Spanish Civil War, such freedom is a form of social control created by the fragmentation of the proletarian unity. For Henein, any collectivity that elides the individual is intrinsically repressive and authoritarian. Despite their activist support for pro-gressive collective efforts, this turn by Henein reflects the Egyptian group's individualist difference from the surrealist mainstream, which was predominantly communist at this point in time.[36] It also shows the Egyptians' kinship with the Villa Seurat and New Apocalypse groups in Paris and Britain. One complex element is the limitations faced by British and Egyptian Marxist groups at this specific time and the critical need to avoid anachronistic readings based on corrections now integrated into critical theory. In particular, texts and approaches on which modern readers would naturally rely would not have been available to these groups (such as Raymond Williams or the sense of cultural hegemony developed by Gramsci [*Prison* 233–38], although Gramsci's ideas did reach the authors in Egypt during the war via Italian anti-fascist groups).[37] Hence, figures like Caudwell were the main sources of such ideas on bourgeois freedom and individualism against which these groups were reacting.

Henein, who founded the Art and Freedom group in Cairo, pro-moted workers' rights and union activities through both groups, yet his manifesto makes his anarchist revisions to Surrealism's com-munism overt: "Our position regarding Marxism is the inverted reflection of that adopted by Marxist groups towards the individual, freedom and the activities arising from literary or artistic creation in general" (Henein, "Manifesto," 150). This work is not included in Henein's *Oeuvres*, which reflects the volume's (and general schol-arship's) exclusion of his anarchist writings and views. His individ-ualist and freedom-oriented vision of Marxism reflects the anti-authoritarian turn to the individual already seen in the Villa Seurat and later repeated by the New Apocalypse and New Romantic authors who expressly identified it as anarchist. This is also the problem-atic conflict over which George Orwell had previously voiced his disagreement. For Henein and those Egyptian artists who followed his manifesto, which was signed by most of the same artists and authors in the Art and Freedom group and the Cairo Surrealist group, this vision is anarchist in all but name:[38]

> Our grievance against Marxism lies not in its leaning towards revolution, but on the contrary, to its taking a starchy, stagnant, reactionary stance towards the revolutionary growth of science and thought....We proclaim that we consider the individual as the only thing of worth, yet today, seemingly, it is under relentless fire from all sides. We declare that the individual is in possession of largely unexplored inner faculties, the most important of which is imagination....
> The individual against State-Tyranny.
> Imagination against the routine of dialectical materialism.
> Freedom against terror in all its forms.
> (Henein, "Manifesto," 151)

The final three exhortations are individualist anarchism in nature and recall Max Stirner more than any other thinker. Henein also critiques the authoritarian "'infallibilism' pervading...both the right and left and that acts as a common denominator for both Marxist and Fascist parties" (150). Such a critique is typical of anti-authoritarian thought. The same tension this position expresses between Marxist analysis and criticism and anarchist notions that reject economism or the reduction of the individual to a product of conditions continues through Albert Cossery across his very long career as well as in the Art and Freedom group's Egyptian activities, which often supported workers but shunned the Marxist organizations.

For the anarchist Cossery's works to be translated by Harold Edwards at this point in time—Edward's being a faculty member at Faruk University (now Alexandria University) while it was still a branch campus of King Fuad University (now Cairo University)—is politically striking, as is the parallel translation project taken up at the same time by the British medic and intelligence officer Erik de Mauny, who also translated from Russian and whose wife was Egyptian. Most of the Art and Freedom group fled Egypt after the war, relocating to Paris, due to political persecution. Moreover, Waller included Cossery in his *Middle East Anthology* using a story excerpted from *The House of Certain Death* as translated by his co-editor de Mauny, and both were familiar with Cossery's *Men God Forgot*, a story from which had previously appeared published in Fraser's *Orientations* in Edwards's translation. For Waller and de Mauny, "The Postman Gets His Own Back" (58–73) became a central prose work in their *Middle East Anthology* between the contributions of the two editors. De Mauny's translation of Cossery was for intended publication in England by *Poetry London*, so the interests in his works was obviously strong. Cossery's work was also placed by Waller and de Mauny between two stories by Stefano Terra, whom both Waller and Fraser knew well and with whom Fraser worked in intelligence and propaganda. Terra is the pseudonym of Giulio Tavernari, the Italian anti-fascist activist who edited the journal *Quaderni di Giustizia e libertà* (*Papers of Justice and Freedom*) in Cairo in affiliation with the Italian Justice and Freedom movement, which had already supported the anarchists in the Spanish Civil War in Catalonia. Tavernari later served Italian radio in Belgrade at the same time as Lawrence Durrell's postwar service in Yugoslavia, both of them working against Tito's communist regime. Through the same network, Hamish Henderson, who served in Egypt and associated himself with Fraser, served alongside the Italian anti-fascists in North Africa, was a part of the Italian campaign, and read Antonio Gramsci's *Prison Letters* when it first appeared, which led him to begin his several translation projects for the work in 1947. His translation, however, did not appear in a finished form until 1974 in the *New Edinburgh Review* and then as a book in 1988 now published by Pluto Press. Gramsci's work notably decouples Marxism from interpretations aligned with economism or economic determinism and anti-humanism. Fraser and Henderson shared a particular Scottish bond, and their surviving letters from 1945 show a correspondence that had existed for quite some time (Henderson 6).[39] Fraser's letters focus on the gossip of their shared personal friends, Durrell, Tambimuttu, Ruth Spiers, and John Gawsworth, all of whom figure prominently in the mutual publication engagements between *The Booster*, *Delta*, *Personal Landscape*, and *Poetry London*.

When Lawrence Durrell, Robin Fedden, and Bernard Spencer together founded a new poetry periodical in Cairo in 1941, at least in

part with Terence Tiller, they selected Spencer (who had greater stability at the time) to manage the correspondence, and they included
a startling range of writers associated with this same broad network.
Personal Landscape began in January 1942 with an issue comprised entirely of works by its three editors as well as a single review by Tiller. In
the artistic context already outlined for wartime Cairo and its pre-
existing stance with regard to Surrealism, Marxism, and anarchism,
Durrell opens the journal with an anti-manifesto, the first point of
which sets out a tension between the social collective and the artistic
individual (as well as the third entity, the artistic product): "Neither
poet nor public is really interested in the poem itself but in aspects of
it" ("Ideas [I]" 3). Against this, Durrell offers the creative individual
saying, "The poet is interested in the Personal aspect: the poem as an
aspect of himself" whereas "The public is interested in the Vicarious
aspect; that is to say 'the universal application', which is an illusion
that grows round a poem once the logical meaning is clear and the
syntax ceases to puzzle" ("Ideas [I]" 3).[40]

These may seem peculiar lines with which to open a poetry journal during wartime amidst the intense politicization of art underway
in Cairo. It is especially peculiar for an ostensibly reactionary author
serving in the British intelligence services who was already deeply
tied to currents of surrealist art and anarchist revisions to Surrealism
prior to the war (Gifford, "Anarchist" 65), who would publish in
George Woodcock's *NOW* through the then infamous and imprisoned anarchist Freedom Press (Durrell, "Elegy" 30–32), and who
had produced anti-fascist propaganda in Athens prior to the Nazi
invasion (Stephanides, *Autumn* 75–77). It is an even more peculiar and
provocative introductory anti-manifesto when the startling network
of authors involved is taken into account.[41] However, Durrell's trinity
of individual, society, and artwork returns in the second "Ideas about
Poems [II]," which begins with a quotation from his own poetry
and explains "Nonsense is never just nonsense; it is more like good
sense with all the logic removed. At its highest point poetry makes
use of nonsense in order to indicate a level of experience beyond the
causality principle" (2). This becomes Durrell's more serious poetic
assertion: "Logic, syntax, is a causal instrument, inadequate for the
task of describing the whole of reality. Poems don't describe" (2).

When further clarity is added in the fourth issue of the first volume, still within 1942, Fraser's work had already been included. Moreover, Fraser's inclusion expressly acknowledges *The White Horseman* where he had previously published "City of Benares" as part of the post-surrealist New Apocalypse group in London. Although they joked at the expense of the New Apocalypse, Fraser demonstrates that they were all familiar with the movement and that the poets involved had all interacted prior to the war (*Stranger* 124–25). Spencer contributed the third "Ideas about Poems [III],"[42] but Durrell added to the same issue his second printed comment on his notion of the Heraldic Universe. The "Heraldic Universe" is a personal conception of his artistic work first articulated in a letter to Henry Miller as a rebuttal to Herbert Read's temporary endorsement of Marxism as a component of his support for Surrealism during the 1936 London International Surrealist Exhibition. The same letter has been tied to Miller's anarchism and close working relationship with Durrell. In "The Heraldic Universe," Durrell returns to the themes above to contend, "Logic tries to describe the world; but it is never found adequate for the task" and "Describing, logic limits. Its law is causality" (7). Against this function of logic, causality, and syntax, Durrell sets his ideal of poetry: "Poetry by an associative approach transcends its own syntax in order not to describe but to be the cause of apprehension in others," which allows Durrell to define the Heraldic Universe as a notion (8). This concept is discussed widely in critical work on Durrell, though never with a politicized context. The revision, then, occurs from rereading his closing line to this short contribution: "'Art' then is only the smoked glass through which we can look at the dangerous sun" (8). The same sentence appeared in his previous published comments on the Heraldic Universe in *Delta* in an article dedicated to Miller's *Hamlet* book. In anticipation of his argument that Shakespeare's Prince Hamlet is caught in conflict- ed performances of a social self (the Prince) and a personal self (Hamlet), Durrell tells Miller, "the self, which you used as a defense against the novel terrors of this heraldic universe, as one might use smoked glass to look at the sun, is diffusing itself: it is less necessary" (Durrell, "Hamlet" 41). The revision shows that for Durrell, the Ego as a defense is less necessary because it has taken on its indepen- dence rather than being a product of circumstance in which the

"Ego" signifies alienation. The Ego, like the blazing sun, cannot be seen directly, yet the Ego and art are deeply bound. This I/Art bond is a unifying theme in this network of authors (41).

Theorizing this individual *self* versus economic determinism or the stabilizing *Ego* is akin to the problems explored by Henein and Cossery's "LONG LIVE DEGENERATE ART!" and particularly its subsequent imperative in Henein's follow-up manifesto for the group, "The individual against State-Tyranny. / Imagination against the routine of dialectical materialism. / Freedom against terror in all its forms" (Henein, "Manifesto" 151). Theorizing this problem of the self is a task for another chapter in this book; however, its kinship to the problems being explored by Henein and Cossery cannot be overlooked. In the same sense, Durrell's role providing the first three critical visions for *Personal Landscape* is paralleled by the journal's namesake poem written by the pacifist Fedden. In Durrell's critical articulation, the "Personal aspect" of the poem is the poet's vision of it as a revelation of self as his *own*, independent of any context, against which struggle the social interpretation with its "universal application" (presumably a Marxist sense of the ascendancy of the social) and the reality of the poem's existence as an artistic artifact unto itself. This *personal* principle (not impersonal) is a striking statement for a young poet who had T.S. Eliot as his correspondent during the war and as his editor and mentor at Faber & Faber.[43] Within these tensions, syntax and logic create causality that reduces the self to a product of the social caused by "'the universal application,' which is an illusion that grows round a poem once the logical meaning is clear and the syntax ceases to puzzle," and in resistance to this universal application, "the individual is the only thing of worth…[and] is in possession of largely unexplored inner faculties, the most important of which is imagination" ("Ideas [I]" 3; Henein, "Manifesto" 151). In his poetry of this period, Durrell's resistance to the standardizing influence of syntax and the social unity implicit in a common syntax also stresses the personal vision, which marks Durrell's revision of the Auden generation's stylistic and political views as well as its dominance in England and America. Even to the end of his long career, Durrell's attitude remained the same regarding "the poetic sickness of syntax" ("From the Elephant's" 4), and although syntactic complexity is not a shared trait across this group of authors, they did all stylistically respond to an anti-authoritarian impulse held in tandem with a privileging of the personal.

For Durrell, however, this vision of syntax is not independent of precursors or broader context. Durrell's readings in Nietzsche at this time were significant, and his surrealist short story "Zero" begins with a lengthy quotation from the philosopher ("Zero" is the first segment, though chronologically produced and published second, in his *Zero and Asylum in the Snow*, both of which were initially published in *Seven* and republished by Circle Editions in Berkeley, California, after Durrell had produced his own private printing on Rhodes). In Durrell's heavy reliance on Nietzsche for concepts of language and selfhood (Gifford, "Durrell's *Revolt*" 111–12), he displays the same interests as James Joyce had for Nietzsche and Stirner. In relation to anarchism, as demonstrated persuasively by David Kadlec, this functions as a rationale for Joyce's disturbances of syntax and logic in poetic language, and I contend the same results appear in Durrell's works:

> Nietzsche carried [in *A Genealogy of Morals*] Stirner's argument a step further, suggesting that appetites themselves were not attributes of the individual subject but rather the foundational phenomena that produced the traces of agency upon which the false notion of a static subject was based. In terms of grammar, Stirner's anarchistic project had involved a scaling back of the generalized nominal categories upon which political and religious structures were built. Beneath the calcified general nouns of the state could be found the more germinal particular nouns of the subject....Nietzsche conceived general and particularized nominal subjects themselves as fictions produced by false assignations of causality....For Nietzsche there was from the very beginning no thing that grows hungry. There were rather expressions of hunger, and these expressions were falsely contoured by grammar. (116–17)

There is a striking kinship between Kadlec's vision here of Joyce's anarchist interests in Stirner and grammar with Durrell's use of Nietzsche in his later novel sequence, *The Revolt of Aphrodite* (Gifford,

"Durrell's *Revolt*" 124). The subject I to the verb think is disrupted in a parallel to Descartes such that thought occurs and the subject remains elusive or the product of language. The freedom of thinking and being remains, but the stabilized subject (itself a means of control) is not held in the same position or accorded the same function.

This syntactic problem is precisely the challenge posed by the *Personal Landscape* poets to which Derek Stanford was attracted during the war. He dedicates a good deal of his discussion of Durrell in *The Freedom of Poetry*, published immediately after the war, to this critical concept at the heart of Durrell's works at the time, and he in large part simply reprints Durrell's commentary from *Personal Landscape* (Stanford, *Freedom* 124–25). For Stanford, as an anarchist at this time as well as a conscientious objector during the war, it is also important to notice how his attention to Durrell's discussion of causality and syntax in conflict with the individual flows into the anarchist resistance to syntax, resistance to the propagandistic clarity one finds in Auden, and the ruptured syntax allowed or even needed in Surrealism. In many respects, this rupture of syntax, logic, and causality in favour of the independence of the self and artistic independence is at the heart of the Villa Seurat's influence on the English post-Surrealists, the New Apocalypse, and the broadly Personalist group as a whole.

This is also a strong example of the limitations of Tolley's political castration of these various groups of the 1940s since he notes from Stanford the same importance of syntax and logic to Durrell's discussions but can only relate it to Modernism as an aesthetic rather than a critical decision:

> The equation of "logic" and "syntax" is reflected in Durrell's poetry. Of William Empson, he said: "his real contribution to poetry is in the logical way in which he has disturbed syntax to force multiple meanings upon the structure of words. He is the real space-time poet" [Durrell, *Key* 198]. Poetry, Durrell felt, is akin to nonsense—"like good sense with all the logic removed" ["Ideas [II]" 2]. Distorted or incomplete syntax is frequent in Durrell's poetry. It is a step outside the bounds of "good sense," to allow "play"—or the play of the imagination.
> (Tolley, *Poetry* 46)

These things may be true, but Tolley's articulation offers only a very partial interpretation of the role of this stylistic component of Durrell's works and its relation to his surrealist writings while interacting with Miller through the Villa Seurat, such as while producing *The Black Book* and "Asylum in the Snow." This exemplifies a further trouble in Tolley's attempt to neatly tie off this critical problem: the endless division of movements and moments in order to elide continuity of thought. For Tolley,

> Durrell sees distortion (the "semantic disturbance") as a characteristic of modern writing in both prose and verse, and he makes it a part of his own work. Indeed, no British poet of the forties carries on so strongly the ironic inheritance of Anglo-American modernism as does Durrell. Yet Durrell's irony, as his distrust for logic might lead one to expect, is not the controlled, distanced irony of so much British writing. The Durrell of *The Black Book* remains. (*Poetry* 47)

The closing quip misleads since these traits are exactly the same as the Durrell of *The Black Book*, without contradiction. The modernist component of Durrell's challenge to syntax also seems inapt since it is marked as a resistance to the inheritance from Auden and Eliot together. The fragmentation found in Eliot and Pound or the Imagists might indeed be kindred with regard to style, but it is certainly not the same in conception. It is also distinct from the stream of consciousness in prose to be found in Henry James, James Joyce, and Virginia Woolf since Durrell also adopts from D.H. Lawrence (as does Miller), a distrust of the stable Ego and its allotropes (Durrell, *Key* 45, 63; quoting Lawrence, *Letters* 183).

The relationships between Durrell's anti-manifestos and the other movements in London are important to note at this point. In his retrospective *How I See Apocalypse*, Treece offers a reconsideration of the New Apocalypse via Hendry that is strikingly similar:

> [Hendry] has also said, "Apocalypse occurs where expression breaks through the structure of language, to become more *organic*"...This development from socialism to anarchism

is further emphasized when Hendry writes, "Logic (i.e., Totalitarian or Capitalistic), machine-made logic, has resulted from our fear of ourselves, fear of our uncontrolled energy, being translated into fear of the outside world." And the solution he finds is the one which Read arrives at, by a different route, which is, "Each man has his own space, his own orientation, which must be encouraged or adapted if we are to attain the wholeness we are seeking." But there is no place for the individual in the Machine States and Apocalypse is, above all things, anti-mechanistic. Freud says, "The myth is the step by which the individual emerges from the group psychology," and Fraser rightly observes, "The Apocalyptic writer will be on the side of the myth, the living and organic expression of human need, against the object-machine—the attempt by Newspapers, Government rhetoric, and systematic organization to manipulate men as mere parts of a huge State Machine." (76–77)

While the theoretical consideration of the impact of such notions on selfhood must be left for another chapter, the timeline is crucial to a narrative history, as is marking this continuity of thought between Treece, Hendry, and Durrell. Durrell's first articulations of the Heraldic Universe using these terms occurs in 1936 in his correspondence with Miller at the point when Miller's letters to Read (with Durrell copied on both sides of the correspondence) turned to the problem of the individual and Surrealism's communist politics. Durrell's comments were a rebuttal to Read's short-lived endorsement of Marxism during the 1936 London Surrealist Exhibition, and he returned to them while discussing Miller's works in *Delta* in ("Hamlet" 41) in 1938. These same issues are infused in Miller's works as well as his unpublished but widely distributed book on D.H. Lawrence. Both were then appearing in the journals consumed by and most closely aligned with the New Apocalypse, through which *Delta* was distributed, only after which Hendry writes his comments following after the 1941 first issue of *Transformation*.

To this timeline, it must be added that Hendry's comments also relate closely to his intimate work with Treece, and Treece's comments on Miller are deeply indebted to Durrell, as evidenced in his essay "Enquire within upon Everything," which precedes Miller's "Finale" in *Kingdom Come*'s autumn 1943 issue (the same year in which Nicholas Moore published his monograph on Miller). Treece quotes the sentence from Durrell's essay that immediate follows on Durrell's comments about the self in Miller's writings used as a defense mechanism against the non-syntactic and illogical terrain of personal creativity, the sentence that Durrell subsequently repeated in his *Personal Landscape* essay on the Heraldic Universe (Durrell, "Hamlet" 41; Durrell, "Heraldic" 8; Treece, "Enquire" 13). Treece's lengthy quotations from Durrell define Treece's approach to and understanding of Miller. From this, Treece's most pointed query is how to interpret Miller's use of the term "*egotism*. I would like to have him explain exactly what he means by the word" (Treece, "Enquire" 14). Treece, like Harold Bloom's attempted strong poet, turns on Miller at the mid-point of his essay, but not without further revealing his points of greatest influence. He falls back to the terminology used by Orwell in *Inside the Whale* and by Kathleen Raine, to cast the pacifism of the Villa Seurat group as "defeatism" (17), which contrasts with Treece's ultimate decision to serve in the military. This is, almost certainly, the bitter point of conflict between the different groups in England rather than their having simply *been* different groups as argued by Tolley: conflict between the pacifists and those who opted to serve and reject conscientious objection. This division underlies the conflicts in their reviews of each other's works, not any difference in terms of aesthetic school, shared influences, or anarchist views on authority. Treece then makes his alternative known by advocating Read's vision, though without knowing Miller's role in provoking Read to write the very works to which Treece turns.[44]

Shortly after, G.S. Fraser wrote to Treece from Egypt near to the end of the war after having read the most recent publications from the Apocalyptic-cum-New-Romantic poets under Hendry and Treece's joint editorial work. This follows on Fraser's extensive interactions with the *Personal Landscape* poets and his own republication of "The City of Benares" in their journal (after its first publication in *The White Horseman*). Fraser's published letter expresses a feeling very much like that articulated above by Treece (quoting Hendry), a feeling that demonstrates Fraser's continuing close reading of such works and the link between the London poets and that those in Cairo:

I never enter any great centre of our war organization—a
headquarters with its enormous corridors, a barracks enclosing
the Spanish cruelty of its square, or even the huge mess
where, as in an enormous third-class waiting room, so many
strangers eat together—without a shuddering sense of personal
impotence; I expect at any moment a thousand fingers to point,
whistles to blow, and I expect then to be brought, like a Kafka
character, before some tribunal in a small, shabby room that
will condemn me to unexampled penalties for the crime of
being myself....Moreover, one is guilty in being oneself. (Fraser,
"Letter to Henry" 165)

This sentiment is remarkably akin to Henry Miller's, but again, Fraser
was a civilian unlike Treece, and had not gone to the war to fight,
which is perhaps why he was more able to function in the *Personal
Landscape* group (which included Fedden as an outspoken pacifist)
than, for instance, John Waller.

Fraser's surprising kinship of thought to Miller is striking when he
considers the role of the artist in society and the importance of the
individual person. This is particularly so when we recall that his criticism of the Left does not come from a conservative inclination but
rather from that of a pacifist working alongside anti-fascists the likes
of Giulio Tavernari and outspoken Marxists like Hamish Henderson:

The popular Journalists of the Left are already explaining that
atrocities on our side are inevitable—you cannot make an
omelette without breaking eggs, and so forth....I can't manage
to care enough about the omelette: Cruelty still appalls me
more than anything else. But to be responsible to one's own
conscience only, to one's sense that atrocities are atrocious, is
difficult and painful; It means that so many types of success,
and not only cheap success, must be rejected....I don't believe
that the most brilliant achievements of a civilisation that in the
last reckoning rests upon torture can outweigh, or even alleviate,
the horrors. The degradation remains degradation. The pain
remains pain. (Fraser, "Letter to Henry" 166)

This is much akin to Miller's discussion with Read prior to his declaring for anarchism, or what Miller would articulate at the same time as Fraser in *Murder the Murderer*, an essay for which Durrell sent high praise from Egypt on August 22, 1944 (*Durrell–Miller Letters* 173–75), prior to Fraser's letter being written to Treece:

> Thank you for the essay. IT IS TERRIFIC. I haven't read anything of yours for so long that the impact of it came with something of the pristine clearness I first felt when I opened Tropic....Incidentally in England they are beginning to wake up to you—not to mention Egypt. (173)

Fraser's likelihood to have read the work at the same time is suggested by Miller's comment on December 28, 1941 to Durrell that "The other day a typewritten excerpt from a book by Fraser (about my skull portrait) came—but no letter with it. I'm sure you addressed the envelope" (152). Likewise, Waller recounts Fraser borrowing (and losing) works by Miller in the Ministry of Information Middle East reference library in Cairo ("Athens" 269). The anarchist component of Miller's argument was recognizable enough to lead Marguerite Young (who later collaborated with Anaïs Nin) in the 1945 *Conscientious Objector* to compare Miller's essay (even while disagreeing with parts of it) to Alex Comfort's novel *The Power House*. Stanford in London also identifies it as an anarchist work ("Independent" 62–64).

Miller's essay is unabashed in its anarchist allusions and frame of reference. It is not possible to know definitively if Fraser saw Miller's essay through Durrell, although we do know Durrell had planned to share it with at least George Seferis, and Fraser was in some form of correspondence with Miller via Durrell, and theirs are kindred visions. Where Fraser objects to atrocities in the name of necessity or good ends and emphasizes one's sole obligation to one's conscience, Miller offers an anecdote of a man seeking repentance for murder who only finds it in sacrificing his own recuperation for the sake of saving others: the murderer seeking atonement for his crimes in the allegory decides to sacrifice his own recovery to save someone else who is being attacked. For Miller,

There are murders and *murders* then. There is the kind that enslaves and the kind that liberates. But the final objective is to murder the murderer. The last act in the drama of "the Ego and his own" is to murder one's own murderous self. The man who with the fifty-third murder renounces all hope of salvation is savéd. To commit murder in full consciousness of the enormity of the crime is an act of liberation. It is heroic, and only those are capable of it who have purified their hearts of murder. Murder sanctioned by the Church, the State, or the community is murder just the same. Authority is the voice of confusion. The only authority is the individual conscience. To murder through fear, or love of country, is as bad as to murder from anger or greed. To murder one has to have clean hands and a pure heart. (Murder 41)

The notion of "the Ego and his own" is direct from the famous anarchist Max Stirner, as is the emphasis on "authority" as the obligation to obey "the Church, the State, or the community" without recourse to "the individual conscience." Various ways of conceiving of this position will be taken up in the next chapter, but the issue at stake here is the kinship between Miller's views and those spreading through the Personal Landscape poets to the London-based New Apocalypse. For Fraser, at the same time, with or without direct influence from Miller, the similarity of their notions is striking and recalls the tensions over Caudwell in the volume to which he contributed for the New Apocalypse:

> Does not freedom, I mean responsible freedom which is the only sort worth talking about, depend upon the creation of an interior order (perhaps, for personality, what form or what total intention is for a poem)? If we had this sense of interior order would the outward mechanical order terrify us so much? Would we feel so impotent in the face of it? (Fraser, "Letter to Henry" 167)

This sense of freedom, though no longer taken up by Treece in his response letter to Fraser after his enlistment in the Air Force (170–75), demonstrates the ongoing thread of anti-authoritarian thought in the Cairo literary circles, as well as Fraser's attempts to reconcile it with the anarchism espoused by the New Apocalypse.

This bears further analysis as a way of retrospectively retracing the common thread in the production of *Personal Landscape*. Fraser continues his exploration of the now common problems faced by the personalist group as a whole and articulates a response that must be individualist and anti-authoritarian, even if it takes up no other explicit name:

> As an individual, he is a fiction; as a member of Society, with a capital S, he is a fiction; both the individual and society are logical constructions from the experiences of quite small groups....We need a society in which groups can defend themselves; in which the obedience of the individual to the State is conditional on the State's respect for the rights of the group. This personalist and pluralist philosophy is as far as possible from being an individualistic one; with nothing between himself and the power of the State, taken as Absolute, the individual becomes impotent and unscrupulous. Faced with the might of the lion, he adopts the servility of the jackal or the cunning of the fox. ("Letter to Henry" 170)

Fraser then becomes more specific in his comments to Treece:

> By politics in a human sense, I think we can say now, we mean a political system which will allow him to preserve his honour and his dignity, his sense of responsible freedom. This seems to me to be the morality of politics that we must adopt. It means loneliness, as we were lonely in 1940. It is very far from implying an aloofness to politics—it is a morality very full, of practical compulsions. (170)

Alas, the response from Treece is commonplace and quasi-reactionary even while mentioning the anarchism of their New Apocalyptic visions, and Treece puts much of this tone to his then demanding military service. This is certainly the case, and the change in Treece is both marked and permanent. Nevertheless, to see such a conceptualization of the individual in a social world in the midst of violence and the use of authority to justify violent action is striking when Fraser's personal proximity to Miller's essay on the same is recalled along with the narrative thread running from Miller and Read's very fecund correspondence on the same topics and Fraser's role in articulating the New Apocalypse's anarchism.

Writing from Egypt at the end of the war, Fraser also openly acknowledges that the New Apocalypse's ideas, and his own contributions to them, were "a fertile but anarchic theory of the image" (Fraser, "Letter to Henry" 168). At the same moment, he blends the London and Cairo terminologies to show that they overlap: "this mythic [a key term to the New Apocalypse]—or in our Cairo jargon, this 'amusing' character" (168). In this rich letter, he also demonstrates that not only did the Cairo writers have access to the anthologies of the Apocalypse and New Romanticism, they also had *Kingdom Come*, including Treece's essay in it on Miller (168).

What, then, is the vision of *Personal Landscape*, the peculiar periodical produced by Durrell shortly after his close interactions with Miller in the Villa Seurat, Bernard Spencer who had previously edited *Oxford Poetry* with Stephen Spender in 1930, and the pacifist Robin Fedden? The first and most obvious point for attention is its titular proclamation for the "Personal" amidst the social obligations of war. Moreover, the title was adopted a full year prior to Treece and Schimanski's "Personalist literature" recalibration in the first issue of *Transformation* in London. Apart from Durrell's focus on logic and syntax in relation to the creative individual in his "Ideas about Poems" pieces and related prose in the journal, we are also drawn to attend to Spencer's concerns about "violence of sun and its worship; / Of money and its worship" ("Delos" 6) in one of the first set of his poems that opens the first issue. In the poem, the same conflated "violence" of worship and money is bound to slavery and the market, with "Wealth" and "money" opening and closing the first four lines. Amidst the poetic image of a personal visit to Delos, the struggle is scarcely concealed, yet this social exterior to the poet is never allowed to openly intrude in the world of the poem. Fedden is, likewise, "Not gripping sword" ("Camp" 9) and cannot distinguish between the wartime desert landscape and that of a lover: "I cannot disentangle your arms / From the body of the day," the light is like her hands, and "soft the contours of the hill" ("Personal" 8). The same first issue holds Durrell's three poems, with "To Argos" employing the disjoined syntax and image that Valentine Cunningham might call surrealist metaphor and a loss of history, myth, and allusion that leads him to lament, "And this is what breaks the heart" ("To Argos" 12).

This may strike a reader first as a quietist form of Personalism that retreats from the war, yet inspection shows the suffering of war is never far from the surface of these poems—Durrell's Argos and Spencer's Delos both having been visited under the imminent threat of invasion in Greece. This, precisely, is their poignance, without which the poem's effect is lost. The subsequent issues of *Personal Landscape* also thicken the challenge with the inclusion of, and high praise given to, Elie Papadimitriou, a Greek poet writing of her experiences of the massacre at Smyrna in 1922. Papadimitriou was also an ardent Marxist, acknowledged as such, and her long poem (present in several excerpts) is, for the journal's editors, "one of the most important of recent productions in modern Greek" (Durrell, "Editor's Note" 7). The appearance of Papadimitriou also presages Spencer's later inclusion of his own "The Behaviour of Money" (15–16). The arrival of Dorian Cooke's works in the fourth issue further cements the ties to the origins of the New Apocalypse, as per Keery's outlining of Cooke's central role ("Burning [7]" 45–49), and Cooke's works continued to unify the quasi-surrealist and political ambitions, as did his translations for the journal. Herbert Howarth, who had appeared across *The Booster* and *Delta* in Durrell's earlier endeavours, also contributed from his teaching post in Cairo an Arabic co-translation he had completed with Ibrahim Shukrallah. Both men would certainly have been in contact with Durrell while working in the Press Office of the British Council during the war. Their translation in *Personal Landscape* was the early product of a project that became Howarth and Shakrullah's postwar book *Images from the Arab World*.

This left *Personal Landscape* in 1945 retrospectively aligning its inception "at a time when propaganda colours all perspectives" as a periodical that "emphasized those 'personal landscapes', which lie obstinately outside national and political frontiers" ("A Change" 2).

Durrell was already relocated to Alexandria and was preparing for a further relocation to Rhodes. Spencer and Fedden were also facing relocation, and for Spencer as with Durrell, this was the result of representing the British government abroad during European reconstruction. Fedden was returning to London, and his stated aim in the final volume was "An anthology from *Personal Landscape*... [that] will bring together much of the best work that we have published" ("A Change" 2). The book, naturally, was published by Tambimuttu through the Editions Poetry London imprint where Fraser was already caging for a job between Tambi and his assistant Nicholas Moore, who was planning to return to Cambridge. Even in closing, *Personal Landscape* retained the same well-trod paths and avenues away from "propaganda" and "outside national and political frontiers."

Egypt, Paris, and London to New York, Big Sur, and Berkeley: The San Francisco Renaissance

In this ferment, Henry Miller interacted with Robert Duncan in New York before both of them relocated to the West Coast near to San Francisco. Duncan included Durrell, Miller, and Nin in *Experimental Review* at the same time and emphasized Miller's anarchism in his reviews for the same issues (Symmes 79). Moreover, once he moved to California, Miller then lived in the artist commune created by Jean Varda, the same commune in which the Canadian writer Elizabeth Smart was living when she first met George Barker, leading to her novel *By Grand Central Station I Sat Down and Wept*. Smart already knew Varda intimately in Cassis in 1938, and she had first contacted Barker through her correspondence with Durrell, who had included her poetry in *Delta* in 1939 in Paris ("Comforter" 17) and who had passed it along to the editors of *Seven* in Cambridge ("Three" 22–24).[45] This was her first entry to the British literary community developing from English post-Surrealism that would publish her novel after Miller had tried to have it published through the same press bringing out his *The Colossus of Maroussi* in the same year.[46] Miller also supported the Berkeley-based *Circle* magazine, which George Leite launched in 1944. This new literary journal developed out of his participation in

Kenneth Rexroth's San Francisco Libertarian Circle (later Anarchist Circle), which included an active reading group and overlapped significantly with Varda's commune.[47]

Circle's print run quickly shows the wide network of collaborators, especially if we take into account Rexroth's anthology The New British Poets, which was published in 1948 and focuses mainly on this same anarchist group. Rexroth discusses this group extensively in his Introduction through their politics, which mirrored his own (viii, xxiv, xxviii). Despite the differences between American and British experiences of surrealist art, Circle magazine immediately endorsed an anarchic Surrealism akin to English Surrealism: "We believe that the surrealists, in the progressive tradition, have these valid qualities" (Leite, Editorial n. pag.).[48] Moreover, in closing his first editorial, Leite turns to Miller's struggles with censorship and borrows directly from Miller's contemporaneous essay Murder the Murderer, and Miller's letter supporting the journal also provides its illustrations and first text:

> It is one of our major hopes in this world-wide struggle for
> freedom that there will be included a possible freedom of
> literary expression....We have all been made aware of the power
> of censorship in the last few months....In 1934 Hitler's aesthetic
> differed from many of the artists of his country; he was obvious,
> he burned the offending work. (Leite, Editorial n. pag.)

Miller's comments were published in the same year as this issue of Circle and distributed earlier in typed carbon copies as far as Egypt where it was read by Durrell and Fraser, as is already noted, and who then wrote about it for the English New Apocalypse. Miller's Murder the Murderer similarly blurs the authoritarian repressiveness of both Nazi and Allied states, differing by degree but not in authoritarian means. Miller writes, "Some say...that you would never be allowed to write as you do if you were living under a Nazi regime. No doubt I wouldn't. But then neither am I allowed to write such books in England and America" (Murder 11). Leite would later live with Miller and featured him across the journal's run.

Circle quickly allied itself to Robert Duncan's defunct Ritual and Experimental Review, the new journal Ark, and to Miller's network through

the Big Sur anarchist commune. By the fifth issue, *Circle* announced
its intention to publish the first of the Circle Editions in the coming
fall of 1945. The *Circle* double issue of 1946 opens auspiciously with
Duncan's major poem "The Years as Catches" (1–4) then includes
Georges Henein's "There Are No Pointless Jests" (126–27), which
is translated from French by none other than Ithell Colquhoun, the
wife of Toni del Renzio, who produced the anarcho-surrealist journal
Arson in 1942 and published with his wife in Alex Comfort's *New Road*
at the same time as *Circle* (Renzio, "Morgenroth" 228). Henein, as has
already been noted in relation to the *Personal Landscape* poets, was affiliated with both the English poets in Egypt and was a major figure in
Egyptian Surrealism and anarchist politics, and in 1964 Durrell would
lament not having been able to include Henein in *Personal Landscape* in
Cairo when he wrote an obituary for Bernard Spencer ("Bernard" 44).
Yet, the same issue that contains Henein's poetry was *Circle*'s last issue
for a time. In 1946, it ceased publication for two years to focus on
the Circle Editions imprint. Among the first books was Cossery's *Men
God Forgot* in 1946. The issue containing Henein also contains Miller's
review and promotion of Cossery's novel, likely written at the same
time as the materials that later formed his Introduction to the 1955
City Lights edition (Miller, "Novels of" 181–83). He also demonstrably read it in detail and noticed it is "the sort of book that precedes
revolutions, and begets revolution, if the tongue of man possesses any
power[, yet]…they do not speak like the professional agitators indoc-
trinated with Marxism" (182). Miller also praises Cossery's book as
"this terrible breviary, dispatched to us from Alexandria by Lawrence
Durrell" (Miller, Rev. of *Men* 136). Durrell left Alexandria a year prior,
which dates Miller's comments to early 1945, which also tells us when
the materials would have originally reached Leite for publication.
Moreover, Cossery's surviving correspondence with Durrell suggests
a far more extensive relationship than has been previously recognized, thanking Durrell for both his friendship and for the money
Durrell had sent him. Durrell defended Cossery when the American
secret services thought he might be a spy, and Cossery recounts, "I
remember, when he arrived from Greece—it was at the time that
the Germans were invading and all the British people living there
were reluctant to go to Cairo—he sent the English translations of my

novels to America to be published" (Nouri n. pag.). This implies that Henein's and Cossery's works arrived at the same time and from the same source and network: Alexandria to Berkeley, Edwards, Howarth, and Waller to Durrell and Fraser to Miller to Leite.[49]

The same timeframe applies to Durrell's strikingly experimental *Two Excursions into Reality: Zero and Asylum in the Snow*, which Durrell had reprinted himself on Rhodes in 1946 (following their first appearance in Nicholas Moore's *Seven* prior to the war), but this short story pair only appeared through Circle Editions in 1947 after a failed publication attempt by Duncan. Although the proofs are lost, there is still a surviving contract (privately held) for the first American edition of Durrell's *The Black Book* as well. Duncan had also already undertaken to publish *The Black Book* (along with Durrell's *Zero* and *Asylum in the Snow*) in 1941 and had advertised them for sale in *Experimental Review*. After Duncan's failed project, Durrell signed the contract with *Circle* for the novel in Alexandria on September 24, 1945 and Leite signed his on November 20, 1945, with a copy from Curtis Brown dispatched to Leite on January 3, 1946, precisely the same timeframe as his production of Cossery's novel. The Circle Edition of *The Black Book* reached the proof stage and was advertised but again failed to appear. Of course, Durrell's work was already advertised in the magazine ahead of the contract. In this manner, just as *Seven* printed the unpublished materials from *Delta*, *Circle* published and undertook to publish the unfinished projects from Duncan's *Experimental Review*. In both instances, the legacy of the anarchist revision to English post-Surrealism initiated in the Villa Seurat is clear.

At the same time, Duncan offers a kindred problem in "Toward an African Elegy," which was published in *Circle* in the summer of 1948 after John Crowe Ransom's famous rejection of the poem for *The Kenyon Review*. Duncan's "The Homosexual in Society" appeared in *Politics* in August 1944, after which Ransom revoked his offer of publication—Leite had wanted to publish the resulting correspondence along with the poem in *Circle*, which Duncan had refused, and most scholars, including Michael Davidson, see this as beginning the breakdown in their friendship (39). In contrast, in Duncan's letters to Sanders Russell,[50] with whom he had edited *Experimental Review*, Duncan records selling his printing press (in order to buy a painting by Robert De Niro, Sr.) and that

CIRCLE is publishing this…coming issue The African Elegy and a correspondence which I had with John Crowe Ransom about my article in POLITICS on the homosexual and the homosexual elements in the above poem.[51] But CIRCLE suffers as far as I am concerned from its Editorial policy—well, in short, from its editor who doesn't see at all what I am doing. His enthusiasm is so damnd [sic] mistaken. (Letter to Sanders n. pag.)

He follows this up a week or so later by writing,

Leite has written me an exceedingly winning letter—winning by its rather surprising maturity of tone and countenance; the result of which is, specifically, that he is printing the African Elegy and the correspondence with approval. I shall read the proofs carefully myself etc. The result, generally, is that I no longer am minded to boycott CIRCLE and shall make what contribution I can to him in the future. (n. pag.)

However, the point of their disagreement is clearly interpretive and not personal or political. For Duncan, in his letters to Ransom, "The theme of the poem is not homosexuality; nor does the darkness stand for homosexuality" (Letter to Ransom, n. pag.), which means his gesture to the unknown is not simply the "unbewusst" or re-pressed unconscious. For Duncan, "The dark continent in the poem is not what one hides, but what is hidden from one….It would be rather astounding in an overt homosexual that what was held back, imprisoned in the unconscious, was the homosexual desire" (n. pag.). In this context, Duncan's poem presents "in jungles / of my body…/ Moves / I. I. I." such that this fragile selfhood and its substitutional dreamwork presents the darkness of "The halls of Africa we seek in dreams / as barriers of dream against the deep" ("Toward" 96). This is to say, the dreamt of desire is itself a substitutive gratification of we know not what, for which the Ego is yet another substitutive gratifica-tion or form of control and mastery. The kinship to Durrell's Heraldic Universe comment is indirect yet reflects both poets' kindred notions of the self. "I. I. I." cannot be overlooked or cast as a product of con-ditions, though it is an embodied "I" capable of change, development, and self-revision, and the libidinal drives of this "I" shelter it by creating a barrier against a further limitation on self-knowledge. Duncan's assertion seems to move the self to some other location that is not contiguous with desire or the containing Ego.

This "needful desire" of the body can be both a path to freedom as well as a means of containment. Through the desublimation of sexual desire conjoined with regulation of the means of satisfaction in a capitalist economy (repressive desublimation), the modern "one-dimensional" society transforms the corporeal and previously contained drives of the body into yet more insidious forms of domination—one might satisfy desire through interpellation as the consuming subject regulated by a capitalist economy and thereby fetishize desire itself. Alternatively, when such needful desire bursts the stabilizing boundaries of the Ego, the interpellation of the subject within a regulatory economy cannot function, and in Eve Kosofsky Sedgwick's sense, "sexual desire is an unpredictably powerful solvent of stable identities" (85). Duncan renders this notion as "a man's sexuality is a natural factor in a biological economy larger and deeper than his own human will" (Duncan, "Homosexual" 38), much as Durrell describes sexual desire in 1957 by noting "we had been trapped in the projection of a will too powerful and too deliberate to be human" (Justine 18–19). In this group of authors, Duncan is the most nuanced in his capacity to suggest this regulatory capacity in desublimation.

This is hardly a new problem to anarchist discourse. As Allan Antliff argues in relation to Stirner's work and his importance to Man Ray (one of Miller's close friends in Paris), "Stirner deemed the very notion of an 'I' to be a form of metaphysical alienation from the self" (Antliff, Anarchist 77) such that the "I" is a fixed construction of absolutes whereas the "self" is a transforming yet autonomous experience of being: the "absolute" Ego versus the finite and transitory Ego. The latter may seem a peculiar preference for a philosophy seeking self-determining autonomy, given that the same self is subject to revision or even rediscovery, but it again returns to praxis rather than essentialisms or categorizations and logics to which the self must submit in order to be known. In Durrell's phrasing, "in thinking of [identity] as a stable thing we are trying to put a lid on a box with no sides" ("Kneller" 163–64), or for Duncan we find a group of persons "who have been willing rather than to struggle toward self-recognition, to sell their product, to convert their deepest feelings into marketable oddities and sentimentalities" ("Homosexual" 40) through the regulation of desires that contradict the stability-seeking Ego. For Miller in the context of the Second World War, "the fight is for life, to have it more abundantly, and the fact [is] that millions are now ready to fight for something they have ignominiously surrendered for the greater part of their lives" ("Open" 157).

In this sense, Duncan's "Toward an African Elegy" and Durrell's *The Black Book* and "Asylum in the Snow" and Cossery's "The Postman Gets His Own Back" offer examples of how the various critical histories retraced here could lead to an actual practice of rereading, which is detailed in the final chapter of this book. Duncan's "I. I. I." works in a manner akin to Durrell's titling of the sections of *The Black Book* as "Ego and Id," "Ego," and again "Ego and Id" with no superego. Cossery demonstrates a kindred concern through his postman and laundryman being "bellicose" in any stabilized and social form of identity yet free when they turn to an unknowable interiority that carries the "distress of a far-off world" and "for ever, afraid of the wide and vast unknown" ("Postman" 73), which is why Miller describes Cossery's work as "the sort...that precedes revolutions and begets revolution" ("Novels of" 182). In all three works, the "I" is disturbed in order to displace the ostensible contiguity between the self being its own (the Ego and its own, so to speak) in contrast to the "I" being stable or even knowable. Hence, they explicitly challenge stable notions of selfhood even while disputing the supposition that subjectivity is a product of and is defined by material conditions or that social being determines subjectivity. This is to say, even when self-contemplation generates an order that lacks logical syntax (as with Durrell's conception of poetry) or when the various allotropes of the self (qua D.H. Lawrence) are the only manifestation of it accessible (rather than some pure, unchanging essence), the self is still its own, in Stirner's sense of Ego belonging to itself and no other. Hence, the exercise and experience of freedom is predicated on the self yet does not necessitate stability, knowing, or even any form of certainties with regard to it—freedom is not another manifestation of authority's stabilizing influence on the Ego.

The point of all this is to demonstrate the profoundly international, multipolar nature of the overlooked and misunderstood anarcho-surrealist networks in Late Modernism as well as their rich mutual influences. In summary, Durrell's and Miller's journals *The Booster* and *Delta* initiated an anti-authoritarian-cum-anarchist revision to Surrealism's communist stance following the 1936 London International Surrealist Exhibition, and their revision caught up major figures from Read and Gascoyne to the New Apocalypse and New Romantics under Henry Treece and Alex Comfort. The next year, Henein and Cossery began the same anti-authoritarian revision to Surrealism in Egypt and in reaction to Nazism's "Degenerate Art" exhibition. Durrell, due to the war, was then relocated to Cairo and Alexandria along with many of the British authors who had created the New Apocalypse movement in England as a form of anarchist post-Surrealism following the model created by *The Booster* and *Delta*. In America, Henry Miller returned after visiting Durrell in Greece up until the Nazi invasion and Durrell's evacuation to Egypt via Crete. In the United States, Miller worked with Robert Duncan and Anaïs Nin in New York and Woodstock, where they tried to republish Durrell's surrealist story "Asylum in the Snow" several times as well as *The Black Book*. Both Duncan and Miller then relocated to California and became involved in the network that created the anarchist, surrealist journal *Circle*. In Egypt, Durrell's network engaged with Henein and Cossery,[52] and during the Second World War he sent their works to California to be published in *Circle*, which brought them out beside Duncan's, Durrell's, and Miller's own works. In the meantime, the English post-Surrealists were also publishing them in Egypt and through which they became available to the New Apocalypse and Tambimuttu's *Poetry London*. Two points then arise as the pith of this polemic: (1) the anarchist revision to Surrealism was rampant during World War II and was not fragmentary nor rare, as virtually all prior criticism has contended, and (2) this network of authors was densely interconnected in a manner that fostered mutual support and international distribution of materials despite paper rationing and exclusion from the mainstream media. My further contention, then, is that it is impossible to think about American literature since the San Francisco Renaissance and the Beats without recognizing the origins of these groups' inspirations and their aesthetic models in wartime

London, Paris, Athens, Cairo, and Alexandria. It is not sufficient, for instance, to begin this tracing of origins in the 1950s, as do Nancy M. Grace and Jennie Skerl (1) or R.J. Ellis when noting the Beat issue of Tambimuttu's *Poetry London* in 1960 (Grane and Skerl 146).

All of this is to say, for this section of the "Narrative Itinerary," the local "Cult of Sex and Anarchy" in California, as it was described in the famously scathing *Harper's Magazine* story of 1947, was more accurately a reaction, at least in part, to Egyptian art's rejection of European fascism and Nazism mediated through British anti-authoritarians and anarchists. We open the pages of the American avant-garde to discover that the punctuation and drops of ink are made up of seeds from London, Athens, and Cairo.

But this is still not the entire story, and *Circle* marks more than a migration of materials from Cairo to California. With Miller's departure from Paris after the closure of *Delta*, and with the end of the Villa Seurat group as a geographically localized endeavour, many of *Delta* and *The Booster*'s authors began migrations as well. Elizabeth Smart had appeared in the final issue with her uncollected poem "Comforter, Where, Where is Your Comforting?" (17) and through Durrell began contact with David Gascoyne's recently departed roommate, George Barker.[53] She would again appear with three poems the next year in the final issue of *Seven*. She would cross paths with Miller again in California, this time during her turbulent travels with Barker across America, as recounted in her visceral novella-cum-prose poem *By Grand Central Station I Sat Down and Wept*, a book published by Tambimuttu immediately after the war through Editions Poetry London. The two met after Smart had already encountered Kenneth Rexroth while washing her socks in a public fountain (Hamalian 135); he intuited her difficult situation and shortly realized the challenge of her affair with Barker and Barker's ongoing relationship with his wife while the three lived near Big Sur. As Miller recounts, "The romance which inspired the book took place at Anderson Creek in the days when Varda ruled the roost" (Miller, *Big Sur* 59). Jean Varda, the painter whom Miller knew in Paris, ran an anarchist artists' colony in Big Sur and had convinced Miller to relocate to the area. It proved to be another node in the larger personalist network, in this instance, reassembling Miller, Varda, and Smart after their time in Paris.

Miller's associates in Big Sur included George Leite, who lived with Miller in his cabin for a time out of poverty. Prior to this, however, Leite had written a letter soliciting contributions for a new periodical to be named *Circle*, Miller's response to which became the first piece in the journal's first issue, Miller's "Open Letter to Small Magazines." Miller advised the young Leite chidingly on how to be an effective acquisitions editor without an acquisitions budget, claiming "In Paris…I ran a magazine ("The Booster," which later became "Delta") and it was the contributors who paid to keep the magazine going" (Miller, "Open Letter to Small" n. pag.). While this was not true, the timing was remarkably apt since Leite was a part of Rexroth's reading group Anarchist Circle, through which the magazine was launched, later becoming Circle Editions, and later still Leite opened daliel's bookstore. Rexroth even designed the cover image of the third issue of *Circle* (Hamalian 152). Miller had such a group as well, though it did not emphasize political activism.[54] The Anarchist Circle (originally Libertarian Circle) is remarkable for having been organized by Rexroth and including the young Robert Duncan who had returned from James Cooney's commune in Woodstock, New York, where he was the editor of a small magazine title *Experimental Review* publishing Durrell, Miller, and Nin from Paris while Miller worked as the European editor for Cooney's own pacifist magazine *Phoenix*.[55] Duncan had already endeavoured to publish Durrell's surrealist short story pair "Asylum in the Snow" and "Zero," both of which first appeared in *Seven* via Nicholas Moore and John Goodland, and were advertised as part of the Booster Broadsides that did not appear in Paris. Miller had also carried out a lengthy correspondence regarding American publication by Duncan of Durrell's *The Black Book*, the novel having had an equally significant impact on the young Duncan as it did Gascoyne in Paris and Dylan Thomas in London at the same time.

Duncan's projects to publish Durrell and Miller did not come to fruition apart from the three issues of and supplement to *Experimental Review*, but his arrival in Berkeley and acquaintance with Leite eventually led to Circle Editions' publication of these aborted projects as *Two Excursions into Reality: Zero and Asylum in the Snow* and at least the production of proofs for *The Black Book*, which was agreed to in contract but was never produced, either due to censorship or lack of funds. It was advertised as available for order yet never appeared. Miller recounts correcting the proofs in his correspondence with the French professor Wallace Fowlie (Miller, *Letters* 109, 122),[56] who himself was a contributor to the New Apocalypse's *Transformation Four* with an essay on Antoine de Saint Exupéry. Although Duncan is often separated from these projects through *Circle* and Circle Editions, in the context of discussing Duncan's Anarchist Circle meeting in San Francisco, Ellen Tallman recounts in her memoir that "Henry Miller, who occasionally attended, had a group of his own in Big Sur where there was less contention (so we heard), but none of the big gathering, fund-raisers, great music, and food that the San Francisco group had" (64).

This period is rife with examples of Durrell and Miller's mutual promotion, in particular Miller's activities promoting the publication of authors of a "personalist" disposition in like-minded periodicals. Although it did not come to fruition, their interactions with Edward Dahlberg's anarchist *Twice A Year* give telling examples of the typical pattern. Dahlberg, the anarchist editor of *Twice A Year*, during the final few years of the 1930s "undertook to introduce certain new voices as yet unheard in America. Perhaps the most notable of these is Henry Miller...Miller in turn interested Lawrence Durrell in *Twice A Year*" (Wasserstrom xx), and he appears to have been the spark interesting Mrs. Norman and Dahlberg in Patchen's work as well (Bush 261). Dhalberg and Herbert Read were also, notably, good friends and regular correspondents after 1945. This pattern recurs well into the 1950s for both Durrell and Miller relating to journals as far apart as Yale University's *Chimera* or the *T'ien Hsia Monthly* in Singapore. Moreover, according to William Wasserstrom, "Durrell wrote to Mrs. Norman saying that Miller urged him to send work, and...'I am gathering nuts for you: poets & young people...' He recommended David Gascoyne, Patrick Evans, George Barker, and Dylan Thomas" (xx). Durrell's correspondence, which was Wasserstrom's primary resource from the papers of *Twice A Year*, leads him to assert this constituted "a loosely organized group that wrote mainly for *Delta*, edited in Paris by Durrell, Miller, and Alfred Perlès, or for *Seven* ('independent, apocalyptic and experimental'), edited in Cambridge by Nicholas Moore, these writers shared Mrs. Norman's beliefs" (xx).

Moore published "The Imaginative" in the fall–winter issue of 1940,

and Miller republished his Balzac essay from Twice A Year in Henry
Treece's *Transformation Four*, as did Nin for her story "Birth," originally
in *The Booster*, then Twice A Year, and thence to Treece, all via Miller. In
this manner, Miller consistently recirculates his network through stra-
tegic channels that encourage further traffic along particular pathways:
predominantly anarchist and post-surrealist progressive pathways,
such as "Mrs. Norman's beliefs" carried out through the anarchist
Dahlberg's editorship.

Casting backward from the 1944 founding of *Circle*, we find a four-
year anticipation. Apart from Miller's and Durrell's letters of support
published in Cooney's *Phoenix*, the second issue of *Experimental Review*
from 1940 includes several works of Villa Seurat origins: Nin's "House
of Incest," Durrell's "The Sermon," and Miller's review of Kenneth
Patchen's *The Journal of Albion Moonlight*. Patchen's works would later be
championed by Gascoyne and Comfort through Wrey Gardiner's
Grey Walls Press in their edition of his *Outlaw of the Lowest Planet* as well
as through Gardiner's *Poetry Quarterly* through the same press, which
also featured a lengthy essay by Gascoyne on Patchen's relationship
to Dada. This English interest in Patchen was significantly later than
Miller's essay and Duncan's subsequent supplementary issue on
Patchen, but Miller is very likely the origin of English periodicals'
familiarity with the American poet, which recurs in Comfort's *Poetry
Folios*. The third issue of Duncan's *Experimental Review* from Woodstock
then included further works by Patchen as well as pieces by all three
of the Villa Seurat group: Nin's "The Story of Pierre," Durrell's "Ten
Poems," and three excerpts from Miller's *Tropic of Capricorn*, as well as
advertisements for Duncan's unproduced edition of Durrell:

> LAWRENCE DURRELL, ASYLUM IN THE SNOW
> Two long prose pieces, *Asylum in the Snow* and *Zero*. Designed
> With jacket and title pages by VIRGINIA ADMIRAL.
> Publication date: January 20th, 1941. $1.75 (n. pag.)

Admiral was a significant painter and wife to Robert De Niro Sr.,
with whom Duncan had a relationship. Duncan also had an intimate
relationship with Nin near this time. His direct personal contact in
New York was with Nin, but his previous correspondence was with

Miller, and his publishing focus was on Durrell, for whom he wrote "An Ark for Lawrence Durrell," which takes up a focus on organic objects common to Durrell's poetry of this period.[57] The relationship with Nin may be a factor in the relative exclusion of this period from studies of Duncan, a portion of which have focused (rightly) on his importance as a pre-Stonewall gay rights figure, although more recent scholarship had not shied away from the topic.

Apart from Miller, Duncan, Cooney, and Leite's anarchism, a common position that should by now be almost expected is articulated by Duncan in his pseudonymous review of Miller's *Tropic of Capricorn*, which had only been published in Paris but would be excerpted for the subsequent issue of *Experimental Review*. For Duncan,

> From the meridian of Dada Miller has moved into the free world. He is a revolutionist who holds no betrayal, for he has no desire to replace the prison which he has destroyed with another prison which he likes better. Politically he has no politics. Having come at last into the real world he is an anarchist. Anyone reading over the foregoing passage will see clearly why the Marxist surrealists are afraid of Miller. (Symmes 78–79)

The same undercurrent of a politics of the unpolitical that resists the Marxist ambitions of Surrealism and redirects them to an anarcho-personalist post-Surrealism recur in America through Duncan's interactions with Miller. This also contextualizes Duncan's growing interest in Patchen, whose work led to a symposium issue as the final supplement of *Experimental Review* in 1941.

Duncan was also in correspondence with Rexroth in San Francisco at this time, with whom Miller was also in contact, and this was the same period in which Rexroth grew to know Elizabeth Smart, and through her George Barker. Rexroth would not compile his influential *The New British Poets* anthology until 1947, but the material was already being brought to him through these contacts. As Richard Cándida Smith argues, "Rexroth deliberately chose poets ignored by the Eliot-Auden-Spender circle and therefore generally unknown in the United States" (47), but he also deliberately chose those among the network of authors with whom he had the most personal contact and through whom his own works were being published abroad. Miller was an unhesitating advocate for Patchen's works, and his literary network reached in two directions, creating a means for British writers to contact Duncan and Rexroth as well as for Rexroth to contact a great many British writers and their periodicals.

In 1943, Rexroth first met Smart in California and Miller relocated to Big Sur where he also renewed his friendship with Smart through Varda's artists colony. Varda had been Smart's lover and Miller's good friend in Paris only three years earlier. Until the autumn of the same year, Comfort's *Poetry Folios* (issues 1 through 4, 1942–43) included only British poets, though it had begun to foster contact with South American writers through *Revista Agonia* in Buenos Aires. Comfort's *New Road* of the same year, through Grey Walls Press, was likewise entirely British apart from the Surrealism section and a handful of foreigners living in London, such as Tambimuttu. The same applies to Wrey Gardiner's *Poetry Quarterly*. However, by the undated fifth issue of *Poetry Folios* later in 1943, Patchen has appeared with two poems, "The Lions of Fire Shall Have Their Hunting" and "Instruction for Angels." Comfort also adds, to the back cover of the chapbook, "The poems of Kenneth Patchen are printed by kind permission of the author and Editors of RETORT. Further work by this writer will appear in future FOLIOS." *Retort: An Anarchist Review* had begun publication in 1942 in New York. The only mutual contact between Comfort and Patchen was Miller, and Patchen's works rapidly began to appear from this point forward in the various periodicals affiliated with the personalist movement in general in Britain. By 1944, *New Road* was reprinting material from Jean Giono's "Refusal to Obey" that had originally appeared in Cooney's *Phoenix*. By early in 1946, in its ninth issue, *Poetry Folios* began to include Rexroth, including his seminal anarchist poems "Climbing Milestone Mountain August 22nd, 1937" and a long excerpt from "The Phoenix and the Tortoise," by a large margin the longest poem published in the complete run of *Poetry Folios*. Finally, the common cause of their anarchism or anti-authoritarian views was articulated openly by Rexroth in 1947 when he wrote of the British poets. When praising Savage and Woodcock as "the most remarkable of the young men who came first to prominence during the War," he adds of the group, "it is significant that they are all anarchists, 'personalists,' and pacifists. In his critical book, *What I Mean by Apocalypse* Treece also calls himself an anarchist" (Rexroth, Introduction xxviii). From Smart and Varda to Miller to Treece to Rexroth, the network's knots tightened to firm bonds running like cables from California to New York to London to Cairo.

In this vein, it is deeply tempting to unify Rexroth's vision of "autocthonous" poetry as a movement with the principles developing in the New Apocalypse at the same time. For Rexroth, the auto-cthonous movement, as a form of poetic immediacy rather than formal rigour, was defined by four principles: "personal witness against the permanent war state...A decentering of European tradition... Personal contact with raw nature...[and] religious faith" (Cándida Smith 48–49). Set next to the Apocalypse's vision of personalist anti-war protest favouring freedom, a return to Celtic traditions, organic form, and reinvigorating myth, the kindred nature of their vision of anarchism seems strong, though Rexroth appears to have only discovered their works at the same time as Miller's arrival in Big Sur. The further temptation is to query a relationship between the Apocalypse's vision of myth expressed by Fraser and Hendry as a potential precursor to Robert Duncan's much later and more nuanced conception of myth expressed in *The Truth and Life of Myth: An Essay in Essential Autobiography*: "The poetic imagination faces the challenge of finding a structure that will be the complex story of all the stories felt to be true, a myth in which something like the variety of man's experi-ence of what is real may be contained" (11–12). The temptation is increased by Duncan's inclusion of a new form of Romanticism in his discussion of myth such that "The very word 'Romantic' is, in literary and social criticism today, pejorative. But it is in the Romantic vein— to which I see my own work as clearly belonging—that the two worlds... mythological vision and folklorish phantasy, are wedded in a phantas-magoria...the spiritual romance" (38).

Lastly, while Durrell is the only poet in this group who does not explicitly endorse anarchism, in Duncan's anarchist sensibilities a unification of these sympathetic visions of poetry emerges:

> My politics which was, in the tradition of Emerson and
> Thoreau, and then near too to the spirit I read in Vanzetti's

letters, anarchist where Pound was so committed to the cause of
Fascism. It seemed to me that I saw in Pound the artist wanting
to have the state a work of art, as Plato had once wanted a
philosopher's state. I was not, anyway, that trusting of order and
coercion, whether political or that other inner political coercion
that Freud saw in the superego. (Duncan and H.D. 36)

This blending of external and internal coercive authority, whether
through Freudian guilt or political power, remains the "personalist"
challenge to all four groups of authors, whether they identified as anarchist or not. This is the backbone of their collaboration. It was equally a challenge to the *Personal Landscape* poets, the proto-San Francisco
Renaissance, the New Apocalypse, and the Villa Seurat group. Much
like Duncan's resistance to organized political dissent and the author-·
itarian potential in both the left and right, Durrell's first invocation of
the Heraldic Universe and refutation of Read's endorsement of communism during the 1936 London International Surrealist Exhibition
asserts (in echo of Read's language in his published speech),

> Let's look at the manifestoes. Begins a political discussion. The
> artist's place in society. A definite lean leftward. Well what's
> wrong with that? Nothing, provided politics are not going to
> be confused with art. I'm tired of political people. They have
> confused the inner struggle with the outer one....Politics is
> an art that deals in averages. Art is a man that deals in people.
> (Durrell and Miller 18; Miller and Read 89)

In the instances across these personalist views, the pre-eminence of
the individual and internal, personal struggle is consistent. It impacts
both politics and aesthetics, including form, order, organization, and
syntax.

The American component of this movement developed in a direct
though often overlooked lineage. Antliff recounts "former Woodstock
resident and anarchist poet Robert Duncan helped found a weekly
discussion group called the Libertarian Circle," and this group
enjoyed not only Duncan's direct contact with the Villa Seurat group
and ideals through Durrell and Miller: "The Circle began in 1946,

when Duncan and Philip Lamantia proposed founding an 'open and above-board' anarchist discussion group to fellow anarchist Kenneth Rexroth...; with his backing, the project prospered...[and] moved to the top floor of a building occupied by the Jewish anarchist group Arbeiter Ring" (Antliff, *Anarchy* 117). Rexroth's support was vital, as were his own ties to the English anarchist post-surrealist groups and to Miller and Durrell.

In this context, Rexroth makes grand claims that have gone un-heeded in the critical literature, and his link between the British and American writers is persuasive, particular from his inside view:

> There are only two writers of fiction who could be called part of the contemporary San Francisco group—Henry Miller, who stays close to home in Big Sur, and Jack Kerouac, who lives here only occasionally. Kerouac is a lot like Miller, a lot like Celine of *Guignol's Band*, a little like Lawrence Durrell's *Black Book*. (Rexroth, "San Francisco" 215)

The stylistic affinities between Miller, Durrell, and Kerouac are strik-ing, though such a comparison has not received scholarly attention. Duncan noticed similar parallels and wrote to Denise Levertoff (who published her first works in Wrey Gardiner's *Poetry Quarterly*) that Kerouac sounds like Miller and Saroyan (whom Miller published in *The Booster*) (Duncan and Levertoff 119). More importantly, while Miller is loosely acknowledged as an influence on the American Beat movement, the role of the generation of English authors tied to the personalist movement is utterly overlooked, yet it lends a vital inter-nationalism and a clearer politics to the Beats. Again, from Rexroth's perspective,

> Anarchism, conscientious objection, war resistance, were more popular with young English writers than with the Americans, and there was considerable contact during and just after the war between San Francisco and London. Writers like Alex Comfort, D.S. Savage, George Woodcock, Herbert Read were widely read. The first magazines to publish the new San Francisco school were *Horizon*, [Wrey Gardiner and Nicholas Moore's] *Poetry*

Quarterly, [Alex Comfort's] *Poetry Folios*. This has all died out, not
because the Californians have changed, but because the British
have. A kind of hopeless inertia—atomophobia—has settled
upon the British *avant-garde*. (214–15)

Rexroth's framework draws out the transatlantic relationships that
informed this Pacific coast group of writers, and the atomophobia
he refers to is not only the threat of atomic war and the atomization
of the group by wide geographical relocations; it also reflects the
silencing of this generation by the senior Auden group and High
Modernists after the war's end.

By the time *Circle* reached its fourth issue in 1944, it was announ-
cing work by Nicholas Moore, Miller's good friend Michael Fraenkel
(with whom Miller had written the *Hamlet* correspondence), and the
Untide Press, which was publishing George Woodcock from England.
It was also including in its pages further works by Miller, Nin, Miller's
friend Wallace Fowlie (who was not otherwise previously tied to the .
San Francisco Renaissance poets but was publishing with the British
New Apocalypse through Miller[58]), as well as Duncan's close friend
Sanders Russell. Russell's description under the list of contributors
casts him as "the editor of Experimental Review, one of the first
American magazines to become aware of Henry Miller's genius" (73),
and the subsequent advertising page lists Miller's *Murder the Murderer*
as available for order through Leite's co-editor, Bern Porter. The only
advertisement for Yale's *Chimera* also advertises its inclusion of Miller's
"Criticism," which presages Durrell's materials reaching it from
Rhodes the next year.

The beginning of the final year of the war then featured both prose
and poetry works by Moore in the fifth issue of *Circle* while he was
preparing to print works by Patchen in England. Moore had also just
published his book *New Poetry* including the anarchist Paul Goodman
as well as translations from Italian by G.S. Fraser (who was working
with Hamish Henderson at the time, who would translate Gramsci)
and Durrell's "Coptic Poem" on the same page as Goodman (Durrell,
"Coptic" 7).[59] The same issue also announces the intention of *Circle*
to publish the first of the Circle Editions in the coming fall of 1945,
Abraham Rattner's *When We Were Together*, which never appeared. The

double issue (number 7–8) of 1946 opens auspiciously with Duncan's "The Years as Catches" then included Georges Henein's "There Are No Pointless Jests." Henein, as has already been noted in relation to the *Personal Landscape* poets, was affiliated with both the English poets in Egypt and was a major figure in Egyptian Surrealism and anarchist politics. *Circle* then turned to Circle Editions, and among the first publications in this imprint was another Egyptian work—Albert Cossery's *Men God Forgot*, which appeared in 1946. Again, the issue containing Georges Henein also contains Miller's promotion of Cossery's book in his "Books Tangent to Circle."

The final 1945 issue, number 6, features Miller again discussing Surrealism and revolution, as well as Comfort's poetry on pacifism. The issue opens, however, with a revealing manifesto from the "Activist Group" led by Lawrence Hart that Leite provides with a generous "Editor's Note":

> This group has made an attempt to control poetic structure through a surface of brilliant notation, imagery and connotative statement. The problems dealt with in this work are the same problem about which the disputes have been raging among the Surrealists, Apocalyptics, Imagists, Traditionalists and the many other movements that compose the literary scene of this century.
>
> Although the attitude in this survey should not be taken as the critical stand of the editors of Circle, the questions and problems raised are the very ones in which Circle is most interested. (Leite, "Editor's" 1)

The "problem" and "disputes" that return Leite's attention to the New Apocalypse among others is the titular "order" in the collectively written "Ideas of Order in Experimental Poetry." Where the New Apocalypse calls for "organic form" and authorial order or control in post-surrealist practices, the Activist Group sees individual control through language.

Hart is also keen to promote his distinction between a "connotative" versus "denotative" organization of meaning that structure and conscious control over surrealist imagery such that denotative words will be formulated in statements, statements into larger structures of denotative or literal meaning—the syllogism, etc.—and those perhaps into philosophical formulas or other ideological formulas representing comprehensive systems of understanding....[This system's antithesis is] Images, and other connotative phrases, combine in more involved patterns of connotative meaning, and finally may be formulated in comprehensive patterns of esthetic intuition. That is, a complex of understanding regarding the world and the individual experience in it need not appear as a completed philosophy. It may be more valuable as a completed esthetic intuition. (Hart et al. 3–4).

In this vision, authority is aligned with denotative meanings, such that "dictionaries are used primarily for denotative meanings, with only shades of connotation added. There are no dictionaries of connotative meanings" (4) and denotation leads to, in Hart's opening table, a "comprehensive rationalistic philosophy" that he aligns with ideology and socially defined meaning (3). The alternative is a personal sense of meaning bound to the individual and interpretation, that is, connotative meanings that are subject to change and revision: "connotative poetry, especially in associational techniques, is often condemned as lacking in logical order—a condemnation quite beside the point. Because order is not necessarily the order of logic, and meaning is not necessarily logical meaning" (4). This he calls "associational poetry."

Apart from the titular kinship between "Ideas about Poems" and "Ideas of Order in Experimental Poetry," the Activist Group's work also recalls Durrell's anti-manifestos in *Personal Landscape*: "Logic tries to describe the world....Describing, logic limits. Its law is causality" (Durrell, "Heraldic" 7). The same passage to which Stanford was so deeply attracted is again akin to Hart's "associational poetry": "Poetry by an associative approach transcends its own syntax in order not to describe but to be the cause of apprehension in others" (Durrell, "Heraldic" 7). Hart's kindred notion is an "esthetic intuition" that is able to create understanding, only by associative techniques, of "a complex of understanding regarding the world and the individual experience" (Hart et al. 4). This distinction between poetry as a "cause of apprehension" or an "esthetic intuition" rather than a denotative communication in both poetic visions seems slim and the kinship keen. Likewise, a further comparison can begin with Hart's sense that the aesthetic-cum-connotative component of meaning in experimental poetry resists traditional notions of logic such that poetic meaning and poetic order are not necessarily the logical forms of meaning and order (Hart et al. 4). For the counterpart in Durrell's vision, we see poetry as "Transcending logic[;] it invades a realm where unreason reigns, and where the relations between ideas are sympathetic and mysterious—affective—rather than causal, objective, substitutional" (Durrell, "Heraldic" 7). From Durrell's description, it is only a very small leap to Hart's "dictionaries are used primarily for denotative meanings, with only shades of connotation added. There are no dictionaries of connotative meanings" (4). To understand Hart's connotative meanings as poetical "relations between ideas [that] are sympathetic and mysterious—affective—rather than causal, objective, substitutional" (Durrell, "Heraldic" 7) is easy, and this ease marks the appeal of both authors to Leite's magazine. The rationale for their links and sympathies is clear.

The final issue of Circle in 1946, number 9, closes the journal's run by opening with Durrell's "Eight Aspects of Melissa," which is a sequence of eight poems about Egyptian landscapes. The biographical statement about contributors lists Durrell's titles incorrectly and has him returned to Corfu after the war, which indicates it was compiled some time closer to early 1945 or late 1944 since the contract from Durrell for the Circle Editions publication of The Black Book predates the issue and would have gone through his home on Rhodes. In any case it would be prior to March 1, 1945 when Durrell wrote to Miller informing him that he was waiting for his posting to Rhodes (while ironically jabbing at the ending of war leading to the success of monopoly capitalism) (Durrell–Miller Letters 180). Circle then had two years of defining conflicts and activities during which publication of the periodical was suspended.

By the time Circle resumed publication, perhaps in part to re- but Mildred Edie Brady's scathing article "The New Cult of Sex and Anarchy" in the April 1947 issue of Harper's Magazine, it was

1948—Circle Editions was actively producing books, and transatlantic correspondence was working smoothly. It was a new postwar world with new critiques. Brady comments on "The English poet Lawrence Durrell, for example, who until recently published an avant-garde poetry review in Cairo, called *Personal Landscape*, not only understood *Circle* but published in it and still does now and then" (Brady 318), and she goes on to reference Woodcock's *NOW* in London, associating the entire group with anarchism and salvation through sex. While it is difficult to feel great sympathy for all that Brady is pursuing, her contention that Miller set the avant-garde literary scene in coastal California aflame when he arrived in Big Sur is justified, and from it she argues, "They read his uncensored books published in the United States (*Cosmological Eye*, *Colossus of Maroussi*, *Sunday After the War*, *Air-Conditioned Nightmare*, etc.) and from them imbibed an engaging potpourri of mysticism, egoism, sexualism, surrealism, and anarchism" (319). The first title, notably, contains Miller's "An Open Letter to Surrealists Everywhere," the same text that so strongly influenced Gascoyne and the English post-Surrealists, causing them to abandon their communist position held through the 1936 London International Surrealist Exhibition. Despite her vitriol and the eventual dismissal of her argument, Brady was quite right in noticing the kinships and concerns shared among these groups. Brady's article, however, took a paternal tone toward the American avant-garde, dismissing it as childish and fraudulent, binding it to Wilhelm Reich's theory of orgonomy. Brady's assertion that "Wilhelm Reich, whose *Function of the Orgasm* is probably the most widely read and frequently quoted contemporary writing in this group" (293) is obviously false, as are her claims that Reich was widely published and praised in the related avant-garde periodicals.

When *Circle* resumed in 1948, it began with a rebuttal to Brady. The contents of this issue also feature Comfort's "Two Enemies of Society" and Duncan's "Toward an African Elegy," the former's novel *The Powerhouse* being advertised along with the latter's famous *Heavenly City, Earthly City*, as published by Bern Porter, the co-editor of *Circle*. Comfort's future role through *The Joy of Sex* was, of course, unanticipated. Leite's and Porter's editorial for the 1948 tenth issue, is pointed, calling Brady's article "the libelous mud thrown last year in HARPER'S MAGAZINE" (n. pag.).

Immediately prior to this resurgence of *Circle*, Rexroth completed what is perhaps the most productive and influential project linking the British Personalist group(s) to the San Francisco Renaissance, his *The New British Poets*, which has already been mentioned briefly. Rexroth was particularly sensitive to the political and personal vision of the poets he selected, almost exclusively from the post-Auden generation, and with Miller nearby,[60] he was also remarkably capable of spotting the prose-writer's influence. For Dylan Thomas, amidst the long list of influences and youthful readings, he notes "translated Surrealism, 'science fiction,' horror tales, sex books, occultism, Shakespeare, Blake, Lawrence, Henry Miller" (xviii), and though it is little know, Thomas kept his copy of Miller in the oven in order for it to be out of sight. Thomas was indeed deeply struck by his readings of Miller and feared meeting the man in person, as is described in the chapter section on Apocalypse.

Indeed, for the generation as a whole, in Rexroth's estimation, a

> major influence which is difficult to measure is that of Henry Miller. All over the world Miller has acted as the liberator of a generation. Not since Ibsen has an author had so catalytic an effect, nor has the reaction produced by his catalysis been so violent....No other person of his generation has had so great an influence. (xxiv)

This is high praise indeed considering the generation in question, but Rexroth is not simply flattering a friend; he sees the matter in expressly politicized terms that relate to Miller's anarchism as well as that of the poets Rexroth foregrounds in his anthology. To Rexroth, Miller was important to a generation that was called to serve and die in a war that pitted three authoritarian forms of government against each other, and he was a catalyst precisely because these young poets were disillusioned during their youthful period of imaginative en-thusiasms and grand visions. Works like *Tropic of Cancer* and *Murder the Murderer* appealed because

> Miller expressed their disbelief, and their emergent beliefs, not just their distrust of the putative aims of their governments,

but their rejection of the whole social lie of a diseased and tawdry civilization, and their hope to found a new foundation for life in a cleansed and redeemed love relationship. There were other things to be found in Miller, too—his apocalyptic style,...and, most important, his rejection of the State and all other complexes of power and irresponsibility as evil hoaxes. (Rexroth, Introduction xxiv)

There can be no mistaking the political context of Rexroth's comments and his personal friendship with Miller as the basis for being able to make them overtly, but the networked relations implicit in "his apocalyptic style" must also draw attention since the New Apocalypse poets are anthologized in Rexroth's book. Rexroth's personal familiarity shows through in his ability to sidestep the question of "defeatism" that plagued the British discourse after Orwell's *Inside the Whale* cast Miller's pacifism through the term. For Rexroth, "There is another side of Miller, his quietism, his ability to bend in the storm, his shunning of the violence" (xxv), and for Rexroth unlike Orwell, these words are not derogations.

This sense of quietism, which Miller discusses openly in his letters, in particular those with Durrell, is an astute observation for Rexroth. It is rendered more astute when he rightly observes, despite the violence of the language in the literary works under discussion, "It is this aspect of Miller [quietism] which is most pronounced in the work of his friend Lawrence Durrell" (xxv). Rexroth goes on from this point to offer particularly high praise to the interior and personal vision of Durrell's *The Black Book* and his poetry during the war. What Rexroth could almost certainly not have know (apart from confirmation through Miller) was the degree to which quietism influenced Durrell's novels prior to *The Black Book*, in particular the pseudonymous *Panic Spring*, in which his characters carry on long discussions of quietism.[61]

To this remarkable insight, Rexroth adds the slyly informative note, "Miller was not quite alone. In England at least, one other older man spoke out, clearly and forcefully, Herbert Read...[who was] always searching for an organic life in an organic society" (xxv–xxvi), to which he adds, "This is also Berdyaev's philosophy" (xxvii). Nikolai

Berdyaev was part of Miller's understanding of Dostoevsky and re-inforces his anarchist beliefs. Berdyaev's *Dostoevsky's World View* was first translated into English in 1934 while he was living in Paris, as was Miller, and Miller quickly refers to it. Whether they knew each other or not is unknown, but Berdyaev certainly knew Miller's works as well at the time (Carlisle 20). As Keery has noted in John Goodland's formative influences while thinking through what would become the New Apocalypse,

> Goodland's journal [diary] contains numerous quotations from Nikolai Berdyaev, and the route by which he arrived at his work can be retraced (by contrast, Thomas makes no appearance before 1939). A list of "The Ten Books that have influenced me most in the last Year" (1937) includes D.H. Lawrence's *Apocalypse*, but also Aldous Huxley's *Brave New World* (1932), which carries an epigraph in French from "Berdiaeff," transcribed in full by Goodland around June 1937. He then proceeded to read *Freedom and the Spirit* (1935), from which he transcribes a series of quotations later the same year. ("Burning [7]" 49)

This confluence of notes around a single concept leads Keery to unify how Goodland would have understood the language of Apocalypse in his various readings:

> It was Goodland who read the recently published *Solitude and Society* in the autumn of 1938, when a spark must have flown between Berdyaev's "inner apocalypse" and the deployment of the [Apocalypse] word by Durrell via Lawrence and Miller. ("Burning [7]" 49)

For Rexroth to intuit the relationship is so unlikely (even with his encyclopedic reading) that we must assume Miller's conversations with him were a factor. The unification, by Rexroth, of the political-poetic vision of Read, Miller, and Berdyaev, however, demonstrates the growing recognition of the shared origins of the Personalist group as a coherent movement rather than a series of distinct and unrelated groups. When he turns to Albert Schweitzer's "reverence for life" as "a key term in [his] philosophy" taken up by Read, he is also turning to one of Miller's touchstones.

These combinations are perceptive for Rexroth and also draw together the disparate threads seen in the various periodicals explored in this chapter. He anticipates yet more by casting the generation as Romantic and drawing forward Denise Levertof for special notice, and the comment that makes the transatlantic relationship stand out is again one that conjoins. Rexroth's observations could just as well be applied to Leite, his, and Duncan's Libertarian Circle in San Francisco and the publishing activities of *Circle* and Circle Editions:

> The religious personalism and political anarchism which
> provide the dominant ideology of the movement is still young
> as a Weltanschauung. It is not something taken over from
> their bureaucratic betters by poetic fellow travellers, but has
> been developed, in situ and from the heart by Read, Comfort,
> Woodcock, Savage, Treece, and the rest, as they went along.
> So it can still stand an enormous amount of critical shaping.
> Its relations with the orthodox "anarchist movement," a
> rather doctrinaire body at the best…, are still to be defined.
> Contemporary English thought has avoided the diffuse, eclectic,
> heterodox religiosity represented by Huxley, Heard, Isherwood
> and other Anglo-Hollywood mystics. (Rexroth xxx)

Rexroth's various networks in the San Francisco Renaissance, most particularly through Leite and Duncan, merit the same observation as avoiding the Anglo-Hollywood generation drawn from the High Modernists and the Auden group. By referring to the English anarchist authors as personalist and anarchist, he expresses the core commonality to be found with those actively producing new works in Big Sur and Berkeley. Hence, not only did the San Francisco Renaissance take up the pre-war interests of Egyptian anarchists, they did so through their other great influence, the English post-Surrealists. In both instances, the vehicle again proves to be the group that has been centred around the Villa Seurat in Paris prior to the war.

Shanghai: Between Europe and America

A final locale stretches this network to Asia, though its anti-authoritarian seeds found greater hardship, and any connection is far more speculative than the preceding materials in this chapter. Nonetheless, it is too provocative to exclude. The Shanghai-based literary arts journal *T'ien Hsia Monthly* is less known in Western literary circles today and was closed when the editors fled to Hong Kong during the Japanese invasion of Manchu, but it merits much attention. In 1936, it published Hsiao Kung-Chuan's work on "Anarchism in Chinese Political Thought" (on anarchism and Taoism) and poetry by the major Chinese anarchist Ba Jin whose pseudonym is created from Bakunin's and Kropotkin's names, and by 1938, it had published Durrell, Miller, Perlès, and Read and reviewed Durrell and Miller in relation to English-language Surrealism. Lin Yutang's influence over the magazine was possibly the first point of contact, and Shuang Shen has given the most complete summary of the journal extant (Shen 59–93), though his interests are principally in translation and theories of cosmopolitanism centred on China, and his perspective is inevitably dominated by Jameson's vision of modernity and the bourgeois function of individual identity (64–65). In contrast, the editor of *T'ien Hsia Monthly*, Wen Yuanning,

> believed that individualism...was inevitably compromised during the war. He wrote in an editorial in the March 1940 issue that "war also throws men into crowds....Individuality dies and a mob is born. With the extinction of the individual, literature and culture die too: for the life blood of literature and culture is the individual in his uniqueness." (Shen 68)

This call for the individual amidst clear support for modernist literature (which Wen Yuanning acquired as a passion during his studies in law at Cambridge University) is the point of sympathy between Yuanning and Miller, Read, Perlès, and Durrell. Studying at Cambridge during the same years as Christopher Isherwood would prove a further contact point for Yuanning to the anti-authoritarian networks of the authors he published in Shanghai, but not through the Auden group.

Yuanning visited Cambridge during the Second World War, at the behest of his government, at the same time as the young man he was enticing to report on the war in Europe was contributing post-surrealist short stories to the New Apocalypse's *A Map of Hearts* edited by Henry Treece and Stefan Schimanksi: Hsiao Ch'ien (Xiao Qian).[62] Hsiao Ch'ien recounts this meeting in his later autobiography *Traveller Without a Map*:

> At the end of 1943, just as I was starting work on my Master's thesis, the Chungking government sent a goodwill mission to Britain. The delegation included the important politicians Wang Shijie and Wang Yunwu, and also scholars such as Wen Yuanning....Hu Lin and Wen Yuanning came to visit Cambridge. Hu Lin came right to the point. Sitting down and starting at me through his thick spectacles, he said "I didn't come to Cambridge to see the sights. I came here to get you away." (120)

He was wanted by his government as a reporter on World War II in Europe, and he turned to this task and many others that followed. Hsiao Ch'ien's story for the New Apocalypse, "The Ramshackle Car," begins with the clear political statement, "This incident happened at the beginning of 1937, when China was inert under the stranglehold of the Japanese. People in North China were filled with anger, disgust and gloom" ("Ramshackle" 16). His subsequent 1942 story "Calamity" is closer in tone to what would be expected from Albert Cossery, painting the hopelessness of the lower classes in the city Tuanfeng as it resisted the Japanese in the second Sino-Japanese war—his pathetic focus is an orphaned child abandoned at a train station and the "hundreds of desolate human beings who have survived an undeserved calamity" (Hsiao, "Calamity" 40). He also contributed "The New China Turns to Ibsen" to *Daylight: European Arts and Letters*, and Ibsen's anarchism would not have been missed by the New Apocalypse authors, nor would his references to China needing Ibsen's "healthy individualism" and his belief that due to Ibsen Chinese "Individuals began to assert their right to think and act" (Hsiao, "New" 167). He finally marks his own interests by stating, "One fact that particularly interests me is that Ibsen was an anarchist in youth. The early period of modern Chinese literature was strongly anarchist in character. It expressed a vehement indignation with this clumsily created world and a rosy paradise where the individual is free" ("New" 170). He adds further clarity by noticing "to the great displeasure of the Marxists, that the tide immediately following Ibsen's individualism was romantic" (180).

The Wen Yuanning who accompanied Hu Lin to persuade Hsiao Ch'ien to leave Cambridge and report on the war for China was the same man who had edited *T'ien Hsia Monthly*, publishing articles on anarchism as well as works by some of the principle person- alist authors. Steven Tsang's recent research on Cold War relations between the Republic of China and the United Kingdom again returns to these two figures. Wen Yuanning taught at National Peking University and became an ambassador to Greece in July 1947 (visiting Cairo en route), a post he would hold for twenty years. As Tsang points out, "Ambassador Wen Yuan-ning, a longstanding Anglophile, was able to keep on 'very friendly personal terms' with his British colleagues in Greece" (54). This closeness is remarkable since Durrell took up his post on Rhodes during the accretion of the Dodecanese Islands to Greece from Britain during the same years as Yuanning's arrival in Greece after publishing Durrell in Shanghai. Like Hsiao Ch'ien's visit to San Francisco in 1945, however, there is no record of contact with the other poets whose works circulated in the personalist network, and it must remain a matter of specu- lation. What does remain of his correspondence with E.M. Forster (with whom he was good friends), after Hsiao burned much of it in fear of reprisals during the Cultural Revolution, records Forster self-identifying as an anarchist to Hsiao and discussing Ibsen with him (Hsiao Ch'ien, *Traveller* 116).

Hsiao Kung-Chuan's article on anarchism in *T'ien Hsia Monthly* (249– 63) argues for a kinship between anarchism and Taoism in China (a kinship also noted by many anarchists [Marshall 53–60]), and this was particularly linked to Kropotkin's ideas. As Charlotte Furth argues,

Like the reformers of 1898, both groups of anarchists saw themselves as internationalists. However, by 1907 internationalism was less simply a development of the traditional East Asian cosmopolitan ideal of "all under heaven" (*t'ien-hsia*) and more a contemporary protest against both the anti-Manchu and anti-imperialist nationalist movements which had grown up so powerfully since the 1890s. (73–74)

This leads Furth to the most specific intervention,

The anarchists rejection of "wealth and power" as national defence priorities in the face of imperialism, more than any other single issue, provoked criticism from readers of both magazines. To answer, the anarchists drew upon Kropotkin against Darwin and Spencer, arguing that analogies from the group life of animals show that human social evolution is propelled by intra-species cooperation rather than by strife. (74)

Arif Dirlik has argued as well that Kropotkin's vision of anarchism was particularly helpful to Chinese anarchists due to its focus on social transformation (Dirlik, *Anarchism* 14). Dirlik pursues the same topic, and uses the *T'ien Hsia Monthly's* anarchist work in "Vision and Revolution" as well (123–65).

While too little is known of this specific connection, it is sufficient to provoke interest for further research and indicates the scope of the networks discussed across this chapter.

Summary

The core point of this chapter has been to stress the commonalities through correspondence, modes of expression, and mutual publication that exist among the various individualist-cum-personalist groups of the 1940s, most of whom began to be active in the mid- to late 1930s. Although this generation has been largely cast as diffuse and its groups as unrelated, the evidence gathered here is sufficient to historicize a broad anti-authoritarian network of authors active over the years of the Second World War. They were scattered across the globe yet continued to nurture strings of attachment and interaction as well as influence, much of which originated in the Villa Seurat in Paris, most iconically seen in Henry Miller's correspondence with Herbert Read culminating in their discussion of the London International Surrealist Exhibition of 1936.

3

Authority's Apocalypse
Theories of Personalism

Anti-authoritarian Theory

In his 1962 definitional text, and perhaps the most widely used
modern outline of anarchism, George Woodcock asserts unequivo-
cally, "the anarchists not only reject political action as such, but also
attack reformism—the idea that society can be changed by piecemeal
measures—and deny the theory of a transitional period between the
capitalist state and the anarchic society" (*Anarchism* 29). Yet Noam
Chomsky, perhaps the most popular living anarchist figure, could
assert only eight years later,

> at every stage of our history our concern must be to dismantle
> those forms of authority and oppression that survive from
> an era when they might have been justified...but that now
> contribute to...material and cultural deficit. If so, there will be
> no doctrine of social change fixed for the present and future,
> nor even, necessarily a specific and unchanging concept of the
> goals towards which social change should tend. (118–19)

This relatively straightforward issue, which is itself very largely framed
in relation to Marxist thought on utopianism and revolution, has
elicited antithetical yet equally anarchist responses from numerous
anarchist figures. The first casts the anti-authoritarian spirit as one
that must engender a quasi-messianic rupture to a utopian future,
perhaps in relation to Walter Benjamin, and the second adopts a

gradual development of an anti-authoritarian society that is not yet even able to conceive of its eventual form or specific goals. David Stafford casts these views as part of a common vision since "the dilemma...between apocalyptic revolution producing on its morrow the perfectly functioning anarchist society on the one hand...and seeking personal salvation on the other,...[shows how] revolution and reform were extremes on a scale of evolution" (111). Another well-known break is anticipated by Murray Bookchin, who argues for "social anarchism" rather than "lifestyle anarchism," which he sees as too individualized and fragmentary:

> While *autonomy* is associated with the presumably self-sovereign individual, *freedom* dialectically interweaves the individual with the collective....When applied to the individual, *freedom* thus preserves a social or collective interpretation of that individual's origins and development as a self. In "freedom," individual selfhood does not stand opposed to or apart from the collective but is significantly formed...by his or her own social existence. Freedom thus does not subsume the individual's liberty but denotes its actualization. (Bookchin 12–13)

This is, in miniature, Bookchin's method for engendering a Marxist anarchism founded on communitarian values and opposed to individualist anarchism or its perversion into capitalist libertarianism (in the American use of the word). Bookchin's labels for these different forms of anarchism have spread much dissent and disagreement among those who might otherwise find themselves with a greater amount in common were they to articulate their concerns differently. For David Weir, in his Jamesonian study of Modernism *Anarchy and Culture*, Bookchin's ideas demonstrate that "the collectivist model of anarchism...belongs to the heritage of the Enlightenment, while the autonomists have more in common with the ideological counterstream of romanticism" (266)—both ideas that will return in this chapter.

David Miller, who is not sympathetic to anarchism but does attempt to discuss its various forms, notes here too that

Philosophical anarchism entails the view that the state has no right to tell me or anyone else how to behave. One can believe this and respond in a wholly passive way, evading inconvenient or immoral state dictates whenever possible and complying with them when forced to do so, but taking no positive action to get rid of the state and having no constructive view about what might take its place. (15)

Rather than clarifying the meaning of anarchism, Miller's great success in this study lies in demonstrating his own perspective by shaping his materials into a straw man. While "philosophical anarchism" may indeed allow for a quietist or passive view, this is an emphasis on the non-political and non-state possibilities and not simply the absence of a "constructive view." Living in the interstices of state exercises of power is indeed itself the "constructive view about what might take its place." This failure to understand the context of his materials culminates at the end of his brief exegesis on philosophical anarchism when he attempts to philosophically refute the possibility of ethically rejecting authority as a rebuttal to Robert Paul Wolff's In Defense of Anarchism (29). He invents a fictional scenario in which submission to authority is the only means to fulfilling one's ethical beliefs, which he then holds as proof that "none of the ethical theories considered gives conclusive reasons for rejecting authority... [because] none of them succeeds" (29). Miller's contention fails in its inability to distinguish between obeying a command because one deems it just or necessary versus obeying a command because the figure issuing it has authority via a natural or just expectation of obedience. Obedience and authority are not an obversion. An anarchist could obey directions on a continual basis—the distinction would lie in the absence of authority per se or a just expectation of obedience, a point that Wolff takes great pains to make and that Miller takes equally great pains to avoid in his straw man since it would derail the framework of his study, which is principally empirical and historical in orientation rather than philosophical.

A revealing conflict appears in relation to philosophical anarchism and the various responses it has from those with different views, in particular those who condemn reformism. According to Ruth Kinna, philosophical anarchism has

> its most famous modern statement i[n] Robert Paul Wolff's
> In Defense of Anarchism. Wolff's version purported to provide a
> "pure theory" of anarchism without any consideration of "the
> material, social, or psychological conditions under which
> anarchism might be a feasible mode of social organization."
> In other words, it identified anarchism with a commitment
> to individual decision-making (sometimes called private
> judgement) and divorced this commitment from the struggle
> to realize a particular socio-economic arrangement. Walter
> had a pithier view. Philosophical anarchism described a
> partial commitment to anarchy, the idea that "society without
> government was attractive...but not really possible...anarchism
> in the head but not in the heart." (19)

Colin Ward expresses much the same sentiment in his informal "very short guide" for Oxford as well (62, 66–68). This bias, however, directly misquotes Wolff who admits, "this essay suffers from two major inadequacies....On the side of practical application, I have said almost nothing about the materials, social, or psychological conditions" (Wolff viii), yet far from suggesting anarchism was not possible, Wolff claims only a few sentences prior, "The third chapter sketches, in a rather impressionistic, Hegelian way, the reasons for my lingering hope that a solution can be found; it concludes with some brief, quite utopian suggestions of ways in which an anarchic society might actually function" (viii). The dispute with Wolff is widespread, and the general trend is to include him in the Randian anarcho-capitalist group with Murray Rothbard, which Wolff himself rejects and which is made clear by his serious interest in Marx. The latter is a more likely source of the antipathy, though Wolff does admit to being chagrined and even shocked at the praise given his work by right libertarians such that he rethought its viability. Despite his explicit rejection of their view, his works are frequently cited by so-called "anarcho-capitalists" or right-wing libertarians. Wolff's position is more simply social anarchism of a reformist rather than revolutionary orientation and particularly oriented toward an anti-authoritarian interpretation of Marxist critiques of capitalism. Although he acknowledges the unholy anti-authoritarian kinship with right-wing libertarians, in particular the possibility of limited collaborative resistance against the imperialist state, he rejects their turn away from mutual aid, their acceptance of capitalism, and their displacement of the state by corporatism. In this, his views are anti-authoritarian rather than simply anti-statist.

Such chasms are common in anarchist discourse, even between "essential" thinkers, and they certainly recur amidst the poets discussed here and their struggles as the avant-garde after Auden. A list could be easily drawn pointing to discontinuities between Peter Kropotkin and Max Stirner or Pierre-Joseph Proudhon and Leo Tolstoy. Yet, both Woodcock and Chomsky are, in this instance as exemplars, equally grounded in agitating for an anti-authoritarian praxis and the experience of freedom in the here and now (though not in the everyday present projected onto them by much Marxist theory). As Paul Goodman wrote, "There cannot be a history of anarchism in the sense of establishing a permanent state of things called 'anarchist.' It is always a continual coping with the next situation, and a vigilance to make sure that past freedoms are not lost and do not turn into the opposite" (39). These differences allow for dissent that might make two individuals seem utterly unlike in viewpoint, without a common perspective, yet their underlying emphasis on lived freedom and elided authority also creates an enormously flexible commonality that allows for productive interactions in the here and now and in varied circumstances, both well-known and unanticipated. As David Kadlec has pointedly noticed,

> Since the late 1960s, a range of poststructuralist critics—
> Marxists, feminists, postcolonialists, and even some "pure"
> deconstructionists—have shared a tacit belief that radicalism
> must be progressive. Supported by Marxist premises that have
> traditionally merged anarchistic with bourgeois "individualism,"
> progressivist assumptions have kept us from according
> anarchism its historical role in the formation of modernist
> aesthetics. (2)

Kadlec goes on, as does Allan Antliff in visual arts (*Anarchist* 1), to demonstrate the formative role of anarchism in Modernism. This is despite the same calcified attitudes over fears relating to the term "anarchism," as well as Marxist derogations of the anti-authoritarian impulse as essentially bourgeois. Both trepidations over terms and the epithet of bourgeoisdom have stifled widespread response in the mainstream scholarship on Modernism, including Kadlec's and illustrated in his dissociation of "progressive" from "anarchist."

Nonetheless, the same issue of freedom as a bourgeois form of false consciousness is a fertile critique from Marxists against the anti-state freedom represented by anarchism, and it is one that Marxist perspectives traditionally essentialize into bourgeois freedom, as has been discussed in relation to Christopher Caudwell. Such views have provoked major misrepresentations of anarchism and continue in the hegemonic voices of Marxist criticism. This is the approach taken by Frederic Jameson in his blending of Lacan and Wilhelm Reich such that he casts the notion of "the 'self' and the Ego as defense mechanism, into which modern individuals (most often bourgeois individuals) tended to entrench or immure themselves...The depersonalization of the subject—a breaking down of the fortress of the Ego and the self— might also constitute a liberation" (*Singular* 133–44), a notion he aligns with "anarchist movements" (134). The distinction, however, is in Jameson's proposal that this inward turn must, yet again, be conceived as a product of material conditions:

> At best, there stirs here everywhere an apocalyptic
> dissatisfaction with subjectivity itself and the older forms of
> the self....This then is the sense in which I propose to consider
> modernist "subjectivity" as allegorical of the transformation of
> the world itself, and therefore is what is called revolution....All
> the anecdotal psychologies in which it finds itself dressed—in
> their stylistic, cultural and characterological differences—have
> in common that they evoke a momentum that cannot find
> resolution within the self, but that must be completed by
> a Utopian and revolutionary transmutation of the world of
> actuality itself. (135–36)

For Jameson, this allegorizing of the "I" and its own as a product of social processes, an "I" that must abandon itself to fulfill its social function, is the natural byproduct of his personal belief in "at least one clear dividing line between the modern and the postmodern, namely, the refusal of concepts of self-consciousness, reflexivity, irony or self-reference in the postmodern aesthetic" (92–93). Christopher Prendergast glosses this moment in Jameson's work helpfully in a manner that sets the contrast between perspectives more sharply:

> Modernist subjectivity has, therefore, nothing to do with the ideological cliché of the "inward turn." It is rather about a crisis of subjectivity and a related crisis of representation. It is not so much that the self is there to be "explored" as that it is overwhelmed by "an apocalyptic dissatisfaction with subjectivity itself." The drive is to "mutation" and "transfiguration" of the system of subjectivity, linked to the telos of "a Utopian and revolutionary transmutation of the world of actuality itself." It is what came to be called "depersonalization," the tones of which are first heard in the fiction of Flaubert and the poetry of Mallarmé and Rilke. (106)

Prendergast's view will be tantalizingly close to that developed in the Late Modernist authors studied here, in particular Duncan, Durrell, and Miller, as well as in the Apocalypse's characteristic language that implies the potential for a utopian break from the present. However, the notion of the "I" in Jameson and its intention is ultimately incompatible via his insistence that

> this also coincides with the disappearance of the slogan of freedom, whether in its bourgeois or anarchist sense: the feeling that the biological individual can no longer enjoy individualism as in the entrepreneurial stage of capitalism, but that he or she is integrated into a larger collective or institutional structure seems to me common both to contemporary conservative neo-Confuscianism (of all types) as much as to the Marxist tradition,...[which renders] the individual consciousness... conceptual[ly] incoheren[t]. (Singular 93)

Naturally, Jameson avoids confronting the alternative perspective offered by Herbert Marcuse on the same, limiting his only comment to a footnote outlining Lacan's rejection of the same notion of "liberation" used by Marcuse while concomitantly rejecting Lacan as well. The same pattern recurs in his discussion of Maurice Blanchot's writings about Henry Miller, in which Miller is elided. For Jameson, the anarchist alternative is no easy straw man, so he avoids noting its work in the field and almost even its existence.

Jameson's work is, thus, exemplary; he culminates and extends the Marxist reconfiguration of anarchism through a range of argumentative misdirections. Jameson's principle discussion of anarchism arises in *Archaeologies of the Future*, in which he emphasizes

> a certain anarchism, indeed, by emphasizing a freedom from
> state power which does not so much involve a seizure and
> destruction of the latter as the exploration of zones and enclaves
> beyond its reach, would seem to valorize a life in the present
> and in the everyday....Consciousness is in that sense the realm
> of the existential; the self is the domain of history, personal or
> otherwise. (213)

Hence, for Jameson, anarchism becomes part of the interstices of power, defined and shaped by the powers around and between which it operates. Indeed, for Jameson, there is a pronounced defense *against* anarchism and frequent blending of it with exploitative capitalism through his perception of its emphasis on the everyday and the present (as forms of false consciousness and bourgeois freedom), such that "The third stage of capitalism...seemed to...enable a return to non-socialist utopias, such as those of Nozick's anarchism or those implicit in that romance of finance capital to be found in cyberpunk" (*Archaeologies* 21).

Weir has used Jameson to consider anarchism and Modernism in this same context. For Weir, however, the framework and outcomes are different from those of this study, and he shifts to Jameson's seminal work on a critical distinction via Marxist theory on the distinction between the conditions that produce Modernism versus postmodernism. He contends,

> Jameson's seminal description [of postmodernism] sees
> "aesthetic production today...integrated into commodity
> production generally." To this observation we can add that
> politics is likewise susceptible to capitalist packaging. Indeed,
> *anarchism* would be the missing term in Jameson's construct
> of postmodernism when he notes "the explosion of modern
> literature into a host of distinct private styles and mannerisms
> has been followed by a linguistic fragmentation of social life
> itself." (Weir 264)

Weir's, and Jameson's, consistent alignment of anarchism with late stage capitalism is itself more a demonstration of their own ideological perspective than it is an argument. The misrepresentation of the left libertarian tradition of anarchism as being a laissez faire capitalist model of Tea Party right-wing libertarianism is a distinctly American perspective and entails recasting the *subject* of analysis in order to make it amenable to the *mode* of analysis, rather than vice versa. In other words, this model cannot interpret its subject matter.

Furthermore, since Treece in earlier chapters has already led the discussion into fantastic fiction, Jameson's discussions of the utopian in literature also becomes entwined, though obviously the utopic in fantasy remains markedly distinct from science fiction, Jameson's main focus. However, this shift makes the ideological load of such arguments far more visible, in particular their influence on developing critical traditions. When discussing Ursula Le Guin's novel *The Lathe of Heaven*, Jameson reveals his own schema clearly and the ways that his Marxist paradigm blocks him from engaging with Le Guin's anarchism as discussed in the overt content of her work:

> The ideological content of Le Guin's novel is clear, although its
> political resonance is ambiguous: from the central position of
> her mystical Taoism, the effort to "reform" and to ameliorate, to
> transform society in a liberal or revolutionary way is seen, after
> the fashion of Edmund Burke, as a dangerous expression of
> individual hubris and a destructive tampering with the rhythms
> of "nature." Politically, of course, this ideological message may
> be read either as the liberal's anxiety in the face of a genuinely

revolutionary transformation of society or as the expression of more conservative misgivings about the New Deal-type reformism and do-goodism of the welfare state. (Jameson, *Archaeologies* 293)

The hidden content here is Le Guin's long-held and explicit anarchism, with which Jameson would clearly prefer to not engage. Instead, he casts it as "liberal," "conservative," or "mystical." In other words, Jameson cannot see the explicit because it contradicts his interpretive paradigm (or else he misrepresents it), hence any anarchist revolutionary transformation of society must become, for Jameson, precisely what he mocks as reductive in Caudwell: bourgeois freedom and thereby reformism.

However, there is more to this story. Jameson footnotes his reference to conservatism to a description in more damning terms. He contends that Le Guin (while refusing to use her name, so great is his distaste) engages in "counterrevolutionary anti-utopianism" in "her nasty little fable 'The Ones Who Walk Away From Omelas'" (*Archaeologies* 293). Le Guin's short story is, of course, no such thing— she provokes a revolutionary move of leaving behind Omelas, a society built on the advancement of the many through the torture of the few. Jameson is, however, exactly correct that Le Guin's works are "anti-utopian" since utopia would be, for the anarchist, an impossibility built on delusion and surrender to authority or symbolic overcomings that sacrifice one's individuality: a living death to avoid life *versus* death. The truth of the conflict, however, is abundantly clear to Jameson during this rather bitter note. One hundred and thirty pages earlier he annotated the truth of the matter when he describes "The Ones Who Walk Away From Omelas" as Le Guin's "decidedly anti-Utopian attack on socialism" (159). In fact, Jameson had been picking away at Le Guin for thirty years by the time he would write this note, and Peter Fitting had already critiqued Jameson's refusal to recognize Le Guin's very clear political references:

Instead of writing about Le Guin's use of Bakunin or the feasibility of the Anneresti system for assigning work, instead of critiquing the sexual politics…Jameson argues that

> "...[Le Guin's work] can be reproached for the poverty of its
> political concepts and the naivete of its view of present-day
> world history...and the conventionality of Le Guin's own
> liberalism." (Fitting, "Concept" 10)

While Jameson's contributions to the discourse of utopia is trailblaz-
ing, his own rejections need careful review since they form aporias in
his work centred around the anti-authoritarian or anarchist contents
of his subject matter, and they likewise occlude any focus on the
individual. Most importantly, Jameson's position is not the result of
an articulated disagreement or basis for rejecting such difference—it
is a rejection of the topic, which becomes a myopia and eventually a
misrepresentation for the sake of critical expediency. Failing to notice
this, regardless of the choice one eventually makes, creates only blind-
ness to the issue rather than a genuine resolution or at least mutual
comprehension.

   In *The Political Unconscious*, Jameson also uses his quick alignment of
anarchism with other issues as a means of dismissing any need for
direct consideration. For instance, when he encounters "the theory of
desire," he immediately casts it as "a metaphysic and a myth," yet a
metaphysic with an impact on the world as

> an essential feature of the great mass revolts of the 1960s in
> Eastern and Western Europe as well as in China and the United
> States...Such myths must be carefully reexamined. If they
> have affinities with Marxism, they have even greater ones with
> anarchism, with whose vital renewal today a contemporary
> Marxist must also come to terms. (Jameson, *Political* 52–53)

This leads Jameson to contend, "desire must always be transgressive,
must always have a repressive norm or law...Yet it is a commonplace
that transgressions, presupposing the laws or norms or taboos against
which they function, thereby end up precisely reconfirming such
laws" (53). This commonplace, however, is not so simple. In this,
we seem to return to Foucault's repressive hypothesis, which post-
anarchist thought would reject (Cohn, "Postanarchism Post" par. 23).
The implication, moreover, cannot stand: that this dualism defines

anarchism due to the theory of desire's affinities with anarchism but does not relate to Marxism, to which it must have affinities of a different nature. This serves the same function as Jameson's recurrent alignment of anarchism with the postmodern (Jameson, *Archaeologies* 56, 196; Call, "Postmodern" 89), which ultimately implies (though only very rarely states) that his conceptualization of the individual and of freedom has altered little in general outline from Caudwell's, even while developing a great deal more definitional nuance. Jameson's views on Caudwell as an essentially "light" thinker are also well-known, or as he frames it, "destined more for use in night school rather than in the graduate seminar" (*Marxism and Form* ix). My personal experience has seen equally critical discourse in both continuing studies and the graduate seminar, so I cannot easily accept his distinction, and in any case, Jameson's distinction is itself the product of and functions within the logic of the very class consciousness it attempts to critique.

By summarizing Paul Goodman and Gustav Landauer, Jesse Cohn argues the contrast to Jameson's definition of the transgressive as a function of the dominant. Rather than Jameson's "commonplace" belief that transgressions reconfirm law and thereby anarchism reconfirms authority, Cohn articulates the insufficiency of the inherited laws or norms, for instance in language itself, to respond to the needs of the continually arising newness of circumstances predicated on contingency or the needful desires of individuals. In Cohn's sense, the individual works and acts within the productive tension between various contingencies rather than reductively being defined within a determinist false binary. Cohn has also defined the conflicting definitional approaches between Jameson and Baudrillard with regard to anti-representationalism (Cohn, *Anarchism* 51–54) and has stressed an anarchist, inductive interpretational paradigm in which "we do not need to approach any given text armed with predetermined categories that we read it against—e.g., the categories of class, gender, race, etc.; instead, we seek to enter a dialogue with the text, not only to critique it from an external perspective seen as superior, but to reconstruct our perspective with the aid of the text itself" (Cohn, "What is Anarchist" 117).

These are among the pressing debates of the moment that shape how a contemporary reader turns to and frames the personalist

groups of writers—it is a rereading that likely shapes how we understand their anti-authoritarian vision as well as if we understand it.
Much like Orwell's and Hynes's view of literary history and criticism,
we have a theoretical tradition that impairs our capacity to understand what the personalist authors have explicitly stated.

The Personalist Rationale

I am attempting to write a systematic and logical argument about what
I mean by "anarchism" or the term "personalist" in this book, yet
both are contested and local terms. Both are also terms that amount to
the same thing though with significantly different cultural associations
and preconceived biases—clearly my intentions of systematic thought
and order run contrary to the very poetic intentions I seek to clarify
and for which I seek to foster understanding. If any appropriate meas-
ure could be offered, it would be interpretive and contingent on each
reader. This is not, however, possible without a far greater effort than I
am capable of offering in this project, so I ask my reader's forgiveness
for employing a method contrary to my intentions but akin to my
personal practice, which seems the only way to proceed. It will also
necessitate a "personal" reading sequence that traces one, but not the,
reading path into these texts and their critical perspective.

Michael Moorcock, the anarchist, literary novelist, pulp fantasy
writer, and rock musician is a surprising reference here to theorize
the work of the various personalist groups and figures discussed so
far. Yet, Moorcock also wrote introductions to Henry Treece's postwar
writings—high adventure fantasy novels—and in doing so he must
have disappointed fantasy fans drawn to the book by the naked female
figure (seen from behind and ridiculously 1980s in style despite the
pre-Roman setting). Moorcock steadfastly discusses only personalist
ideals, anarchist politics, the literary scene of the year of his own birth,
1939, and the birth of the New Apocalypse ("Introduction" 2–4). As
astonishing as it must be for the typical pulp reader, Moorcock's
focus in introducing Treece's fantasy novel *The Great Captains* is to recall
G.S. Fraser's theoretical overview of Surrealism as a dialectical pro-
genitor of the New Apocalypse in *The White Horseman*, in which "This

Apocalyptic Movement found its first real expression" (Moorcock, "Introduction" 3). This is a striking intervention: to place the critical exegesis of the New Apocalypse's anarchist critique of the object-machine in modern culture directly into the hands of the common reader, despite its wildly unsuitable clash with what the reader would expect to be escapist pulp. Moorcock's ambition is plainly to align the birth of the modern fantasy genre via Treece and Mervyn Peake (who published alongside Treece and was also engaged as a poet in the New Romanticism) with their core concerns over freedom, tradition, power, and authority. From this perspective, the imaginative free-dom of fantastic literature "was one of the few 'admissable' forms in which the romantic imagination was allowed to flourish" (Moorcock, "Introduction" 4), and hence the "creative imagination" is for Moorcock set in conflict with "the well-bred populism of Auden or Day-Lewis" because the common reader may have "equated [Treece and Peake's Romanticism] with their limited experience of degenerate romanticism (Nazism and so on) and the threat of chaos" (Moorcock, "Introduction" 2). The striking part of this commentary is that it draws the fantasy novel reader into an interpretive freedom and appreciation for individual imaginative experience that aligns closely with Treece's (and Moorcock's) anarchism. And contrary to Jameson's suggestion, night course readers (or even junior high school students) took up these arguments for pleasure in their fantasy novel readings.

Moorcock, then, is an inside figure in some respects. He also provides me with a cautionary as he discusses the reactionary com-ponent of fantasy fiction in his seminal "Starship Stormtroopers":

> I attack these books [authoritarian fantastic fiction] because they are the favourite reading of so many radicals. I attack the books not for their superficial fascination with quasi-medieval social systems (à la Frank Herbert). Fiction about kings and queens is not necessarily royalist fiction any more than fiction about anarchists is likely to be libertarian fiction. As a writer I have produced a good many fantastic romances in which kings and queens, lords and ladies, figure largely—yet I am an avowed anti-monarchist. *Catch 22* never seemed to me to be in favour of militarism. And just because many of Heinlein's characters

are soldiers or ex-soldiers I don't automatically assume he must therefore be in favour of war. It depends what use you make of such characters in a story and what, in the final analysis, you are saying. (Moorcock, "Starship" 191)

In an unexpected manner, Moorcock's view betrays the importance of form for the New Apocalypse writers. Anarchism, or more generally the anti-authoritarian worldview that informed their works, cannot be embedded explicitly in the content in a reliable fashion, whether poetry or pulp prose, and if it could, it may be subjected to overt censorship or significant bias that prevents it from being read. This is especially true of pulp fantasy, although the poetic avant-garde also faced more prosaic editorial authority unlike Moorcock's. Yet, the anti-authoritarian spirit could be built invisibly into form and process, which is precisely how Moorcock interprets both Treece and Peake, and anticipates Robert Duncan and John Cage. This approach to form and process guides my work in this chapter, not the associative and representative method in the previous chapter.

What, then, can be embedded from anarchist philosophies into formal structures, practices, and aesthetics? Even asking the question seems to invoke the potential for individual responses, and this is also the answer. As Antliff has shown, significant interests in "organic form" (Antliff, "Open" 6–7) were adopted by anarchist artists as a way of reflecting both the artist and the audience in the artistic process, such that creation and interpretation are autonomous activities undertaken in relation to that third object given priority by Durrell in his "Ideas about Poems": the artistic object or work itself (Durrell, "Ideas [I]" 3).

In short, by finding out what these groups believed, we begin to discover how they produced their art—the relations among thought, form, and praxis.

Core Commonalities of the Personalist Group

Entirely apart from what discussions exist or might exist, the problem still remains of what *was* said, and by such, I mean what expression of anti-authoritarian interests appear to be either shared among this group or appear to be major personal idiosyncrasies. They certainly had idiosyncrasies as well as differences, but across these they shared an anti-authoritarian vision of their poetic praxis and engagement with the world.

I have already detailed Miller's anarchism as expressed in his *Murder the Murderer* and "An Open Letter to Surrealists Everywhere" as well as the New Apocalypse self-descriptions in their various manifestos (to which I will return below) (Fraser, "Apocalypse" 3–31; Hendry, "Art" 140–50; Treece, *How* 14, 22). Therefore, I will suffice here with repeating their crucial turn on authority, their implicit rejection of what Foucault would term later the "repressive hypothesis" in *The Will to Knowledge*, and their quietist turn to the individual. Kenneth Rexroth's anarcho-pacifism is well documented in the same way as is Herbert Read's. The explications that follow build from this foundation and particularly focus on the anti-authoritarian ideas in these groups that had a demonstrable impact on the other members.

As I have shown elsewhere, the descriptions of the Heraldic Universe that Durrell articulates derive directly from his partnership with Miller in a correspondence with Read that concerned communism and anarchism (Gifford, "Anarchist" 61–63). In reaction to the copy of Read's speech from the 1936 London International Surrealist Exhibition, a speech that Miller sent to Durrell with Read's letter, Durrell responded, "*This* manifesto would be a lot clearer if these brave young revolutionaries started by defining what they mean by art. To begin with, they seem to mean Marx" (Durrell and Miller 18). Read concludes his uncharacteristically pro-communist speech with the statement that Surrealism only succeeds "in the degree to which it leads to revolutionary actions" ("Speech" 8) and "work[s] for the transformation of this imperfect world" (13). To this, Durrell responded directly: "A definition of the word surrealism, please," and "I firmly believe in the ideals of cementing reality with the dream, but I do not believe the rest of this stuff. That the artist must be a socialist, for example. That he wants to transform the world. (He wants to transform *men*.)" (Durrell and Miller 18). It was only in this immediate context, for which Miller had established his anarchist vision in contrast to the communist perspective endorsed by Surrealism, that

Durrell offered his first articulation of the Heraldic Universe just a few lines later in the same letter: "Listen, Miller, what I feel about it, is this….What I propose to do, with all deadly solemnity, is to create my HERALDIC UNIVERSE *quite alone*. The foundation is being quietly laid" (18). In this context, Durrell's subsequent anti-rationalist and autonomous articulation of the Heraldic Universe in *Personal Landscape* takes on a new tone: "Describing, logic limits. Its law is causality…. Poetry by an associative approach transcends its own syntax in order not to describe but to be the cause of apprehension in others: Transcending logic it invades a realm where unreason reigns" ("Heraldic" 7). Durrell's other aesthetic comments for the journal, "Ideas about Poems," draw on further loaded terms gesturing to the anarchist New Apocalypse's personalist movement, "The poet is interested in the Personal aspect….That is the only explanation for Personal Landscape now" (3). John Waller, who edited *Bolero* and *Kingdom Come* in Oxford and was published by Durrell in *Personal Landscape*, stated the relation succinctly: "Durrell is likely to found no school. (Indeed the best poetry of 1940 onwards may come to be known as that of brilliant individuals rather than of groups and tendencies.)" ("Lawrence Durrell" 179).

However, this anti-authoritarian component of Durrell's early works came to a head in 1948, shortly after a rapid flurry of publications and attempted publications by anarchist presses and periodicals as well as projects by other authors that he supported through the same literary circle. In 1949, Durrell relocated to Yugoslavia, and in this new position, his anti-Marxist stance was reshaped and intensified. The humanist and anti-Marxist elements of the anarchism envisioned by Miller in works like "An Open Letter to Surrealists Everywhere" took on, for Durrell, a conservative tenor after his sequential postings to Belgrade and then Cyprus, the former of which he regarded as proof of the impoverished outcomes of authoritarian communism. As Durrell wrote to his dear friend Theodore Stephanides while serving in Belgrade in 1949,

> Conditions are rather gloomy here—almost mid-war conditions, overcrowding, poverty: As for Communism—my dear Theodore a short visit here is enough to make one decide that

Capitalism is worth fighting for. Black as it might be, with all
its bloodstains, it is less gloomy and arid and hopeless than this
inert and ghastly police state. (Durrell, *Spirit* 100)

This is hardly unqualified conservatism. Moreover, while he did
not consider it as bad as Yugoslavia under Tito, Durrell's capitalism
remains black and bloodstained, and by 1974 he intimately bound
money to *merde* (*Monsieur* 141) through "Marx's great analysis of our
culture or the Freudian analysis of absolute value as based on infantile
attitudes to excrement. Gold and excrement" (141). The trouble for
the reader here is how to hold in creative tension, perhaps even a *defining* tension, Durrell's lengthy anti-authoritarian ties and anti-Marxist
beliefs, both of which seem to have a significant role in the aesthetic
structure of his works, in conjunction with his service to the British
government. Durrell's comments remained measured after he was
redefined as a British non-patrial without the right to enter or settle
in Britain without a visa, a fact that "thickens" this tension. Moreover,
we must ask whether or not the existing political interpretations of
Durrell's works are sufficient for the breadth of this creative tension.
    This problem surfaces again in Durrell's travel narrative of Yugoslavia,
"Family Portrait," as well as in his discussions of Sadat-era Egypt and the
communist experiences of his friend Gostan Zarian. All three pieces
adamantly reject Marxist forms of government that arose from Soviet
Russia as well as Soviet influences abroad. They also post-date Durrell's
last publications among the anarchist presses and periodicals. However,
in all three Durrell's vision and images return to the village, everyday
life, the materials of rural living, and resistance to exploitative labour
and class—it is surprising to find an anti-Marxist position adopted that
nonetheless questions rural-urban tensions (Gifford, "Real" 15–16)
and the transformation of traditional ways of life by the introduction of
technology and new forms of organization, both quintessential Marxist
areas of attention. To be more exact, it is only if we fail to account for
Durrell's previous anti-authoritarian affiliations and quietist interests
that his rustic, utopian anti-Marxism is surprising. This combination
has confused much previous scholarship, which either casts Durrell as
a reactionary Tory or as an elitist artist without regard for the conditions of labour and life. Both are oversimplifications.

Durrell's only expressly political musings apart from news articles to raise ready cash appear in "No Clue to Living," in which he was invited to consider the role of the artist in contemporary society. Juxtaposed against the activist and formerly communist authors in the series of articles organized by Stephen Spender, Durrell's stance that the public ought to form its own individual opinions without relying on the authority of artists, politicians, or other figureheads is shockingly anti-authoritarian in the comparison to his Auden generation antitheses. In contrast to the earnest protestations of the other authors involved in the project, Durrell contends, "it is very doubtful whether [the artist] has anything to say which could be more original than the other pronouncements by public figures, for apart from his art he is just an ordinary fellow like everyone else, subject to the same bloody flux of rash opinion" ("No Clue" 17–18). The phrase "he is just an ordinary fellow like everyone else" is the leveling force that puts the reading public on par with presidents and popes (17), and to which a poet dare not lecture or opinionate. The poet clearly retains opinions but his public is taught self-reliance without relying on opinionated poets for leadership. The result is much akin to Miller's anarchist revision to the authoritarian communism of the Surrealists. Rather than the notion of an artist's authority as a "public opinionator" (17), which "leads the masses to identify themselves with movie stars and megalomaniacs like Hitler and Mussolini," Miller proposed to abandon leadership because "I am fatuous enough to believe that in living my own life in my own way I am more apt to give life to others" ("Open" 157). Despite the appearance of this piece after Durrell's years in Yugoslavia and the cementing of his anti-Marxist beliefs, Durrell's rejection of "that ineradicable predisposition to legislate for the man next door" demonstrates his desire to emphasize the "limitations of Time, on whose slippery surface neither kings nor empires nor dictators could find more than a precarious and temporary purchase" ("No Clue" 23). Doomed kings, empires, and dictators make a striking combination for an author who was a royal subject, servant of empire, and recent resident in Péron's Argentina and Tito's Yugoslavia. It is difficult to recognize in this Durrell the same man described by biographers and critics as a reactionary,[1] although the complex relations among these differing positions certainly enrich our approach to his major novels and the troubled politics of his travel writings. One immediately thinks of Durrell's comments on T.S. Eliot, who when accused by Durrell of being too interested in esoteric material to be Anglican, responded by saying, "Perhaps they haven't found out about me yet?" (Durrell, "The Other Eliot" 64).

Kinships to how Durrell's poetic peers in London were reading him emerge quickly, though with different terms—their close quality lies in their treatment of the reader's independence rather than in the explicitness of their political commentary. In describing the New Apocalypse, Treece gives a clear political voice to the movement: "the logical outcome of this attitude is a form of anarchism not unlike that of Herbert Read: an anarchism which substitutes equity and natural law for man-made justice and moral code; which distrusts the insensible and dehumanising central machine" (Treece, How 14). Francis Scarfe offers a deeply biased account of the core tenets of the New Apocalypse, though his is the only contemporary document to summarize its actual manifesto. Scarfe reports that Treece, Fraser, and Hendry decided on a list of the main interests of the New Apocalypse after a meeting in 1938:

1. That Man was in need of greater freedom, economic no less than aesthetic, from machines and mechanistic thinking.
2. That no existent political system, Left or Right; no artistic ideology, Surrealism or the political school of Auden, was able to provide this freedom.
3. That the Machine Age had exerted too strong an influence on arts, and had prevented the individual development of Man.
4. That Myth, as a personal means of reintegrating the personality, had been neglected and despised. (Scarfe 155)

To this vision of the Apocalypse, Scarfe adds his own political vision, which reflects his own activities in the Communist Party in Paris and his own dalliances in Surrealism, though very much of a Party line: "I do not think that any poet fully alive to the conditions of our time would disagree with these points, with the possible exception of their political implications, which might leave the writer to be crushed more than ever between the Left and Right" (155–56). He is, however, clearly aware of their position since he also notes, "Apocalypse is, then, a de-mechanizing, or a de-materializing, of Surrealism" (158).

Although he only recounted his definition later, Treece is characteristically clear in his evaluation of the core theoretical tenets of the New Apocalypse:

> The political position of such a movement is clearly Anarchic, an antidote to the left-wing Audenism as much as to right-wing Squirearchy—and especially Anarchic of the sort outlined in Herbert Read's *Philosophy of Anarchism*; that is, a mode of living in which natural law takes over from man-made law (including Marxism, Capitalism, Fascism, and eventually Christianity as we see it practiced to-day.) (*How* 76)

This leads Treece to examine the specifics of his peers' descriptions of Apocalypticism. In this regard, he specifically turns to J.F. Hendry and his contention that

> "Apocalypse occurs where expression breaks through the structure of language, to become more *organic*," and in that word *organic* I see Read's pleas for *natural law*. This development from socialism to anarchism is further emphasized when Hendry writes "Logic (i.e., Totalitarian or Capitalistic), machine-made logic, has resulted from our fear of ourselves, fear of our uncontrolled energy." (Treece, *How* 76)

To these contentions, he adds much later in the same volume, the Apocalypse's distrust of the machine and of authoritarian communalism: "when a man stands alone, without machines and systems, more than that, distrustful of machines and systems, he allows his individual spirit to drive him in a way that he could not do, limited by the spirits of his machine-fellows. He becomes a Romantic" (174). He then doubles this Romanticism and organicism as well as the distrust of the machine and enforced communalism by arguing the Auden generation's period "had been one of Socialism, realism, even, at times, of mechanical Classicism. It was a period typified in poetry by the mechanistic conceits of Auden and Day-Lewis, among the little magazines by the *Left Review*, and by the inception and development of Mass Observation" (174).[2]

Derek Stanford would also elaborate on Treece's vision in the same year as Treece's study was published, and Stanford's understanding as well as his own position at this time was expressly anarchist, though he later revised his views, in particular after his divorce from the poet turned novelist Muriel Spark. Stanford's political summation in *The Freedom of Poetry*, prior to his analysis of the poetic work of Gascoyne, Durrell, and Comfort, borrows from the language of the New Apocalypse expressly: "Today, the forces of mass-production have called into being a robot of flesh. This new slave-figure of mechanization must endlessly repeat his identical act—a kind of static treadmill inferno for the mind. In such a situation, the main concern is the rescue of man from these economic hulks" (14). This discourse of the machine and slavery that carry out a form of economic determinism are then contrasted against the organic, which remedies the machine work of the urban centre because "For the aesthetic libertarian, whose credo consists of freedom and art, the main ground for faith is the simple belief that nature reveals a certain order" (19). Stanford then echoes Henry Miller's "An Open Letter to Surrealists Everywhere" to argue, "The paradox is that man's fear of freedom, the way he excludes himself from fuller life, is in proportion to how much he lacks it" (14). As an almost certainty, Stanford immediately shifts to the discussion of naming and power that opens this book through reference to Lawrence Durrell's "Asylum in the Snow": "So it comes about that he wishes to exist in a world of familiar categories, a world where things have their place and their label, a world of 'fixities and definites.' This well-known, 'stay-put,' inventoried realm is largely the work of intelligence; of what we may term utility-logic, with its ready-made titles and convenient distinctions" (14).

Anarchism by Any Other Name

Anarchism as a political and personal philosophy is distinct from most others in that it cannot be codified or made to submit to citation of authority. It offers no high scriptures or unchangeable tenets since it is subject to radical revision and is reliant on the function of the interpreting and acting individual within any circumstance. An individual outside of a social context has no need of an anarchist philosophy and a group principally identified by its cohesion will resist it, so in every attempt to propose a "core" series of anarchist values, the attempt moves contrary to the practice. Therefore, in very general terms, I will begin with a negative definition and move toward a very loose series of propositions that are suitable to the project at hand. My immediate concern will be distinguishing power from authority; I will set aside the anti-state discourse of anarchism for my purposes here in order to privilege a collaborative vision of the individual *and* (not within) the social. Only from this will I move to the next sections on selfhood and the body, two facts that, in Eve Kosofsky Sedgwick's potent phrasing, prove powerful solvents to stable identities (85).

I am also unable to write this portion of the book without placing myself in relation to my project and thereby troubling the stable identity of my personal pronoun. For this, I am reliant on Tom Morris more than I can easily express. As he notes with regard to the fashionable identification of one's subjectivity or subject position,

> Today, academic convention requires that the author's shaping, puzzled, reflecting self be muted if not eradicated altogether through the verbal and formal polish of published expression. While it is also true that there is a kind of narrowly-conceived "personalism" now in vogue, it seems to be tolerated only to the extent that it remain narrow....
>
> Yet the evidence shows that the critic who denies or even disregards the fundamental, generating impress of his own individuated, embodied experience potentially opens up criticism to a tendency whereby the place of the vital, mutable, and individually human is diminished amidst abandoned nature. (9)

Morris's context is the 1980s scene in literary criticism, one in which the self-definition through various labels was fashionable, "narrow," and nearly necessary for academic work even while reactionary popular culture grew. Our meanings of Personalism obviously differ, but I take Morris's distinction between academic self-identification and individuated existence seriously. In contrast to the multiplication of definitional labels that restrict the scope of a chaotically developing individual, one who may not even have an adequately full self-understanding to give stable definitions, I would much prefer to adopt Morris's second option: a critic who accepts the mutable and limited framework within which his or her work is developed. Rather than self-identifying, I prefer to express the limitations of my own position and its susceptibility to change. If I am reasonably successful, this chapter will acknowledge how the "human origins and audience...suggests correctly that the whole project remains incomplete, in progress, and impatient with conventional demands for tidy systematizing and comprehensiveness. Rather it is an amenable vehicle to facilitate independent thought attuned to re-visioning" (Morris 8). In this sense, I aim to provide a work of use rather than a work of authority, especially as I engage in stating my subject position, per se. A good deal of the point is to indicate the protean nature of this position and the negotiations it necessitates.

To insert my position of observation, which is also my position in relation to this project, I first read Morris after being given a copy of his book by a retiring professor, Jerry Zaslove. I returned to Simon Fraser University for a post-baccalaureate degree program while completing my MA thesis in part to study with him before his retirement, and Morris's book (in tandem with other issues of Paunch and Wayne Burns's reminiscences on teaching) made a profound impact on me in the summer before I began my PHD studies. I travelled to Greece, my first time outside of North America, glancingly encountered the thriving anarchist community on Corfu, and began a different life than I had known before. When I returned, however, I set aside these books amidst the standardizing and competitive rigours of a doctoral program. I hardly touched the books again over the next ten years.

When I returned to Morris's Bursting the Foundations, it was as a book of solace while I cared for a dear friend in the imminence of her death, and Morris's recollections of his own life in the landscapes of my childhood in tandem with a vision of the terrifying yet most profoundly personal frailties of corporeality drew me back to my readings with Zaslove, reading that centred on the individual, the body, death, and power. I was deeply humbled. Morris's unflinching recognition of the cost of genuine life as genuine death was imminent to me, and it in turn sent me back to Alex Comfort's poetry, which I had encountered during my doctoral work after hearing of Comfort's death in 2000 during my course with Zaslove. I still cannot help finding it an unfair bargain—real death for real life—yet it is one I would choose over the alternatives, unhesitatingly. This is to say, genuinely embracing being oneself means embracing the limitedness and finite existence of that resplendent existence without recourse to another power. Regardless of one's faith(s), being oneself entails not being another's, and in this, having an ending. In Comfort's 1940s critical work, this means, "Fascism is the attempt to summate the destructive impulses and to use them as a basis for a society. It teaches, logically, contempt for death and suffering in oneself and in others. It teaches that the individual is unreal, and therefore death, the termination of the individual, is unreal also" ("Art" 21). In a more direct sense, he simply contends, "We are living in a madhouse whenever society is allowed to become personalized and regarded as a super-individual" ("Art" 24).

I must also explain that I use Morris's work here not so much for its clarity or convenience, since it is very likely inconvenient for others to find in libraries or bookshops, which is partly the personal point, but expressly because it was the work at hand when I faced the personal circumstances of my own life outside this project, and the lives of those I love, and because it was itself very much a work of circumstances of strife that made me see my own. The same critical views may be found in many anarchist works with kindred aims, but those others do not arise from the same landscapes, childhood memories, and corporeal experiences with which I identify when I walk through the formative locales of my own childhood that overlap with those expressed by Morris for his own.

My comments above orient attention to the individual, even an inarticulate individual with a limited capacity to offer personal experiences for others' interpretations. In this, however, reside the seeds of my first definitional paradigm. By wresting experience and significance, or some would say even meaning, from the social whole to the infinitely limited and extinguishable individual, we enter into the conflicts over power and authority. Both, and authority in particular, are the great consolations against our finitude and inescapable demise, and in this resides a self-deception we might call false consciousness, the capacity to become self-regulating systems of control that give away life without having ever lived it, all to grasp some opiate that might blur the shape of death out of its reality. Yet we come into being socially— I know myself through a language I did not devise and I come into being with others. Clearly, to be oneself or to be one's own is not an ill-conceived refutation of social and communal existence nor to deny that institutions make subjectivity possible. The pressing matter resides in a different conflict or negotiation.

We are never without power, yet we never fail to resist it. For the anarchist, authority does not even exist; it is the quintessence of false consciousness. This may seem a peculiar assertion, but allow me to begin with its negative definitional origins—I consider my terminology very much in the same sense as did Morris:

> I use "libertarian" not in the more popular contemporary
> sense as a call for reduced State-supported "social" programs
> so that corporate and individualist self-interest can have
> more "freedom" to bully life within given political-economic
> structures, but rather as a call for the transformation of culture
> so that, at the very least, every form of economic, political,
> and egoistic bullying becomes impractical and experienced as
> repulsive. I would use the term "anarchist" here if it were not
> for its more narrow political connotations and the automated
> hysteria it evokes. (7)

Resistance to the very term "anarchism" is strong enough that Howard Zinn, in an introduction to Read's *Anarchy and Order*, would make a deliberate point of momentarily misleading his reader in order to avoid the dangerous shoals of word associations: "The word *anarchy* unsettles most people…; it suggests disorder, violence, uncertainty. We have good reason for fearing those conditions, because we have been living with them for a long time, not in anarchist societies…but in exactly those most fearful of anarchy" (Zinn, Introduction ix). As Zinn demonstrates, the terminology arrives with a predetermined connotative value.

Regardless of these perennial problems that can lead to "left libertarian" or the opposite in the variously named postures of the recent American Tea Party looking for anti-state forms of pro-corporate coercion and perpetuation of authority, the problem of anarchism's name and loss in the propaganda war does not alter its anti-authoritarian basis. The distinction made by Proudhon between property and possession led to his misunderstood exhortation, "Property is theft!," which becomes greatly more cogent once property is seen as ownership of another person's possessions, or as is common in my home city, owning your neighbour's home by virtue of said neighbour's rent paying the mortgage. I "own" it by virtue of another person's work to "pay" for it, which I then thieve. Possessions may be a different matter, but such property is not difficult to understand as a form of "theft." Furthermore, apart from anarchism's own name, one of the most frequent misunderstandings pertains to what is even meant by authority in "anti-authoritarian."

The distinction between power and authority in anarchism is both old and new, being perennial and continually re-examined. I draw my definitional work by considering its limitations. Colin Ward classifies Robert Paul Wolff as an "American free-market philosopher" and as part of a "phalanx of authors [who] have provided the 'ideological superstructure' of the swing to the Right in federal and local politics in the United States" (Ward 66). Yet, Wolff teaches Marxism and has written a cogent brief study on Marxist economics as well as a perennially popular defense of anarchism, so Ward's position seems untenable. Nevertheless, it points to Wolff's distance from action rather than critique. But, for the real issue, Wolff has been used by a wide range of right-wing American libertarians, who use Wolff to support an American sense of libertarian capitalism without giving precedence to Wolff's sense of authority rather than cash or freedom as valuable measures. For this reason, Wolff has been critiqued by anarchists like Ward as if he agreed with this interpretation of his work, which Wolff has repeatedly indicated he does not. Such is the ease with which the left or right orientation of libertarian views may be reconstructed by others for their own ends.

Regardless of fashion or personal feelings some may have about his work or social position, Wolff offers a succinct compression of longstanding anarchist attitudes with clarity and the definitional specificity requisite to his profession, and these are useful as a well wrought simplification of the much larger body of literature on the topic. In particular, he does not base anarchism on any definite "freedom" or identity that can be itemized on a checklist nor by the destruction of one form of coercion that resides in the state and its various institutions. Instead, the crux of Wolff's sense of anarchism is the distinction between power and authority in an Enlightenment context and coercion in its myriad forms not simply the statist form:

> Authority is the right to command, and correlatively, the right to be obeyed. It must be distinguished from power, which is the ability to compel compliance, either through the use or threat of force. When I turn over my wallet to a thief who is holding me at gunpoint, I do so because the fate with which he threatens me is worse than the loss of money which I am made to suffer. I grant that he has power over me, but I would hardly suppose that he has *authority*, that is, that he has a right to demand my money and that I have an obligation to give it to him. (Wolff 4)

I take this as a workable distinction between power and authority such that power is around us in our world in both real and symbolic forms, and we encounter its exercise continually. Chomsky replaces "right" with "justifiable." I am powerless in the face of death or the deaths of those I love, and exigent circumstances may call for the exercise of power over me. This limits my will or my ambitions, either by the will of others or the impossibility of resisting the inevitable, yet it is not a matter of *authority* just as death is not a matter or morality—one need not ask if there is a just expectation for mortality to be fulfilled since it is a fact rather than a will or force. Chomsky repeatedly draws on a colloquial example of a parent protecting an unknowing child from self-injury as an exercise of power that is justified, with which few would disagree—yet it is still an exercise of *power*, justifiable or not, which is not entirely the same as *authority*. However, authority as the "right to be obeyed" and the "obligation of others to obey" seems a far more remarkable phenomenon unlikely to accept of a colloquialism or commonplace.[3] Once a person has the capacity for reason, we must ask if authority can exist, barring any temporary suspension of that capacity.

In contrast to reasonable or justifiable exercises of power, if authority is the just right to obedience and the obligation to obey, then I am confronted by Wolff's second succinct problem based on the Enlightenment notion of the individual and the capacity for rational thought and thereby self-determination (even though his position must subsequently disrupt the Enlightenment subject as rational):

> Every man who possesses both free will and reason has an obligation to take responsibility for his actions....The responsible man is not capricious or anarchic, for he does acknowledge himself bound by moral constraints. But he insists that he alone is the judge of those constraints....He may learn from others about his moral obligations, but only in the sense that a mathematician learns from other mathematicians....He does not learn in the sense that one learns from an explorer, by accepting as true his accounts of things one cannot see for oneself. (Wolff 13)

Insofar as we admit of a self-conscious individual capable of self-reflection leading to actions undertaken in the world, this obligation for learning is requisite, as is the distinction between obedience to authority and learning a convincing rationale for a course of action. The Marxist subject would be an altogether different entity shaped entirely by its conditions, and no anarchist position would accept it as a viable or desirable alternative distinct from an inescapable form of false consciousness. The equivalent in Morris's work is equally (yet not *more*) valid: "Criticism assumes a capacity to reason and a conscious desire to do so beyond the dictated terms of given and contingent circumstances" (Morris 39). The capacity for such criticism and critical awareness makes authority as the just and legitimate expectation of obedience impossible, even while the exercise of power may be necessary and rational explanation may yield the same results. The distinction lies in power's exercise being distinct from justness or the legitimacy of authority and rational explanation being distinct from coercion.

For Wolff, then, the Enlightenment notion of a self—that is (1) capable of rationale self-consideration and reflection, (2) inclusive of a notion of the individual with a capacity for moral thought and the consideration of the self and others, and (3) has the ability to determine a course of action based on personal wants, needs, and responsibilities—offers up the irreconcilable conundrum at the heart of the state's "right to be obeyed" or the self's obligation to the state's authority (or any other forms of authority running the gamut from the superego to the nation-state or the church):

> The defining mark of the state is authority, the right to rule. The primary obligation of man is autonomy, the refusal to be ruled. It would seem, then, that there can be no resolution of the conflict between the autonomy of the individual and the putative authority of the state. Insofar as a man fulfills his obligation to make himself the author of his decisions, he will resists the state's claim to have authority over him. That is to say, he will deny that he has a duty to obey the laws of the state *simply because they are the laws*. In that sense, it would seem that anarchism is the only political doctrine consistent with the virtue of autonomy. (Wolff 18)

In Wolff's vision, this implies the pre-eminence of self-determination over self-identity. Simplistically stated, being social or even admitting that social institutions confer identity does not negate the distinction between power and authority; nor does it create a rationale in which authority may function. The Foucauldian sense of productive power, the fallacy of power's "place," and the necessity of power to subjectivity (Foucault 785) are all accepted in anarchist thought without engendering authority (Newman, "Place" 140–42). Self-identity and autonomy are not determining matters in relation to the primacy of self-determination.

Morris offers a consistent interpretation of authority contra power in a more casual tone:

> Authority can be said to determine obedience…in a situation where both the subject and object of authority assumes similar

sanctions on or responses to experience. Dictionaries possess
authority...but so do "higher" officials in relation to "lower"
officials within a hierarchical structure accepted by both levels
of officialdom. Power can be understood as the introduction
of force or coercion into a situation calling for obedience
to authority. Some expressions of power sometimes seem
necessary: the adult's forcing of a child away from dangers
which s/he may not perceive. More commonly in history,
power has been joined with violent assault in the experiential
reinforcement of authority. (57–58)

The difference in terminology for Morris is tied to authority, power, and necessity. The authority of a dictionary differs from that of
officials by virtue of power. While the book may be used to justify an
exercise of power, it does not exercise power itself in a way that is
appreciably like an official's exercise of power through his or her office. Authority in Wolff's sense remains separate. Moreover, necessity,
whether in the form of a shared language or mortal frailty, is also distinct from authority. Necessity is of an order distinct from authority,
as is reality—this leaves only the official exercising power.

As a direct consequence, in Wolff's understanding and articulation,

an anarchist may grant the necessity of complying with the law
under certain circumstances for the time being. He may even
doubt that there is any real prospect of eliminating the state as a
human institution. But he will never view the commands of the
state as legitimate, as having a binding moral force. All authority
is equally illegitimate, although of course not therefore equally
worthy or unworthy of support. (18–19)

In this paradigm, what Rexroth recognized as Henry Miller's quietism
takes on a new contextual meaning as "the necessity of complying...
[without] view[ing] the commands of the state as legitimate, as having
a binding moral force" (Wolff 18). Hence, we recognize power and
not authority. Death and, to a lesser degree, taxes are both necessary
to me—authority is not the matter at hand. In many respects, this is
also the quintessence of Miller's quietism.

The Ego and Its Own

In a manner particularly useful for Personalism, with regard to the Marxist and rational positivist tendency to look to social structure rather than deep experiences of the individual, Morris argues that for one to contend

> that the intra-institutional and culturally rational functions of the asylum [qua Foucault] are equivalent to the meaning of the asylum, ignores the destruction of experience often perpetrated within the asylum and on the outside, in culture itself. If seen from within, from the experiential dimension, then the asylum necessitates a radical re-evaluation of apparently "coherent" culture at large. (42)

The inescapable problem here resides in the phrase "are equivalent to," which is to say, the social function equates to meaning without accounting for lived individual experience. If we are to define meaning for the individual without recourse to the individual, then on what basis can this meaning exist without recourse to the authority of the collective? The collective's needs may very well play a role, even an exigent role that necessitates an exercise of power or that renders an unwanted experience inevitable, but the conflation of exigency with authority is the elision of the individual, or for Morris's particular instance, that which "ignores the destruction of experience often perpetrated within the asylum and on the outside, in culture itself" (42). As Morris argues, "if seen from within, from the experiential dimension," the exercises of collective power (without authority) may very well be exigent yet still cannot be called the entirety of "meaning." The individual cannot be elided even amidst the exercise of power. An alternative to this institutional form of meaning, moreover, rests on the "experiential dimension" of an individual caught within social forms and social means of constructing meaning, yet is apart from them insofar as being individual. We are never without society, just as society never acts on an individual without in some way acting upon itself—yet, despite these bonds, the experiences of the subject and object in such relations inextricably differ. This tension stands even as the means of understanding and defining this individual evaporate as we cede priority to the social exertions of power in inscribing meaning. This is to say, if the social inscription of meaning, as an act of power as well as a rationale for further exercises of power (in Foucault's sense of power-knowledge), is recognized as limited to an "outside" of the experiences of such inscriptions, then the individual must be recognized whether or not it may be known or brought into meaning. The supposed self behind this individual also need not be known or brought into meaning in order to occupy a position belonging to itself.

For this self, however, there still remains uncertainty. This has already been seen as a common theme for the various poets of personalist persuasions explored in the previous chapters, perhaps most notably Duncan and Durrell. In comparing his anarchism to Pound's fascism, Duncan wrote to Pound's former lover and protégé, H.D., "I was not, anyway, that trusting of order and coercion, whether political or that other inner political coercion that Freud saw in the super-ego" (Duncan and H.D. 36). I've previously aligned this with Durrell's first formulation of the Heraldic Universe:[4]

> Let's look at the manifestoes. Begins a political discussion. The artist's place in society. A definite lean leftward. Well what's wrong with that? Nothing, provided politics are not going to be confused with art. I'm tired of political people. They have confused the inner struggle with the outer one....Politics is an art that deals in averages. Art is a man that deals in people. (Durrell and Miller 18; Miller and Read 89)

In both instances, the self has no definite proportions, nor any clear claim to being fully self-knowing or autonomous. On the contrary, it is engaged in a struggle against definition and the competition between inner forces of control and dissolution. Herbert Marcuse showed the kindred overlap between the inner and outer struggles through repressive desublimation, the turning of libidinal desire to systems of control that contain the self rather than realize it. For Morris, Durrell's and Duncan's considerations of inner coercion is formulated in Freudian terms, which both poets also used:

Authority and power typically shade off into one another. They are familiars. Here one can distinguish three experiential contexts in which power and authority are manifest: the cultural or institutional context, the interpersonal context (especially family forms), and the inner or psychological context. If power is initially external coercion, authority's adult pre-history is based in what psychoanalysis calls the ego and superego: the ego in its practical engagement of external reality and the superego in its relationship with ambivalently experienced authority/love figures in early life and, later, with tacitly accepted sanctions originating outside the self. The genesis of the superego includes the experience of objective power directed against the self. (Morris 58)

As with Durrell and Duncan resisting the power and perverse presumption of authority exerted by the superego, Morris distinguishes between the exigencies of reality and the construction of authority without first attempting to stabilize or reduce the Ego nor attempting to liberate the Ego from exigencies or its social existence. This is to say, Morris is like Durrell and Duncan insofar as he also resists the superego's tendency to solve anxiety by exerting authority; such a process placates the Ego by neutering it, which neither improves its condition nor resolves the anxiety.

For Morris and Marcuse, then, the "needful desire" of the body can be both a path to anti-authoritarian awareness as well as a means of containment. Through the desublimation of sexual desire conjoined with regulation of the means of satisfaction in a capitalist economy (repressive desublimation), Marcuse would contend that the modern "one-dimensional" society transforms the corporeal and previously contained drives of the body into yet more insidious forms of domination—one might satisfy desire through interpellation as the consuming subject regulated by a capitalist economy and thereby fetishize (in Marx's sense) the desire itself. Alternatively, when such needful desire bursts the stabilizing boundaries of the Ego, the interpellation of the subject within a regulatory economy cannot function, and in Sedgwick's sense, "sexual desire is an unpredictably powerful solvent of stable identities" (Sedgwick 85). This is an anti-authoritarian figuration. Duncan renders this notion as "a man's sexuality is a natural factor in a biological economy larger and deeper than his own human will" ("Homosexual" 38), and for Durrell it becomes a stylistic trait in which stabilizing adjectives fail to appear in relation to the self or textual gaps resist the domination of or reduction to self-expression. Duncan was particularly nuanced in his capacity to recognize the regulatory capacity in desublimation.

Durrell's typical ploy, very likely due to his significant Freudian interests, was to suggest a self that could not be fully self-knowing. This would be accomplished by the symptomatic eruptions of parapraxes in his texts or by removing words, genders, or confusing identity through deep ambiguity. This trend continued across his oeuvre from 1937 to 1985. As an instance, in *The Black Book*, his character Tarquin

> has discovered that he is a homosexual. After examining his diary, having his horoscope cast, his palm read, his prostate fingered, and the bumps on his great bald cranium interpreted.
>
> "From now on it is going to be different. I am going to sleep with whom I want and not let my conditioned self interfere with me....I am that I am, and all that kind of stuff." (Durrell, Black Book 167)

Tarquin's discovery of a self he had not previous known, a discovery made through the needful desire of the body, is first tied to the body's physical traits, but the telling slip is the "conditioned self" that may or may *not* "interfere" with him, revealing the continued rumbling of an unsatisfied unconscious breaking the surface of assent with a parapraxis. We cannot trust Tarquin's discovery to be stable as he moves through the various allotropes of mobile desire. The juxtaposition of the name of God from Exodus 3:14 with "that kind of stuff" reveals a character who does not understand his own statement. His name-cum-identity fails to signify or reveal the self just as the "I am that I am" name of God stands in for what cannot be uttered, although the reader is slyly meant to be able to recognize this whereas Tarquin cannot. The same double valence applies to the discovery of his "authentic" self that the reader likewise recognizes as suspect.

Duncan offers a kindred problem already seen in "Toward an

African Elegy." For Duncan, "The theme of the poem is not homo-sexuality; nor does the darkness stand for homosexuality" (Letter to Ransom n. pag.), which means his gesture to the unknown is not the same "unknown" as Durrell's Tarquin, though their technique is the same. For Duncan, "The dark continent in the poem is not what one hides, but what is hidden from one" (Letter to Ransom n. pag.). In this context, Duncan's poem present "in jungles / of my body... / Moves / I. I. I." such that this fragile selfhood and its substitutional dreamwork that presents the darkness of "The halls of Africa we seek in dreams / as barriers of dream against the deep" (Duncan, "African" 96). The dreamt of desire is itself a substitutive gratification of we know not what, for which the Ego is itself a substitutive gratification.

The important commonality is that "docile and obedient sub-jects" (Seem xx) are disturbed by these corporeal desires issuing from somewhere other than the stable Ego, regardless of whether this fevered dream vision is rendered as "myth," which might be seen in the New Apocalypse; as the attempt to find an unknown self or *Unbewusst Ich* (as so many of Durrell's character's attempt only to fail); Duncan's "the deep"; or as the Anti-Ego in Mark Seem's reading of Henry Miller in relation to Gilles Deleuze and Felix Guattari's *Anti-Oedipus*. In all such instances, the stability of the Ego itself is secondary to the freedom of its self-possession, even amidst its own instability or solvency in the face of desire. Seem calls this "what is nonhuman in man, his desires and his forces" (xix). The trend is for "a politics of desire directed against all that is egoic—and heroic—in man" (xix), but not in an anti-egoism in Stirner's sense, rather with the sense that stabilizing the Ego through the repressive desublimation of desire is accomplished by the same force that drives false conscious-ness or makes one desire one's own repression. Again, Seem's most pressing examples are from Miller's postwar *Sexus*: "The man who looks for security, even in the mind, is like a man who would chop off his limbs in order to have artificial ones which will give him no pain or trouble" (Miller 428; Seem xvi). The origin of this theme for Miller, however, is pre-war in his *Tropic of Cancer* and its mockery of the various desiring machines, for which mechanization horrifically displaces human contact, which is precisely the image with which Elizabeth Smart closes *By Grand Central Station I Sat Down and Wept*, the same image that captured so many writers of the 1930s, ranging from Read and Thomas to Durrell and Duncan to Cossery and Gascoyne. It is not a rejection of Stirner's sense of the Ego and its own but rather a rejection of the stabilization of the Ego, which desire then disrupts. The Ego's self-possession is not in question—only the forces that stabilize it via regulation.

These challenges regarding the self are common across the writers under discussion as well as in anarchist studies. Both Durrell and Miller open explicit challenges to stable notions of selfhood even while disputing the vulgar Marxist supposition that subjectivity is a product of and is defined by material conditions or that social being determines subjectivity. This is to say, even when self-contemplation generates an order that resists logical syntax (as with Durrell's conception of poetry) or when the various allotropes of the self (qua Lawrence) are the only manifestation of it accessible (rather than some pure, unchanging essence), the self is still its own, in Stirner's sense of Ego belonging to itself and no other. Hence, the exercise and experience of freedom is predicated on the self yet does not necessitate stability, knowing, or even any form of certainties with regard to it. Freedom is not another manifestation of authority's stabilizing influence on the Ego—nor is it exempt from necessity or power over it.

For Saul Newman, this relationship between self-knowing (and thereby self-domination by containment and restriction) and freedom is an ongoing challenge:

> Anarchism is a politics and ethics in which power is continually interrogated in the name of human freedom, and in which human existence is posited in the absence of authority. However, this raises the question of whether there is an anarchist subject as such....To explain the desire for self-domination and to develop strategies—ethical and political strategies—to counter it, would be to propose an anarchist theory of subjectivity, or at least a more developed one than can be found in classical anarchist thought. It would also imply a move beyond some of the essentialist and rationalist categories of classical anarchism, a move that elsewhere I have referred to as postanarchism. (Newman, "Voluntary" 39)

The "post" of postanarchism is akin to the "post" in postmodernism, and for the authors to whom the work of this chapter must be brought to bear, the epithet "late" may be preferable: Late Modernism and Later Modernism rather than postanarchism. Hence, in Newman's sense, "Humanism and rationalism resulted in a kind of blind-spot around the question of desire, whose dark, convoluted, self-destructive and irrational nature would be revealed later by psychoanalysis" (39). The seed for anti-essentialist views is in many respects the organic development of classical anarchism, simply brought to bear on the Ego itself, a notion already explicit in the Villa Seurat, Herbert Read, and the San Francisco Renaissance, and also implicit in the New Apocalypse and New Romanticism.

D.H. Lawrence's notion of allotropic selves is one instance of this contest. Both Durrell and Miller refer to Lawrence frequently, invoking his influence on their works, though likewise pointing out their differences, and this notion of the allotrope is one such instance. Lawrence figures in kindred ways among the New Apocalypse (most notably in their name), as well as James Cooney's *Phoenix* and George Leite's *Circle*. As a chemical term, allotropic means "having different physical properties, though unchanged in substance" (*OED*), such as diamonds and coal both being allotropes of carbon. In other words, wildly diverse things are still connected at the level of Lawrence's blood consciousness and relationships are based on neither "coal" nor "diamonds" but on "carbon." More specifically, in his June 15, 1914 letter to Edward Garnett, Lawrence claimed,

> You mustn't look in my novel for the old stable ego of the character. There is another ego, according to whose action the individual is unrecognisable, and passes through, as it were, allotropic states which it needs a deeper sense than any we've been used to exercise, to discover are states of the same single radically-unchanged element. (Like as diamond and coal are the same pure single element of carbon. The ordinary novel would trace the history of the diamond—but I say "diamond, what! This is carbon." And my diamond might be coal or soot, and my theme is carbon.) (Lawrence, *Letters* 183)

This famous passage is not lost on Durrell and Miller, especially given their shared interest in the censored "dirt" of what Lawrence tactfully calls "soot." To the point, this passage's topic illustrates the area where Durrell's and Miller's extension and development from their predecessors is most apparent: the old stable Ego. In 1932, Miller wrote his study of Lawrence, *The World of Lawrence* (published in 1980 but discussed with Denys Val Baker's pacifist journal *Voice: An Anthology of Individualist Writings* in his article "The Tree of Life"). Miller's book was contemporaneous with Anaïs Nin's *D.H. Lawrence: An Unprofessional Study*.[5] Nicholas Moore praises precisely this component of Miller's work in his book about Miller published by Baker's Opus Press. Durrell, in contrast, was outside the trend in the Villa Seurat, and did not pen a study per se of Lawrence, but he did write a preface to Bantam's 1968 edition of *Lady Chatterley's Lover* (vii–xi), and as early at 1936 he wrote to Alan Thomas (his friend and the editor of Durrell's *Spirit of Place*): "it is a qualitative difference in which I blow the Lawrentian trumpet. I [know?] my own kind, I haven't begun. Beside Lawrence, beside Miller, beside Blake. Yes, I am humble, I have hardly started. BUT I AM ON THE SAME TRAM" (*Spirit* 50).

Ian MacNiven has already used Durrell's comments in the passage above to illustrate the relationship between Durrell's, Miller's, and Lawrence's works in his "Lawrence and Durrell: 'On the Same Tram,'" and this is an established element of the criticism. Nonetheless, sharing transit to the same station should not lead us to disregard the "qualitative difference" in how they all play a new tune on the bugle of the novel. This difference resides in the continuity of the allotropic self in contrast to the "warring selves" that Durrell identifies when placing Miller beside Lawrence ("Studies" 49). Lawrence's use of the term "allotropic" derives from two footnotes in F.W.H. Myers's *Human Personality and Its Survival of Bodily Death* (Gibbons 338–41), and it is this "'subliminal self' which represents 'our central and abiding being'" (Gibbons 339). Lawrence promoted what appears to be another frame for the immortal soul, which Durrell and Miller both back away from, though to differing degrees, even if they are not fully successful in totally ridding themselves of "the old stable ego" (Lawrence, *Letters* 183). The continuity of at least the drive, if not an actual self per se, is where Durrell and Miller break from their forebears—if a drive remains for Durrell and Miller, it is divorced from a central and abiding being. Both authors refer to this moment in Lawrence's *Letters* across their careers, but both also make the crucial distinction that the Ego's stability is far less important than, in Stirner's sense, the Ego's *own*, that is, that the Ego is its own and no other's property. Therefore, we see Miller and Durrell arriving at Morris's "I/me" distinction via D.H. Lawrence, and this function of selfhood in the Personalists is crucial. While it would muddy the water to reread these movements through Deleuze, it is worth noting that this parallels his use of both Miller and Lawrence, opening an avenue for further consideration.

To return to the critical "red thread" that opened this chapter, the crux of the disagreement between anarchism and Marxism is not necessarily the historical disagreement over the interposition of a tyranny comprised of the proletariat in revolutionary theory. The more prominent conflict *after* the failure of anarchism in Spain in the 1930s groups under analysis here arose through ways of conceiving of the self or subjectivity rather than a direct means to overthrowing the state. The contemporary inheritance of this tension is usefully demonstrated by Jameson's opening to *Late Marxism* and his strong reading, in Harold Bloom's sense, of Adorno across the book as a whole. For Jameson, via Adorno, "neurosis is simply this boring imprisonment of the self in itself, crippled by its terror of the new and unexpected, carrying its sameness with it wherever it goes, so that it has the protection of feeling" (16). In this vision, sameness equates to stability and thereby to counterrevolutionary forces, whereas the "new" is revolution itself. This "new" is cast in terms surprisingly akin to a break or rupture in history: "how one could go about conceptualizing and imagining what you can by definition not yet imagine or foresee; what has no equivalent in your current experience" (16). Against this radical potential for a reconstruction of human relations and economies "there slowly emerges the counter-image or -mirage of the neurotic self locked utterly into its own 'identity.'...[Hence,] a closed self and a primal flux are...useful in grasping the *function* of the compromise formations...: garden-variety 'psychic identity'" (16). In this vision, the stabilizing notions of identity are a function of social control, a form of false consciousness, that exist only in an essentializing manner. This leads Jameson to perhaps one of his most plain statements of the issue: "Ego is thus, in that larger sense of personal identity [a persistent identity over time], a defense mechanism but also a weapon, an instrument of praxis and survival" (17). This leads him to cast Ego and same as obversions, since the Ego is the compromise function that constructs "personal consciousness [a]s still somehow 'the same'" over time and "as what makes things the same as well as inscribing sameness...on the psyche" (17). This in turn casts the revolutionary project as "undermining that logic of recurrence and of sameness in order to break through to everything sameness excludes," which would be the revolutionary "new" (17). This obversion of the same and the self, which occludes or simply misrepresents the anarchist emphasis on the self's *self-possession* rather than a totalitarian stabilization of the self, allows for Jameson's later return to questions of freedom (77) that develop greater definitional nuance without formulating anything not already found in Caudwell's articulation of bourgeois freedom.

The Body and Its Own

Both the personalist writers and their various theorizations of their practices accord a significant role to embodiment. This appears in the important function they give to sexuality and physical desire, as we find in Miller, Durrell's *The Black Book*, Smart's politicized eroticism, Moore's and Comfort's erotic poetry, Duncan's "deep," or the various desiring and desired bodies presented in *Circle*. Embodiment, however, serves a dual function as both the origin for resistance to authority and also the inevitability of subordination to power. Morris offers a sense of the former, such that the various controls and coercions structured to contain the desiring body (perhaps most markedly in Marcuse's repressive desublimation, for which the satisfaction of desire itself becomes the means to authoritarian control) are rendered visible, for

> if the repressive tampering with the body leads back through
> the core of civilization and beyond, it finds its modern

rationalizing theory in the idea that men and women are
interminably malleable. Modern social scientific discourse
is filled with the language of "conditioning," "shaping,"
"controlling" the individual. Without significant qualification,
one argues from Marx that "social being...determines
consciousness."...In all this the body seems to have become
or remained a non-entity: endlessly pliable, docile, radically
without its own claims, a vehicle of either domination or
despair. (Morris 52)

In this sense, the disembodied subject experiences the transformation of the inescapable body as a form of socialization that engenders
control, standardization, and ultimately leads to cultural hegemony.
The body, with its ruptures of the cultural norm and its transgressive
exigencies, is controlled and rendered hostile to a socialized vision of
the ideologically more pure self. From such an approach to the body,
the ambition becomes "to recover the human as embodied creator a
little this side of all the subsequent and already too imposing words
and theories" (Morris 10).

However, bodies end and have finite limits without regard to
ideology, cultural hegemony, or any exercise of power or needful
desire—in this the limits of social authority and the impossibility
of its strictures are made apparent. Hence, death or the damaged
body become irresistible instances of the individual who has become
autonomous from social control, and such bodies give the lie to
authority. Without reifying transgression, the exigent break of the
body from hegemony creates a rupture toward which recuperation
races, but the endless defeat and incapacity of the body to meet the
perverse demands of the superego ultimately signals its irrecuparable
nature. Authority cannot bid the body to rise from the dead or to
heal its deformities, so alternative forms or regulation are perversely
imposed, though their insufficiency remains irrepressible. Regardless
of authority, I will die and my body sets limits upon my existence.
In relation to these embodied facts, social authority ruptures or
adapts itself symbolically. Of course, around such ruptures we find
assembled a variety of social controls and regulatory institutions,
which are perhaps the most common and the most pervasive controls

of all: controls that allow for embodied desire so long as it follows a path that deepens social standardization, as well as rituals of control that erect barriers and taboos to prevent consideration of the inevitabilities (sleep, defecation, decay, and demise):

> In respect to cultures in general, the most elemental areas
> of fissuring appear to be closely related to the life-cycle of
> the body: birth, puberty, adult sexuality, the rearing of new
> generations, and death. It is as if, just as the body responds
> to a wound by concentrating energy at the point of injury, so
> psyche and culture seem to concentrate energy at those points
> of experiential threat along the life-cycle (Comfort, LaBarre).
> Here the systematics of a culture confront the possibility of
> divergence from the rule, and the final helplessness of all rules
> in death. They are forced to acknowledge a source of meaning
> beyond the rule: in individuated affectivity and embodiedness.
> (Morris 68)

Thereby, death is both the denial of social rule as well as the denial of the agency of the individual but not an agent of authority. Our ultimate limitedness in death is reflected in the exigent bending to authority in life. However, bending to authority in life is not the corollary of death's exigency. Not surprisingly, the utopic becomes repressive insofar as it conquers this terminal necessity and renders it as authority or overcomes it symbolically through authority. The utopic urge is, as Marcuse articulates (Marcuse 254), a form of regulation. Its impossibility engenders its perversion.

In the distinction between social and embodied limits, however, Wolff (in a typical philosophical fashion) finds the possibility of recasting our conceptions of limitedness and achievable ends, thereby making space for individual action. For Wolff, the cliché runs,

> Death and taxes, it is said, are the only certainties in this life; a
> folk maxim which reflects the deep conviction that men cannot
> escape the tyranny of either nature or society. Death will always
> be with us, along with all the other instruments of nature. But
> taxes, along with all the other instruments of social action, are

human products, and hence must in the end submit to the
collective will of a society of rational men of good will. (77–78)

The necessity of death need not beget submission to authority as a
symbolic defense, or as Comfort reminds us, we "do not escape death
by evading it in the renunciation of life" ("Art" 30). This metaphor
is susceptible to extension. For Comfort's *Against Death and Power*, do
we mean that insofar as humans struggle against death or so long as
we find life good, we must also struggle against authority with the
same fixity as our will to live? Does our life instinct match an anti-
authoritarian instinct? No animal likes to be caged, just as no animal
likes to be killed, in both cases precluding a gross manipulation of the
psyche through trauma or the varieties of conditioning and psycho-
sis that can be created by situational events and thereby sadism and
masochism. But cages are only a small step from defenses. For both
Comfort and Wolff, a reformist use of disobedience applies without
the regulating impulse that dangerously accompanies the utopic.
This particular notion of disobedience is such that for Comfort, the
reform of society functions like a tool: "We do not refuse to drive
on the left hand side of the road, or to subscribe to national health
insurance. The sphere of our disobedience is limited to the sphere
in which society exceeds its powers and its usefulness" (Comfort,
"October" 48). This position against conscription led Comfort subsequently to the opinion of his generation that "the awareness of death,
the quasi-priestly but secular attitude, are omnipresent for anyone
who knows contemporary English art and letters" ("Art" 40). This
leads him to a revision of the Marxist aphorism,

> History, in so far as it is the history of power, is…an oscillation
> about a fixed point….We see it as a fluctuating conflict between
> biological freedom and power. One cannot suggest on the
> recorded evidence that man is either "morally better" (however
> that be defined) or politically more capable of forming a society
> which does not involve the abuse of power. ("Art" 41)

The particular chain of reasoning, for Comfort, is important since it
leads him to define the notion of Romanticism that bound together

the New Romantics, the Personalists, and the New Apocalypse (in terms close to those employed by Miller). It is also a chain that makes reformism necessarily limited and freedom an impossibility, and thereby utopia is recognized as purely ideological and ultimately repressive. This allows Comfort to unify "Christian and pagan meta-physicians…, including Marxists, who believe in historical inevitability" ("Art [II]" 57). Against the utopic, recognized as a mechanism and praxis of power, Comfort proposes the New Romantic:

> The romantic has only two basic certainties—the certainty of irresoluble conflict which cannot be won but must be continued, and the certainty that there exists between all human beings who are involved in this conflict an indefeasible responsibility to one another. The romantic has two enemies, Death, and the obedient who, by conformity to power and irresponsibility [as opposed to responsible revolt or disobedience], ally themselves with Death. There is no hint of mysticism in this. ("Art [II]" 57)

In this, corporeality limits freedom while at the same time instigating the discomfort of the individual over the social exercises of power meant to comfort and regulate him. We find either the discontent of a regulated economy of desire, through which the unconscious disturbingly erupts to demonstrate the inherent instability, or discontent with the impossibility of escaping from death. For Comfort, this is the conflict between "responsibility" and "barbarism," and the utopian is ultimately a retreat into barbarism as is repressive socialization. Freedom, then, is the impossible attainment of an exit to this existential position, and faced with that impossibility, the only "responsible" action is to "struggle against those men and institutions who ally themselves with Death against humanity" (58). Insofar as power is generative, in the Foucauldian sense (in which we would wish to distinguish between generative power versus domination), death engenders knowledge or meaning (and not necessarily domination, again in Foucault's perspective). Comfort's Romantic must turn this meaning-generative potential to a responsible end that rejects the domination of utopia and embraces the forms of freedom that do not redeem death through the utopian.

As I have proposed in relation to desire, the disruption of so-cial control and of the stable Ego creates opportunities for a form of subjectivity that negotiates between the transcendental (socially repressive) and the strictly corporeal (internally repressive). Whatever subject may negotiate between these powerful coercions, in its struggle it is its own. In this manner, Comfort's sense of freedom and personality resist the bourgeois false consciousness through self-possession that admits of its failure and limitedness. This admission is itself resistance against what Comfort sees as man's internal maladaptation to life: "He possesses a conscious sense of personality which... renders the emotional realisation of death intolerable and incompatible with continued enjoyment of existence. He therefore attempts universally to deny either that death is real or that his personality is really personal" ("Art" 42). Both the denial of death and the denial of selfhood are too easily amenable to hegemony, giving the double theft of life that will only lead to death and living in repression.

In many respects, time has shown Comfort's prescience in this matter. My own personal experience was turning to Comfort's works only after learning of his death during a course in which we were reading Ernest Becker's *Denial of Death* while I was concomitantly beginning to read in the Terror Management Theory paradigm in cultural psychology. The empirical approach has shown a correlation between the salience of mortality and the propensity to violence, stereotypic thinking, the need for self-esteem through social valuation or belonging, and the limitation of creative thought to the socially valued (Gifford, "Self" 215–21; Williams, Schimel, and Gillespie, "Security" 198–201). In short, it is "the negation of individual personality and responsibility, since...Society is not only a form of abrogating moral responsibility, it is a womb into which one can crawl back and become immortal because unborn" (Comfort, "Art" 43). The metaphor is telling since Orwell's *Inside the Whale* uses this as the primary critique of Henry Miller's unnamed anarchism, and Miller's (and Durrell's) works repeatedly call up "back to the womb" images, largely in relation to their readings of Otto Rank, with whom Nin studied, had an affair, and underwent analysis. Rank was the inspiration for Becker's *Denial of Death*, which was the origin of the Terror Management Theory's hypothesis tested through the mortality salience induction.

So, what is Miller's floating womb?

For Miller, death plays a large role and appears frequently as a problem set in conflict with the individual (Gifford, "'Convinced'" 106–18). In *Tropic of Capricorn*, he introduces mortality and an Ego-generative problem:

> When I was a child and went down in the street for the first time alone and there frozen into the dirty ice of the gutter lay a dead cat, the first time I had looked at death and grasped it. From that moment I knew what it was to be isolated: every object, every living thing and every dead thing led its independent existence. My thoughts too led an independent existence. (*Tropic of Capricorn* 51)

In the passage immediately preceding this, Miller specifically aligns this rising knowledge of death as his own personal future with his discovery of his own individuality as something based on isolation from his social group during lonely walks: "If this then was the true self it was marvelous, and what's more it seemed never to change but always to pick up from the last stop, to continue in the same vein, a vein I had struck when I was a child" (51). As has already been shown, for Miller, this "true self" is unstable, undefinable, and subject to radical transformation, yet it is still his own. The submission of this self to the social world or to state thought explicitly offers him comfort in the face of death, and the return to self-responsibility "pushed me outside the warm, comfortable bloodstream" of "belong[ing] to something" rather than belonging to the self (57). Death, across the novel, draws others to submission in ideology and repressive instances of false consciousness, yet death is itself the disruption of these same ideologies and ways of thinking (15, 170, 172).

Miller sets up his narrator's relationship with the trope of death as one that is rewarding so long as death is fully recognized: "Men are lonely and out of communication with one another because all their inventions speak only of death. Death is the automaton which rules the world of activity. Death is silent, because it has no mouth. Death has never expressed anything" (*Tropic of Capricorn* 290). In this scenario, death is horrific because of its hidden existence, which makes it omnipresent yet invisible and denied. In response, the narrator advocates a more direct invocation of death to conscious awareness through which its disruptive and liberatory potential emerges:

> Death is wonderful too—after life. Only one like myself who has opened his mouth and spoken, only one who has said Yes, Yes, Yes, and again Yes! can open wide his arms to death and know no fear. Death as a reward, yes! Death as a result of fulfillment, yes! Death as a crown and shield, yes! But not death from the roots, isolating men, making them bitter and fearful and lonely, giving them fruitless energy, filling them with a will which can only say No! (290)

This alternative, as preached by the narrator, is juxtaposed against his friend Grover Watrous's experience of repressive religious faith in a form that precludes living (171). A part of the problem for Miller appears to be the difficulty of accepting death, which must be symbolized, while recognizing that this process of symbolization is dangerous and may subsume the individual that it symbolically saves. To be saved from death, one might give up living, which is a poor bargain. This conundrum leads Miller back into the erotic content of the novel and the undeniable embodiment that coincides with the erotic:

> Everything was absolutely clear to me because done in rock crystal; at every egress there was written in big letters ANNIHILATION. The fright of extinction solidified me; the body became itself a piece of ferroconcrete. It was ornamented by a permanent erection in the best taste. I had achieved the state of vacuity so earnestly desired by certain devout members of esoteric cults. I was no more. I was not even a personal hard on. (202)

This continual consciousness of the futurity of the narrator's personal death displaces the artistic ferroconcrete "skyscraper" (56), which is itself a highly phallic construction, with the phallus as the engineered structure meant to outlast "that which was Greek, or Roman, or Egyptian" (56). The vacuity is nonetheless imperfect and must be filled with

some investment of Self since it cannot eliminate the fear of
"ANNIHILATION" by denying the self that would be annihilated.

Miller then turns to the subject that is the object to annihilation as
predicate. He

> became a cage of mirrors reflecting vacuity. But vacuity once
> stoutly posited I was at home and what is called creation was
> merely a job of filling up holes. The trolley conveniently carried
> me about from place to place and in each little side pocket of
> the great vacuum I dropped a ton of poems to wipe out the idea
> of annihilation. (203)

This absence or vacuum must be filled, or in more provocative language it could be described as a "lack." In Miller's vision, this "vacuity"
is filled by an artistic product: "a ton of poems" that deny death (*Tropic
of Capricorn* 203). However, Miller is at the same time aware of the
futility of the activity in relation to death since a "ton of poems" can
only have an impact on the "idea of annihilation" rather than annihilation itself—this symbolic act of artistic creation carries meaning in
relation to the life of the individual but remains symbolic. Comfort's
interpretation of such a scene in Miller would be obvious. "I say all
this, because I believe that in essence art is the act of standing aside
from society" (Comfort, "Art" 28)—a concept he immediately links
to Herbert Read's anarchism, so that "anarchism is real and the standing aside preliminary to creation is not resented to the same degree as
in the societies of clock-faces, whose sole virtue is their unanimity in
error. This virtue [of clock-faced societies rather than anarchist societ-
ies] is a virtue of death. They do not escape death by evading it in the
renunciation of life" (Comfort, "Art" 30). That is, there is no escape
from death but there may be an escape from the attempts to escape.

The construction of a skyscraper, which Miller suggests is also
an act that denies mortality, is also creative in this sense, but it is
less comfortably tied to notions of selfhood defined by nationalism
and domination (Miller, *Tropic of Capricorn* 56). Both Miller's "ton of
poems" and the engineer's skyscraper act as a denial of the inevitable,
yet they differ insofar as Miller's personal product does not provoke
the same violence of nationalism, about which Miller was viscerally

aware when the book was finally published in 1939. The body
and embodiment imply death even amidst desire, and this was a
particularly salient concern during war. In part, then, Miller's concern
is how to answer the meaning-making function of identity without
engendering the self-destruction he saw in the nation—a way to
make life meaningful that also takes away life is counterproductive. A
different form of meaning and self-creation is needed.

The opening pages of *Tropic of Cancer* gave Orwell his whale/womb
analogy, but the role of the body, desire, and corporeality escaped his
notice. As Miller writes about his lover, Tania, his images wander between the corpse and the carnal, and in this the possibility of symbolic self-creation begins to figuratively emerge:

> The world is a cancer eating itself away....I am thinking that
> when the great silence descends upon all and everywhere music
> will at last triumph. When into the womb of time everything is
> again withdrawn chaos will be restored and chaos is the score
> upon which reality is written. You, Tania, are my chaos. It is why
> I sing. It is not even I, it is the world dying, shedding the skin
> of time. I am still alive, kicking in your womb, a reality to write
> upon. (*Tropic of Cancer* 2)

The womb, despite the ease of simply applying a pornographic interpretation, is for Miller tied contrarily to the inevitability of death, the
creation of life, the acceptance of carnal life as rebellion against death,
as well as the retreat from reality into a form of false consciousness or
a constricting self-deception.[6] The same language recurs several times
in relation to the womb as well:

> A fear of living separate, of staying born. The door of the womb
> always on the latch. Dread and longing. Deep in the blood the
> pull of Paradise. The beyond. Always the beyond. It must have
> all started with the navel. They cut the umbilical cord,...and
> you're out in the world, adrift, a ship without a rudder. You
> look at the stars and then you look at your navel. You grow eyes
> everywhere—in the armpits, between your lips, in the roots of
> your hair, on the soles of your feet. Inner-outer, a constant flux,

a shedding of skins, a turning inside out. You...find yourself
in the dead center, and there you slowly rot, slowly crumble to
pieces, get dispersed again. Only your name remains. (*Tropic of
Cancer* 287)

In the same manner, there's "an ache in your belly and your womb
turned inside out" (*Tropic of Cancer* 5), "shedding the skin of time" (2),
"Paris is...the womb...Nobody *dies* here..." (29), and "Paris!...The
very navel of the world to which, like...a cork that has drifted to the
dead center of the ocean,...The cradles of civilization are...the char-
nel house to which the stinking wombs confide their bloody packages
of flesh and bone" (182).

The result is a sense of the womb and the whale very much different
from Orwell's escapist vision. In fact, the only descent into the belly
of the whale that appears in *Tropic of Cancer* is antithetical to Orwell's
interpretations yet very closely aligned with Miller's anarchism and the
problems of death and power articulated later by Comfort. For Miller's
Jonah, the stakes are death and self-determination:

> I began to reflect on the meaning of that inferno which
> Strindberg had so mercilessly depicted....The heroic descent to
> the very bowels of the earth, the dark and fearsome sojourn in
> the belly of the whale, the bloody struggle to liberate himself,
> to emerge clean of the past, a bright, gory sun-god cast up on
> an alien shore....Here, at the very hub of the wheel, one can
> embrace the most fantastic, the most impossible theories;...
> the enigmas take on new meanings, one for every white hair....
> These cold, indifferent faces are the visages of one's keepers....
> The world reveals itself for the mad slaughter-house that it
> is. The treadmill stretches away to infinitude, the hatches are
> closed down tight, logic runs rampant, with bloody cleaver
> flashing. The air is chill and stagnant, the language apocalyptic.
> Not an exit sign anywhere; no issue save death. A blind alley at
> the end of which is a scaffold. (*Tropic of Cancer* 182)

Miller's reflections on the anarchist Strindberg's descent into the
belly of the whale is a confrontation with individuality in a form

that accepts death as the total end fraught with the temptation to retreat or blind oneself, to give oneself (one's only property) over to "one's keepers" in order to avoid the salient awareness of mortality or responsibility for oneself. The objective for Miller is to instead stake freedom on this point of meaninglessness and vulnerability, to make the power of death generative or a form of meaning that does not abrogate freedom while it can be had, even in an existence incapable of exercising it. Such problems have been central to anarchist thought since the 1940s, in particular the stream from Comfort and even in Todd May's *The Political Philosophy of Poststructuralist Anarchism* (1994) and his 2009 work *Death*.

In this sense, the womb and the belly of the whale reflect a complex philosophy for Miller rather than a simple misogynistic obscenity. The notion recurs in his *Hamlet* letters with Michael Fraenkel in a passage taken up later by Deleuze and Guatarri (298–99):

> Why revert to myth?...This ideational rubbish out of which
> our world has erected its cultural edifice is now, by a critical
> irony, being given its poetic immolation, its mythos, through a
> kind of writing which, because it is of the disease and therefore
> beyond, clears the ground for fresh superstructures. (In my own
> mind the thought of "fresh superstructures" is abhorrent, but
> this is merely the awareness of a process and not the process
> itself.) Actually, in process, I believe with each line I write that
> I am scouring the womb, giving it a curette, as it were. Behind
> this process lies the idea not of "edifice" and "superstructure,"
> which is culture and hence false, but of continuous birth,
> renewal, life, life....In myth there is no life for us. Only the
> myth lives in myth. (Miller, *Hamlet* n. pag.)

The inhuman in Milller's sense, here, of the womb makes a clear and quick appeal to Deleuze and Guattari, as does his linkage of such concepts to the state, state thought, and the abstract machine. This again leads to a pointed selection from Miller for Deleuze and Guattari's *Anti-Oedipus* (a sharp contrast to how Miller was used by Jacques Lacan as well): "From the little reading I had done I had observed that the men who were most in life, who were moulding life, who were life itself, ate little, slept little, owned little or nothing. They had no illusions about duty, or the perpetuation of their kith and kin, or the preservation of the State" (Miller, *Sexus* 206; Deleuze and Guattari 29). The same concept reflects Jameson's rejection of Deleuze and leads to the conclusion of this chapter.

This notion of the womb being akin to both death and fecundity is stated most dramatically by Miller, and hence is found resurfacing in the works of other authors and critics, but it is shared amongst this personalist group, from Dylan Thomas's womb/tomb in his earlier works, Durrell's persistent womb imagery in his first novels, to Comfort, the New Apocalypse, and Duncan. For Comfort, when he summarizes his argument in "Art and Social Responsibility," perhaps his principal articulation of his anarchism, he argues that

> man, considered individually, seems to be internally maladapted. He possesses a conscious sense of personality which...renders the emotional realization of death intolerable....The main human refuges in the past (the negation of death) is apparently sealed by scientific research [which makes this refuge unavailable].... Accordingly, the emphasis is laid more than ever before on the negation of the individual personality and responsibility, since to admit that I am an individual I must also admit that I will cease to exist....Society is not only a form of abrogating moral responsibility, it is a womb into which one can crawl back and become immortal because unborn. (Comfort, "Art" 59)

This function of anxiety over death is very much akin to Miller's, and the womb of social belonging (which doubles as the refusal of self-hood) carries the destructive elements of death further. It abrogates the self in order to avoid anxiety, creating a double loss in the denial of death.

Open Form as Anarchist Praxis

The prod or provocation out of such a womb is, for this group of authors, very much the same as that which Deleuze and Guattari suggest and enact by returning to Miller. Like Miller's sense of death provoking one to refuse life through anxiety *and* cajoling one to engage in living, Deleuze and Guattari provoke their reader to active engagement and an antithetical process that resists the primary functions of obedience. For the good reason that these various personalist writers do not pursue Deleuze's ideas and such an anachronism does not work, I will not engage in a Deleuzian reading of their works; however, this point of kinship is vital for the emergence of praxis from theory for this particular group. Prodding and prompting an antithetical reading entails goading a reader into an active position, and this is very much what develops poetically. Whether this is Miller's refusal to clarify meaning, Durrell's gestures to blank pages (*Justine* 214), Treece's poetic failure through overreliance on the symbol, or surrealist metaphor, the reader is placed in a position of complex interpretive responsibility. Antliff has cleanly summarized this relationship between form, content, politics, and subjectivity in a manner that makes this linkage clear—his discussion of Donald Judd's vision of art held in tension with his discussion of Kenneth Patchen produces a vision of art remarkably akin to Durrell's discussion of syntax and the Activist Group's manifesto in *Circle*. Antliff begins with Mary Caroline Richards's poem, which consists of the words "Hands:" and "birds." spaced apart on the page, which he uses to discuss form in relation to content and thereby praxis and coercion:

> The gap between words in Richard's [sic] poem [published
> in the previous issue of *Resistance*] was...successful because
> it stimulated, through form, an opening to creative agency,
> uncoerced and indeterminate, on the part of the reader. Last
> but not least, inscribing this agency poetically ensured that
> congruency of means and ends was realized by poet and reader
> alike, because it also released the writer from any authoritative
> role in the process. (Antliff, "Donald" 182)

This release from coercion can also be found in other forms. As is noted above, Durrell revised the ending of his novel *Justine* to send the reader to a blank page, which he has a character in another book later explain as a tactic to "refer the reader to a blank page in order to throw him back on his own resources—which is where every reader ultimately belongs" (Durrell, *Quartet* 307). Although it is not poetically successful, Treece's heavy reliance on opaque symbols accomplishes the same end by leaving the reader with a poem that does not cohere until the reader intervenes to supply its prophetic or mystical unity between "that stone head," the notched sword, the old witch, the lovers, and finally their secrete hiding "from the owl" (Treece, "Relics" 187). Treece's incoherent poetic image may not offer sufficient aesthetic appeal to recuperate it for anthologies, but its very incoherence is its defining stylistic praxis. The reader must work with the myth and image, not the author, and the author cannot teach a meaning to the reader. Miller combines this same impulse for reader-imminent meaning in a startlingly manner with womb images in his descent into an underground chamber in Mycenae, from which he emerges without having ever entered (*Colossus* 91)—the literal gap on the page has proved a productive aporia for critics to fill through the exercise of their own agency in precisely Miller's anarchist formulation in "An Open Letter to Surrealists Everywhere" in which he prompt others to live life their own way not by being a model but by living his own life in his own way (157).

This abrogation of authority and coercion on the part of the author, appearing in a wide range of forms and through a wide range of methods, is their reflection of their shared anti-authoritarian impulse. The quietist activism appears in its most successful form in Durrell's *Justine* in 1957 in a phrase that is deeply political as well as "an opening to creative agency, uncoerced and indeterminate,…[that] also released the writer from any authoritative role in the process" (Antliff, "Donald" 182):

> I have decided to leave Clea's last letter unanswered. I no longer wish to coerce anyone, to make promises, to think of life in terms of compacts, resolutions, covenants. It will be up to Clea to interpret my silence according to her own needs and desires, to come to me if she has need or not, as the case may be. Does not everything* depend on our interpretation of the silence around us? So that…(Durrell, *Justine* 214)

This passage awakens the urgency for an antithetical reading process in which the author does not inhabit a position of authority. The unnamed narrator resolves himself to silence, mirroring the silence the reader meets at the end of the book, precisely as a way of undoing coercion and obligation. Yet, this is also a prompt for interpretation according to one's own needful desires. This is doubly a call into becoming or self-possession without self-definition. In this "everything*," the reader is sent by a footnote to a blank page to begin this process of interpretation just as the narrator has gone through a process of self-exploration and recuperation. This is the function of silence, from which we call the self into being, contingently and hesitatingly. And finally, the last two words of the passage quoted above are an anti-fascist turn that recuperates Ezra Pound's final words of Canto I "So that" (which Durrell had been rereading at this same time in order to review *Section: Rock-Drill*) so that the reader can have the Pound of his liking after passing through the interpretation of silence.

4

Rereading and Recasting
Miller, Durrell, Smart, and Duncan

The preceding pages may have their own value as a literary history
or as an expression of a personal view of anti-authoritarian
thought, but for literary scholarship, it must be admitted that I have
merely reordered already existing information, albeit in a unique
configuration. There is nothing particularly inventive in either my
redirection of the critical literature surrounding the personalist
authors nor in my summary of their anarchist position in relation
to conflicting trends in critical theory—both bodies of information
were already nascent in the literature. In many respects, in order
to attend to their commonalities and interactions, I have both
foreshortened their arguments and have relied on reconceiving
ideas that are already established elsewhere by more nuanced critics
than me, or at least than I can be in the context of this project. The
value of this book, then, lies in whether or not these reorientations
cohere as a network and provide a vehicle for refreshed interpretive
work in relation to the associated literary materials. Do the
preceding pages provoke new readings useful to scholarship or the
university classroom? Does rethinking the 1930s and 1940s through
this perspective make these overlooked decades more amenable to
pedagogy and literary studies? Would readers now engage these texts
differently? Perhaps most importantly, are overlooked texts not only
remembered but recuperated for a useful purpose?

This final chapter sets out to suggestively sketch potential
reinvigorations of critical readings, primarily with regard to acknowledged major novels such as Henry Miller's *The Colossus of Maroussi* or
Lawrence Durrell's *The Black Book* and Elizabeth Smart's novella *By Grand
Central Station I Sat Down and Wept* or Robert Duncan's poem "An Ark for

Lawrence Durrell," all of which are widely recognized yet rarely taught or brought into the mainstream of critical discourse. I would contend this is largely because they do not neatly fit the established paradigms of Modernism, the Auden group, the Angry Young Men, or the Beats, and also because they are likewise slippery enough that they avoid neatly fitting into the established critiques. Rather than their obscenities or ungainly structure, which do little to prevent the classroom from receiving James Joyce and Ezra Pound or later Margaret Atwood and Michael Ondaatje (all fairly standard fare in the under-graduate classroom despite "obscenities" and complexities of form), I contend the absence of a coherent interpretive schema for the Thirties generation has led to the oversights from which these works suffer. As George Woodcock has said of Miller, such oversights also carry a social and political value: "The real grudge they have against Miller is that he is a dynamic social critic, and that he uses his obscenity as a means of jerking people into consciousness of the corruption in the world where they live. Miller is being persecuted not because his books are obscene, but because they are subversive" (Woodcock, "Editorial" 5–6).

In each instance that follows, my approach is suggestive and rela-tively brief rather than complete. The importance of this project is not to establish a new interpretive paradigm for each text but rather to demonstrate the utility of Personalism as an expansion of the critical work that may be done in further writing, reading, or teaching. If successful, the following recastings and reconsiderations will provoke new work, not define it.

Henry Miller's *The Colossus of Maroussi*

Henry Miller's most successful work is undeniably *Tropic of Cancer*. The book continues to provoke eighty years after its publication and maintains an enormous popular following. However, critics are in relative agreement that the less well-known *The Colossus of Maroussi* is his most beautiful book. As with all of Miller's novels, it is semi-autobiographical, and it recounts his time in Greece at Lawrence Durrell's invitation immediately prior to the Nazi invasion. The book has secured far less critical attention than *Tropic of Cancer* or Miller's other major works, and recent scholarship has largely placed the novel in relation to Greek Modernism and the transformation of philhellenism (Roessel 3, 144). In short, it is predominantly regarded as Miller's "nice" book about travel writing in the Mediterranean sun, but this misses the point. Cathy Gere comes closer to the heart of the matter in *Knossos and the Prophets of Modernism* when she recognizes the essentially pacifist tone of Miller's references to Knossos and Sir Arthur Evans: "The most nakedly pacifist response to Knossos was penned by Henry Miller" who "saw in Knossos the joy that awaited if humanity could only solve the riddle of violence" (153, 230). The tone of this pacifism, however, was already deeply rooted in his book of eleven years earlier, *Tropic of Cancer*, in the images of the womb, mechanization, and violence discussed in the previous chapter. It is surprising, then, to see the consistency of Miller's vision across the early stage of his career from *Tropic of Cancer* in 1934 to sketching *The Colossus of Maroussi* in 1939 and finally publishing it in 1941. Moreover, unlike *Tropic of Cancer*, which faced various bans and censorship that made distribution principally covert, *The Colossus of Maroussi* travelled easily despite its anarchist pacifism, even appearing in the Ministry of Information Middle East research library in Cairo very shortly after its publication, from whence its pacifist vision of post-Surrealism was readily available and read by the English post-Surrealists stationed there during the war.

In a redolence recollecting *Tropic of Cancer*, only this time devoid of sexual hijinks, Miller has a paroxysm of language while ferrying to Athens and meeting up with Americans who argue in favour of the United States' industrialization and capitalist growth:

> Progress was their obsession. More machines, more efficiency, more capital, more comforts—that was their whole talk....I asked them if they realized how empty, restless and miserable the American people were with all their machine-made luxuries and comforts. They were impervious to my sarcasm. What they wanted was success—money, power, a place in the sun....*When would life begin?* I wanted to know. (*Colossus* 8)

Miller, of course, receives no answer, but in a moment of self-reliance supplies one himself:

> When they had all the things which America had, or Germany, or France. Life was made up of things, of machines mainly.... Life without money was an impossibility: one had to have clothes, a good home, a radio, a car, a tennis racquet, and so on. I told them I had none of those things and that I was happy without them, that I had turned my back on America precisely because these things meant nothing to me. (8)

This blending of the machine, money, and desolation differs only from *Tropic of Cancer* in its exclusion of sexuality in its representation, whereas in his first novel it is exemplified by sexuality run amok.[1] For Miller, the remainder of his time in Greece celebrates the rural, the organic, and the mythical. This point repeats several times yet has largely gone unnoticed in criticism:

> We don't need the truth as it is dished up in the daily papers. We need peace and solitude and idleness. If we could all go on strike and honestly disavow all interest in what our neighbor is doing we might get a new lease on life. We might learn to do without telephones and radios and newspapers, without machines of any kind, without factories, without mills, without mines, without explosives, without battleships, without politicians, without lawyers, without canned goods, without gadgets, without razor blades even or cellophane or cigarettes or money. This is a pipe dream, I know. People only go on strike for better working conditions, better wages, better opportunities to become something other than they are. (39)

This crux for Miller's list is to disentangle himself from the bellicosity of the manufactured and machined goods as a path to becoming what he already is rather than something he is not. To emphasize the politics of this vision without politicians and battleships, he immediately turns to his environs to say, "I like...the anarchic character of the landscape" (39). His vision is Apocalyptic, written at the same time as the New Apocalypse was growing from his earlier works, and it indirectly states his political vision.

The crux of the book, then, is Miller's angling toward a moment of quietist peace found only at Epidaurus (67–69). For Miller, his arrival at this location prompts another rebirth, for "It is the morning of the first day of the great peace, the peace of the heart, which comes with surrender. I never knew the meaning of peace until I arrived at Epidaurus" (68). Again hinting at the anarchist components of this peace, the scene follows immediately after Miller's celebration of the Colossus himself, George Katsimabalis, whom he casts as utterly dedicated to self-development (65–66). In his description of what he calls the first inferior form of peace, he conflates non-violence with a cessation of rule: "The peace which most of us know is merely a cessation of hostilities, a truce, an interregnum, a lull, a respite, which is negative" (68). This is an inferior peace, since being between reigns (*interregnum* being a peculiar word choice that signals his equation of rulers with hostility) does not end the fact of rule itself. In contrast, Miller sets up a personalist vision that denies rulers and the drive to rule over others by turning to the Ego and its own: "The peace of the heart is positive and invincible, demanding no conditions, requiring no protection. It just is. If it is a victory it is a peculiar one because it is based entirely on surrender, a voluntary surrender to be sure" (68). This, in turn, leads Miller to the healing function of Epidaurus: "Nature can cure only when man recognizes his place in the world, which is not in Nature, as with the animal, but in the human kingdom, the link between the natural and the divine" (68). This is a fine distinction, and Miller's language struggles over it, but it is articulated using terms that mark his politics as well as the influence his earlier works had on the literary movements running in parallel in Berkeley and London:

> What man wants is peace in order that he may live. Defeating our neighbor doesn't give peace any more than curing cancer brings health. Man doesn't begin to live through triumphing over his enemy nor does he begin to acquire health through endless cures. The joy of life comes through peace, which is not static but dynamic…, even if you have a dozen cars, six butlers, a castle, a private chapel and a bomb-proof vault. Our

diseases are our attachments, be they habits, ideologies, ideals, principles, possessions, phobias, gods, cults, religions, what you please. Good wages can be a disease as much as bad wages. (69)

Much like in his letters to Orwell in which he wrote, "We are in for an era of the bloodiest tyrants the world has ever seen" ("Four" 4) until the whole of existing standards could be eliminated and begun again on a new foundation, Epidaurus symbolizes that foundation, which for Miller arrives through revolutionary transformation rather than reformist progressive development.

The anarchist revolution Miller endorses (72) is again individualist and inward rather than outward and political: "It is man's task to eradicate the homicidal instinct, which is infinite in its ramifications and manifestations....War is only a vast manifestation in dramatic style of the sham, hollow, mock conflicts which take place daily everywhere even in so-called times of peace. Every man contributes his bit to keep the carnage going" (73). Moreover, for Miller, there is no quick answer, though it is certainly individualist and inward in his view: "Man kills through fear—and fear is hydra-headed. Once we start there is no end to it. An eternity would not suffice to vanquish the demons who torture us. *Who put the demons there?* That is for each one to ask himself. Let every man search his own heart" (73).

In these ways, *The Colossus of Maroussi* emerges as a book on the political situation of the Second World War, an anarcho-pacifist intervention, and its core is an anti-authoritarian vision. Arthur Evans's Knossos becomes the core symbol of this form of quietist pacifism. In rethinking Miller, sex and obscenity lose their titillating function and shock value to become pathways to unsettling the machine while privileging the organic.

Lawrence Durrell's *The Black Book*

It may seem at first obvious to read Durrell's early fiction in light of Miller's influence, and in particular *Tropic of Cancer*. This has been, after all, the dominant trope in critical discussions of Durrell's *The Black Book* (MacNiven, "Critical" 11–21; Morrison 254–56). The purpose here, however, is slightly different. I ask, what emerges from the novel when it is read with attention to its milieu and context, in particular its deep appeal to the English post-Surrealists turning from communism to a political and aesthetic practice that gave increasing value to the Ego, the individual, and creative expression? What does such a context make of Durrell's first major novel? While it is true that Sharon Lee Brown can reductively argue that in *The Black Book*, "The question of form was resolved…in Henry Miller fashion" (320) and Richard Pine could summarize Durrell's reading of *Tropic of Cancer* by writing, "In response, he offered Miller a risqué novel of phatasmagoric proportions, *The Black Book*" (*Mindscape* 51), neither description seems much to matter to a critical reading of the work. Such views shut down rather than open up critical exploration. G.S. Fraser, who knew Durrell well, is more tempered in linking *The Black Book* to Miller: "In its frankness it owed something to Durrell's friendship with Henry Miller" (*Lawrence* 11). Fraser, unlike Brown and Pine, was not only of the Apocalypse generation, he was also an admirer of Miller's works during the 1930s and was influenced by Miller's prose himself, perhaps most stirringly in his recollections of a fortnight visit to Paris in 1939 in his autobiography (*Stranger* 97–104). As a consequence, Fraser sees the kinship with Miller as well as the difference, and this difference rang true to the contemporary reviewers of the novel as well. Phillip O'Connor, whose 1938 review of the novel appeared in *Seven* on the facing page to the close of Durrell's "Asylum in the Snow," does not mention Miller and regarded the novel as an indictment of English middle-class values, though his review is largely an indirect response to Hugh Gordon Porteus's deeply sympathetic reading of the novel, and Durrell saw O'Connor's comments as an attack.[2]

Porteus, whose review betrays quite careful reading, aligns the book more with "Ulysses, the Waste Land" (341) and sets its main comparison with Eliot and Joyce as well a contrast against Auden. This remains probably the most adroit review of the novel, and its evaluation is plain: "I hereby proclaim, after a third and fine-combed reading, that it is one of the major books of our time. Get down on your hands and knees to this work, and pray for the poor reviewer. These must be personal comments" (341). The contrast of the novel against his contemporaries and its politics are equally plain for Porteus:

> The Black Book...opens with a Tibetan epigraph: "Where there is
> veneration, Even a dog's tooth emits life." Eliot has written of
> "Those who sharpen the tooth of the dog, meaning Death." So
> far as I can see, Eliot is a death-snob...of a quite different kind
> from the death-snobs described in this book by Durrell; who
> seems to be a life-snob of a quite different kind from the (for
> convenience) "fascist." Durrell seems to be making a film of the
> contemporary Bardo...T.S.E. (341)

This makes a striking contrast to the other critical views of the
novel that follow, and Porteus does not once mention Miller's works.
Regarding the novel as a rebuttal of the "strong poet" Eliot makes
much sense, and the political "fascism" is further detailed in terminology that connects with the British views on Apocalyptic post-
Surrealism of the time: the organic and the mechanical. For Porteus,
when setting Durrell's life-snobbery against his contemporaries,
"Durrell doesn't mention metempsychosis (the bogeyman of Stephen
Daedalus) nor does he pursue the theme to its end (as in Auden's
Ascent of F.6)," which leads Porteus to a close examination of Durrell's
method, pattern, and organization (341). The comparison of method
prompts large claims and strong contrasts echoing the language that
would dominate the then emerging Apocalyptic writers:

> I have mentioned The Waste Land and Ulysses, which make use of
> a similar device. Now when the principle of "the best words
> in the best order" is extended to the "organization" of pattern
> of a considerable book, it is apt to become mechanical rather
> than organic. From this defect The Black Book is more free than
> those two great works; and of it their philosophic certainty,
> pretensions of absolute authority, nor is it so "word-exasperated"
> as either. (341)

These are grand claims for a first review, especially one appearing
in The New English Weekly. The preference for the organic over the
mechanical, the clear difference set up from the French Surrealists,
and the revision to the High Modernists whose strong influence
is still felt all ring true as evaluations, but they differ substantially

from the perspective that would appear in later criticism following after the publication of *The Alexandria Quartet*. The difference is almost certainly prompted by Henry Miller's 1959 essay "The Durrell of *The Black Book* Days," and this seems to have shaped critical responses until D.B.C. Pierre's adept introduction to the newest reprint of the book for Durrell's centenary, in which he very correctly realizes, "Of the influences informing the work, I need only mention the one Durrell himself might name: his friend Henry Miller, instrumental not only through his writing...but also in feeding Durrell some of the surrealist materials woven into the work" (7). This turn to post-Surrealism informing Durrell's novel is in many respects a return to Porteus, and it is a necessary return.

Is the meaningful difference, then, simply one of allusions or comparisons, either to the High Modernists or to Henry Miller? This seems unlikely. Instead, this section considers what Durrell's work would have meant to his contemporaries and how the conflicts with Eliot as well as the organicism of the work would have struck the emerging talents of the English post-Surrealists and the New Apocalypse. The book's deep influence is acknowledged in print by Dylan Thomas, David Gascoyne, Porteus, Elizabeth Smart, George Barker, and Antonia White (Podnieks, *Daily* 347).

The alternative perspective on *The Black Book* emerges when the reader sets aside Miller's obvious impact on it and instead notices the rebuttals to Eliot. The tragic-comic Tarquin bears a remarkable resemblance to J. Alfred Prufrock. He is "pinned to a slab of rufous cork, etherized, like a diseased butterfly" (22), and in case we missed the jab (which Durrell was contractually obliged to offer to Eliot for publication through Faber & Faber), when we return to the same point in time at the close of the novel, "Tarquin is lying on the operating table" (217). This may seem "Unreal!" (122), but the antagonist Death Gregory wishes to give "To my father a copy of *The Waste Land* and a kiss on his uncomprehending, puzzled face" (212), and Tarquin's closing words have him pleaing, "Let us escape together, you and I" (228) despite his etherization on a operating table. The trick is hardly new for Durrell, with a copy of *The Waste Land* surreptitiously and bourgeoisly on display for a seduction scene in his 1937 novel *Panic Spring* (published by Faber & Faber) that echoes

The Fire Sermon section (141–44). Eliot is here indeed, as are Joyce and Lawrence, and as Porteus noted, their transformation for Durrell is decidedly organic: anti-urban, anti-futurist, anti-fascist, and anti-authoritarian. In context, Durrell's novel and its impact on the emerging Apocalyptics leads us to a different sense of his oeuvre.

Fraser gives the first hints at what the English post-Surrealists in general and the New Apocalypse in particular would find so enthralling about Durrell's third novel, though he is not explicit in noting the trends:

> If Miller could not understand all the words in The Black Book, he at once grasped its thematic pattern. The reason why The Black Book may still leave many young readers, as it left the young Dylan Thomas, "sickened and excited" is its dizzying emotional swing....Miller put this very clearly...
>
> > The theme is death and rebirth, the Dionysian theme which I predicted in the Lawrence book must be the theme for the writers to come....
>
> More subtly, Miller put his finger on the recurrent symbolic motif of the book, the motif of a sense of stifling enclosure in the womb, a violent emergence from it, and the danger of the regressive wish to get back...."Another back-to-the-womber's allegory" [that]...recalls some of the prose passages in Auden's The Orators..., a motif which recurs at the end of Auden and Isherwood's The Ascent of F6. (Lawrence 52–53)

Fraser is both terribly right and terribly wrong here. Miller's immediate desire to recast The Black Book in his own image leads to critical shortcomings, in particular the difference over the womb imagery that both authors share but seem to mean in very different ways. Nonetheless, the rebirth component of the womb imagery is important and remains overlooked—it is not a novel of being "inside the whale" so much as it is a novel of rebirth and emergence from the whale. Focusing too strongly on Miller as influence, especially for the obscenities, also occludes the more important commonalities they share through post-Surrealism. Moreover, the "dizzying emotional swing" is likely to be tied to the recurrent image of "enclosure in the womb" and the organic corporeality it evokes rather than resistance against it, as Fraser implies. Lastly, he has set his own evaluation in direct opposition to Porteus's on Auden and Isherwood.

The time frame of the book's reception and influence merits a momentary clarification. David Gascoyne first read the book only very shortly after Miller, finishing it before October 18, 1937.[3] By December of the same year, before meeting Durrell and Miller prior to Christmas, Dylan Thomas wrote to Durrell saying, "I mean to borrow the typescript of the Black Book as soon as I get to London" (Thomas, *Collected Letters* 266). Whether he did so or not is uncertain, but by October 1937 he could have seen the closing pages excerpted in *The Booster* (Durrell, "Black Book" 19–23), and another excerpt appeared in *Seven* in the summer of 1938, a journal Thomas was reading and commenting on elsewhere. Thomas was published in both journals as well. By November 30, 1938, he was asking, "Could you get me a copy of the Black Book? I'll give you all I've written in exchange, odd poems, small books," which would imply he had a reasonable sense of the contents in order to have such a strong interest (Thomas, *Collected Letters* 341). He also reported to Vernon Watkins in the first days of 1939, "Last week I went up to London to meet Henry Miller.... Also Lawrence Durrell. We spent 2 days together, and I returned a convinced wreck. We talked our way through the shabby saloons of nightmare London" (Thomas, *Letters to Vernon* 54).

The connection is reinforced by Thomas's phrasing in February 1939 when we wrote to say, "All at sea on the BB [*Black Book*]. I'm sickened and excited," which secures the date at which he read the novel as coinciding with the birth of his first child. A more judicious approach for scholars is to look to the effects on his language rather than direct comments made to anyone in possession of his most desperately needed commodity: money.[4] In the February 1939 letter, Thomas returns to the language of his 1933–1934 "womb-tomb" period by reporting,

a poem for the new Delta, why not the one you like in the paper of Tambimuttu's, that distinguished Celanese? If not—and perhaps, I hope, as well—here's a new short poem. And I'd rather have the 7/6 than a book-token. My bowels need more than consonants & vowels. When you like, and sooner. Oh, a boy, by the way & womb. Llewelyn. (*Collected Letters* 355)

The recurrence of "womb" is unsurprising for Thomas, especially given the writing of the letter in the immediate aftermath of the birth of his son and first child. However, the appearance in his letters to Durrell at this point is more telling, as are the poems to which he refers: "A Saint About to Fall" (titled "Poem in the Ninth Month" when published by Tambimuttu in the first issue of *Poetry London*) and "Poem (For Caitlin)" (published in the first issue of *Delta*). Both poems contain significant references to the womb, and the image is replete in *The Black Book*. In a sense, by reading Miller and Durrell at this point, and by having been in touch with them since 1937, Thomas was discovering fellow bondsmen, or at least writers taking up a vision kindred to his own works and putting it to a new purpose.

The impact is not unique to Thomas. When Gascoyne first read the typescript of the novel, just prior to Thomas asking to read the same, he responded on October 18, 1937 by linking the novel's journal format to his own personal journals:

> After having read those horrifying journals in "The Black Book," I feel even more diffident about showing you these pages than before. The first part of your book particularly made me feel the writing of journals to be such a miserable hold-in-the-corner sort of game that I hardly dared to open this cahier again....You are an expert on the English Death, and what I have written here seems to deal almost entirely...with precisely that. (Gascoyne, *Paris Journal* 33)

Gascoyne's response carried forward his sense of the English Death, the "death-snobs" identified by Porteus, and links this intimately with his own writing. The surprise, however, is to see him echo the same language as Thomas despite his having no personal reason for doing so, having no particular interest in the womb as an image prior to this nor in relation to his personal life. For Gascoyne,

It seems at the moment as though I were in the draughty and uncomfortable position of being half in the womb and half out of it. Don't ask me whether it's my head or my feet that are in or in which direction I'm moving, because I haven't the faintest idea. One can only try to keep moving all the time, and perhaps if one manages to keep it up long enough, one will find out something. (Gascoyne, *Paris Journal* 31)

For both Gascoyne and Thomas, the influence relates back to the complexity of the womb imagery in *The Black Book*, which develops from Miller's in *Tropic of Cancer* but is moving in a slightly different direction, one that would recur conceptually in the New Apocalypse. In contrast to Fraser's understanding of the womb in *The Black Book* as "a violent emergence from it, and the danger of the regressive wish to get back" (*Lawrence* 52–53), we find precisely Miller's interpretation: "The theme is death and rebirth" (Fraser, *Lawrence* 52), and like Miller, it is an organic process, not a technological nor mechanical re-emergence into the world.

The problem Gascoyne faces, of not knowing how to move forward, is very much a symptom of the cultural moment at the end of the 1930s, but regardless of the direction, it is a rebirth of individuation. That is to say, it is a personal experience and a personal action that marks out the self, even in its indeterminacies and transformations. This problem of the Ego is very much the concern of Durrell's novel—it is set out as a three-volume novel worthy of a Victorian ancestor, with each section titled respectively "Ego and Id," "Ego," and "Ego and Id."[5] The "Ego" section published in the first issue of *Seven* is narrated by the Lawrence Lucifer character, a stand-in for Durrell himself, who is remembering his life in London; in the first and third "Ego and Id" sections he has escaped the city and is living on a Greek island, Corfu, where he is reading the journals of his interlocutor in the narrative. This structure places the conscious self as the author of the text who controls and reshapes the notebooks of his London-based counterpart Herbert Death Gregory, the Id. The creative author who has left behind the English Death is the "Ego," and the implication of the novel's form is that the self only comes into existence through rebirth, hence the function of the womb in the novel.

The rebirth gestured to by both Thomas and Gascoyne follows the same pattern, emphasizing the individual and self-creation for the creative artist, not only woman's creation of another life. The metaphor comes from Miller and significantly revises the perspective constructed by Orwell in *Inside the Whale*. In Durrell's novel, Hilda's womb doubles as "the whale" (Durrell, *Black* 173), and rather than a quietist escape from the world, this personal process leads to artistic rebirth as an individual.[6] This end to Book II anticipates the close of the novel as a whole that affected Gascoyne so deeply:

> If I thought I were going to be born again I should begin to whimper, to pout; imagine leaving this plush-lined niche forever. Another world? Don't be ridiculous. As the foetus is reported to have said: "I have been here so long I've sort of got attached to the old place." Konx Ompax...: the entering into of IS! (Durrell, *Black* 176)

This then leads to the rebirth after a quasi-mythic descent into the underworld, which is of course the Id as well as the passage Gascoyne selects as central to his experience and transformation:

> I am beginning my agony in the garden and there are too many words, and too many things to put into words. In the fantastic proscenium of the ego, when I begin my soliloquy, I shall not choose as Gregory chose. To be or not to be. It is in your capacity as Judas that you have chosen for me. The question has been decided....Born in an empty house, no zodiac...Boy in an ark on a black rock....There is nothing in this enormous six-foot bed but the eyelashes of God moving, delicate as talc; or the warm sticky gum, oozing from the lips of trees. From between your legs leaking, the breathing yolk, the durable, the forever, the enormous Now. (Durrell, *Black* 243–44)

The birth is that of the author, and the world he has chosen to inhabit is rural, his "ark on a black rock" or peasant house in the village Kalami, Corfu. The link between this end of Book III and the ending of Book II is also clear through the echo of "IS!" to "Now." (176, 244), and further repetitions take place for the zodiac, blood, ankles (a personal image of death for Durrell), the gum, and allusions to *Hamlet*.

This function of the womb as a rebirth to creativity and selfhood may seem to reflect an indirect politics in addition to building from Miller, but its anarcho-occultism echoes through the repeated words "Konx Ompax." Ray Morrison has read this invocation as

> the Elusinian mysteries…the words of dismissal for the mystes, the one initiated, at the end of the Great Mysteries held at Eleusis early each autumn. The vision, according to the literature available, is only referred to and never described….Durrell presented Lawrence Lucifer's transformation of self as an "is-ness," a supreme moment of Taoist reality. (323)

This is a misnomer. The most likely function of the allusion is both political and mystical, recalling not the ancient Elusinian mysteries but rather Aleister Crowley's 1907 book *Konx Om Pax: Essays in Light* with its philosophy of Thelema and ethics of Liber AL vel Legis: Do what thou wilt. Durrell's lifelong interest in crackpot materials, largely as fodder for fiction, is well established,[7] and Crowley would have been a sure source for him.[8] Rather than a Taoist transcendence, Durrell seems to mean an embodied rebirth from social containment, imposed *moeurs*, and the most applicable component of Crowley's design: the True Will of the self in harmony with the universe rather than obedient to its own lusts or obedience to authority.[9] The superlative of self in "Ipsissimus" offers a highly useful framework for the novel, its politics, and theme of rebirth to selfhood in this respect. It is little surprise that Derek Stanford otherwise inexplicably called Durrell "a wizard of *The Black Book*; a real dark horse" (*Freedom* 121).

This is also aided biographically. In his letters to Richard Aldington in 1958, Durrell nostalgically thinks back to his days in London before moving to Corfu, writing "the thought of dear old Potocki or dear old Prince Monolulu strolling up the drive would make my heart sink purely by association. That grubby little English world; the Fitzroy Tavern; Nina Hamnett; Aleister Crowley" (Aldington and Durrell 54). This is not simply a ramble, though it does superficially illustrate Durrell's familiarity with Crowley at the time he would have written

The Black Book. It is also distinctly politicized, and the mention of Crowley ends his political discussion in the letter, in which Potocki is expressly identified with his fascist beliefs and "You know, Richard, I believe if you could see what happens in a Fascist state—could see the behaviour of the Cyprus Police, Malaya, Palestine police, you would be scared at the strong vein of brutish fascism the British have in their unconscious" (Aldington and Durrell 54). To this he adds what would be an unmistakably anarchist comment, if it were to come from Miller, but that remains typically indecipherable for Durrell:

> The minute Habeas Corpus goes out, and the hundred jackbooted safeguards which we [the British] have built up, it is astonishing how jackbooted and truculent we become. Ultimately both systems are the same. One-party Government supported by a secret police and army. I had two years of Fascism in Greece under Metaxas; it really didn't differ much from Tito except that it left the economics of the country and didn't smash the middle classes. But the same barren boring demagogy, the same mental route marching...No. I can't go along with people who could wear Per Ardua Ad Buchenwald [Through Adversity to Buchenwald] on their shoulder flashes.... And if I am a Royalist it is in the biological sense—the only political creed possible to a poet I think, who is ultimately only interested in values and not politics at all...Enough. (Aldington and Durrell 54)

Only after this political paroxysm running from the fascist Potocki to the Marxist Roy Fuller, does Durrell then nostalgically return to his haunt at the Fitzroy and Crowley in a clearly politicized perspective. And, lest his comments on being a royalist mislead the reader, his letter to Potocki from Corfu, "Letter from the Land of the Gods" makes it clear that he is a royalist insofar as "I respect the King in you and I respect the King in all men—that is what I mean, I think; and this undercuts all dogma, which is after all only a man-made roughage. / A King for all of us then: and the king in each of us. Would you accept that as a toast?" (n. pag.). In this sense, Durrell's rejection of fascism is tied directly to his rejection of nationalism and

British parliamentary democracy in general, since "Ultimately both systems are the same," which leads him to a royalist view that makes every man a king, which may not be an explicit anarchism but is certainly anti-authoritarian and individualist (and utterly antithetical to royalism in its normative sense[10]), and this is what finally leads him to recall Crowley in the 1930s.

To broaden the appeal such a vision would have, Robert Duncan's strong interest in *The Black Book* is also useful to acknowledge. As has already been noted in the historical reconstruction of this network, Duncan had attempted to publish an American edition of *The Black Book* through the same press on James Cooney's farm where he produced *Experimental Review* and Cooney produced *The Phoenix*, both magazines also having published Durrell at this time. Duncan's own reconfiguration of womb imagery in his later poetry is striking, but perhaps the greatest appeal would be to his "cosmologizing stance," which Anne Dewey describes as "a reconfiguration of historical agency in a public sphere no longer structured by the agency of private individuals" (120). The occult possibilities would also have given a strong appeal to Duncan who had hermetic interests, indirect contact with Thelemic beliefs, owned several works by Crowley (Jarnot 129, 240, 264),[11] and linked his anarchism with "magical strategies" (Hatlen 208).

Durrell's conjoining of a personalist vision of selfhood, escape from the urban cage of modernity, and surrealist metaphor directed consciously would have been a compelling admixture. Knowing this also redirects attention to his writing in a more productive manner than much of the existing scholarship, the largest portion of which either looks to *The Black Book* as a demonstration of Miller's influence or as an anticipation of developing talent that would produce *The Alexandria Quartet* twenty years later. By instead looking at the novel in its own right and in the context of its milieu, its role in the personalist movement stands out.

The anti-communist mockery of *The Black Book* is also prominent when the failed artist and Londoner Herbert Death Gregory announces in his first appearance, "The question with which I trouble myself is the question of the ego, the little me. The I, sitting here in this fuggy room, like a little red-haired, skull-capped Pope,...the droll and abhorrent self!" (32). This egoic enunciation then leads to its mocking conflict: "A lifelong sympathy with Communism has never prevented me from investing safely, hoarding thriftily, and living as finely economic as possible" (38).[12] As if to emphasize Gregory's role as Id to Lawrence Lucifer's Ego, the reader is told his journal "is in the cupboard downstairs" (31) and that its inscription is "*To his most esteemed and best loved self*" (32). To this tension between the self and political postures Durrell adds surrealist metaphor and a refutation of the modernity of the city:[13] "Well, at night I decide it is no use. Escape is the endless theme of our contemplation, escape, escape. The city is beating around me like a foetus, chromium, steel, turbines, rubber, chimneys. The nights are dizzy with fog and the trains run amok" (160). Gregory, in effect, has retreated to the womb in a sense parallel to Orwell's critique of quietism as being "inside the whale," but his is an escape. For Miller, this reflects the womb/tomb concept already discussed:

> We think of the child unborn as living in a state of bliss; we think of death as an escape from life's ills...there are people alive and moving about who live in what is called a state of bliss...Wherein are their lives different then from that of the ordinary run of mankind? To my way of thinking the difference lies in their attitude towards the world, lies in the supreme fact that they have accepted the world as a womb, not a tomb. (Miller, "Enormous Womb" 86)

Lawrence Lucifer's return to the womb differs by virtue of being a path to rebirth not a retreat and form of self-deception or a salve for anxiety. Only once this womb/tomb is clarified, with nods to Dylan Thomas, introducing Miller makes sense, such as his original boost for *The Black Book*: "This book is for those who have staked out a new womb in which to continue the creative life...that super-reality which the poets are creating shred by shred" ("Boost" 18).

The opening question of this section is what emerges from a rereading of *The Black Book* with the Ego, the individual, and an anti-authoritarian politics in mind. Apart from the womb as conduit for artistic rebirth into an egoic role, which grants a rationale for a

specifically conscious or egoic development of surrealist automatism, there remains the political question. Crowley's quasi-anarchistic
visions and the privileging of the individual in this new post-
Surrealism suggest a portion of the novel's politics, as do its jeers at
communism. Its most intense allusive reference, however, must also
be recast to complete the cycle. *The Black Book* is replete with allusions
to Shakespeare's *Hamlet*, as are all of Durrell's works at the time, apart
from his claims to have read across the whole of the Elizabethans
before 1935 (an accomplishment he at least approximated). These
readings led to his works allusively caging from Cicely Bumtrinket to
Momus to Howell's *Instructions for Forrainne Travell*.[14] More to the point
here, Durrell dwelt extensively on the revision hypothesis for *Hamlet*
and the Quartos. The view he finally adopted was the division of the
prince from Hamlet: two men functioning in public and private lives.
Rather than a surrealist bifurcated mind, what Durrell conjectured
was one Hamlet who functions in the political office of prince and
another consumed by a personal struggle through grief and self-
development (Durrell, "Prince" 271–73). This is the Hamlet the reader
encounters in *The Black Book*—one torn between the social world and
the personal one imagined through rebirth and cultivation of the
creative self.[15]

This is the reinvigorated *Black Book*. Like the Prince and Hamlet in
Durrell's interpretation, two different men each in the First Quarto
and First Folio, we find one figure defined by (yet hiding from) his
obligations to the state, and another madly exploring an inner realm
in search of *personal* rebirth without a care for his service to the state.
Death Gregory hides from his social role, struggles over the death of
Ophelia/Gracie, and is ultimately a failure in retreat. Lawrence Lucifer,
unlike Hamlet, leaves Elsinore, and explores his individual rebirth as
a creative individual liberated from the perverse obligations of the
superego and without the crutch or defense mechanism of the stable,
fixed Ego. The womb magically doubles as the tomb to which one
retreats from life and the passage to rebirth from the Ego of old. This
rebirth, birth, and fecundity is also the link from Miller to Durrell as
well as from Durrell to Elizabeth Smart.

Elizabeth Smart's *By Grand Central Station I Sat Down and Wept*

Smart's novella or prose poem *By Grand Central Station I Sat Down and Wept* remains a cult classic of Canadian literature and carries a significant popular following, but its ties to her milieu remain remarkably unexplored in criticism. This is despite the predominantly biographical approaches taken to reading her magnum opus. Her work is the most dramatically transformed by recontextualization. The book's poetic diction and densely allusive structure may seem ripe for a criticism of emotional excess, but it is also a consciously contained and revised quasi-surrealist experiment with diction approaching the effects of automatic writing rather than simply an emotional paroxysm on the page. The emotional excess and syntactical race to express them are also densely allusive and thereby show a careful craft and control. Biographically, we know that Smart met her lover, George Barker, through her correspondence with Durrell. Moreover, we know Smart had significant and ongoing contact with Miller as well as an intense sexual relationship with Miller's friend in Paris, Jean Varda—both Miller and Smart would later live in Varda's Big Sur anarchist commune, and this is the setting for the striking coastal landscapes at the opening of *By Grand Central Station*. Much, indeed, is known. This makes it all the more remarkable that the contextual sense of Smart's novella in the English post-surrealist movement, which is based on its specific revisions to Surrealism through the Villa Seurat group, has gone entirely unnoticed in the critical literature. This section seeks to reframe and thereby reinvigorate Smart's remarkable book.

Much is made of the titular allusion in Smart's work to Psalm 137:1, "By the rivers of Babylon, there we sat down, yea, we wept, when we remembered Zion." Notably, this allusion emphasizes the book's function as a remembrance, but it is less a remembrance of one specific love than it is a remembrance of a city, a home, and lost period of time. Simply noticing this function of the allusion reshapes our attention to Smart's work provocatively and revises established critical readings. She is rebuilding a lost era, a lost home. In the Psalm we see a recollection of Zion by the Jews after their expulsion by the invading Babylonians, and this is followed by the articulation of the nature of the song (or novella) that follows: "For there our captors demanded of us songs, and our tormentors mirth, saying 'Sing us one of the songs of Zion'" (Psalm 137:3). Smart's novel, then, is such a song of Zion after war, except her city is the 1930s and 1940s moment rather than a specific location.

But allusion is very much the matter. Smart's allusion to William Blake's poem "The Question Answered" makes sudden sense of her otherwise confusing comments, "[he] was livid with hate of our lineaments of gratified desire" and "Witches were burnt at the stake, all over New England, just for love, just for wearing the lineaments of gratified desire" (Smart, By Grand 50, 97). Durrell uses the same allusion in his 1957 novel Balthazar (110) as a reference to both his own and his protagonist's initials, L.G.D. This was a trick he first began in 1935 with his novel Pied Piper of Lovers and continued in The Black Book, both works that would have been obscure to those who had not known him during this period and virtually unavailable after the war or even by 1945 when Smart published By Grand Central Station through Editions Poetry London, edited by their mutual friend Tambimuttu.

It may seem a stretch to link Smart's allusion to Blake to Durrell's allusion to the same, even if we accept the reminder that Durrell first put her in contact with Barker, the lover whose lineaments she wears, and that she was reading The Black Book in late 1939 after a significant correspondence with Durrell to discuss and share their poetry.[16] However, the link is cemented by a further shared allusion. Durrell's first novel repeatedly alludes to the obscure Middle English poem "Quia Amore Langueo," and his protagonist Walsh sings a musical setting of the poem in a dramatic scene that provides the crisis of this middle section of the novel (Pied 203–05). Smart uses the same phrase, writing, "I am without words. I am without thoughts. But quia amore langueo. I am dying for love. This is the language of love" (By Grand 109) near the end of her book. This is only a part of the allusion, however, and the phrase is densely tied to another repeated image across the close of the novel: the apple plucked from the same poem. For Smart's narrator, writing of her injurious love and the vaginal wound this affair has left in her (in a direct parallel to the wounded Christ in the poem "Quia Amore Langueo"), "the apples (which ben ripe in my gardayne) fall only toward that" (89). The apples are a direct quotation from the poem. The same parallel to Christ recurs with the same allusion in the final scenes as well, no fewer than four times: "My love is crucified on a floating cross....My love has a bandage like a bowel of pain...But it is not the wound that chokes him" (107). This then flows through another repetition of the title of the poem "Quia Amore Langueo" (109) and thence to the organic image of the apples of her garden: "His hand of sympathy goes out to me, soft as a dove, his cheek like early apples....With resurrection in his eyeballs" (110) and finally on the closing page of the work, "Go into your garden, for your apples are ripe" (112). All are direct allusions to the poem she discovered through Durrell's first novel, *Pied Piper of Lovers*.

Such linkages by allusion to Durrell may seem merely convenient, though the ankle and snow imagery of his "Asylum in the Snow" recurs as well (Smart, *By Grand* 73–74). These connections become yet more dense: Miller's golden shit scene in *Tropic of Cancer* (97) is also linked by allusion (Smart, *By Grand* 75); Miller's style in the novel recurs as an echo in Smart (81); Durrell's magma of history and the enormous Now in *The Black Book* (176, 244) appears in allusion as well (Smart, *By Grand* 79, 65); and Smart overtly cites Dylan Thomas's short story collection *The Burning Baby*, an excerpt from which he had published in Durrell and Miller's periodical *Delta* as "Prologue to an Adventure," a text that had a deep effect on the New Apocalypse (Smart, *By Grand* 109) and a magazine in which her own poetry first appeared.

Allusion is very much the matter of Smart's *By Grand Central Station I Sat Down and Wept*, both to these works and many, many others. Allusion, however, only informs the reader of Smart's own readings, and the meaning of an allusion may be ambiguous. Nevertheless, allusion is only a formal technique through which she codes her social critique. The important shift is that this social critique and its allusive frame-work brings her work into a new context and makes it intelligible through the same anti-authoritarian-cum-anarchist paradigm as the New Apocalypse and Villa Seurat writers endorsed. The politics of Smart's various comparisons and allusions then stand out:

> The determination of early statesmen who were mild but individual...No great neon face has been superimposed over

their minor but memorable history. Nor has the blood of the early settlers, spilt in feud and heroism, yet been bottled by a Coca-Cola firm and sold as ten-cent tradition. (57)

The blurring of the state and commercialism is clear, but the addition of an anarchist or anti-authoritarian perspective broadens the rationale for combining the state and commercialism—both are anti-individual and hegemonic. Smart also takes up the contest between the individual and the nation: "There have been men who have been more remembered than nations" (64), only to set her dismissal of "my dear country" (64) in contrast to an extended emphasis on the personal and individual on the facing page in a string of first-person pronouns culminating in another parallel to Durrell's *The Black Book* through the "now" (65).[17] These anti-state gestures (67–69) recur in a juxtaposition of the bloodied corpses of soldiers against the blood of her giving birth to a son.

This then brings the politics of Smart's novel to the fore and re-invigorates our capacity for readings that move beyond biographical essentialisms and romantic excess or worse—the ongoing misogynistic tendency to see Smart as an overwrought hysteric or reductively as a martyr of love, whether this interpretive failing was meant in help or harm. The industrial modernity of the state and its war-machine is set as the opposite of the individual standing for and expressing an organic and anti-authoritarian humanism. This is Smart's grand contrast in *By Grand Central Station*, and it is precisely the same conflict articulated in the anarchist works of the New Apocalypse authors who had themselves developed out of Miller's and Durrell's reconstruction of English post-Surrealism. This is doubled since it was a deep influence on George Barker's post-surrealist poetry as well.

This suddenly makes a great deal of sense from Smart's otherwise inexplicable avoidance of war and politics through an unpolitical stance that extols the organic, fecund, and reproductive in relief: "a lot of statesmen will emerge twirling their moustaches, and see the birth-blood, and know that they have been foiled" (66). The undoing of the state by the organic reproduction of the body reflects very closely the then widespread views of the New Apocalypse. She follows this in an anti-capitalist vein by setting her own reproductive seed as salvation, for "I shall still have a pocketful of rye, whose currency no Foreign Exchange can control, nor value be diminished by transplantation" (67). Thereby, Smart is the agent of organic growth, not some passive, fallow field to be ploughed for the planting of a cash crop. Her pocket of seeds undoes the landowner.

The conclusion of the novel and its titular allusion now come to life as an anti-industrial organic focus on the individual in an Apocalyptic embodied vein: "By Grand Central Station I sat down and wept: / I will not be placated by the mechanical motions of existence....It lit up Grand Central Station like a Judgment Day" (103). The unborn child is the Christ of this Apocalypse coming to wash away the urban world of industrialized warfare such that "I am going to have a child, so all my dreams are of water" surrounds the watered city "When Lexington Avenue dissolved in my tears, and the houses and the neon lights and the nebulae fell jumbled into the flood, that child was the naked new-born babe striding the blast....The grief trumpets its triumph" (104).

This unmistakably Apocalyptic frame then returns to the allusions seen in the Durrell-originating "Quia Amore Langeuo" and an anarcho-pacifist vision of the Second World War. From this war, and through this allusion, Smart's narrator is awakening, and in this context her love story allegorically figures. For the war, her lover "sees the huge bird of catastrophe fly by. Both its wings are lined with the daily paper. Five million other voices are shrieking too....All martyrdoms are in vain. He is drowning in the blood of too much sacrifice. / Lay aside the weapons, love, for all battles are lost" (111). The final organic call comes from Smart's pinching of Durrell's allusion when she repeats, "Go into your garden, for your apples are ripe" (112), a phrase that ends this natural argument in the text before its final tragedy and recalls her own use of the apple as a figure for endless fecundity through generations in a fallen world (89, 110). This cues the reader for the postwar world of inescapable modernity in the nuclear age that ends the novel:[18]

> Odours of disinfectant wipe out love and tears. With rush
> and thunder the early workers overrun the world they have
> inherited, tramping out the stains of the wailing, bleeding

past....I myself prefer Boulder Dam to Chartres Cathedral. I prefer dogs to children. I prefer corncobs to the genitals of the male. Everything's hotsy-totsy, dandy, everything's OK. It's in the bag. It can't miss. (112)

This dystopic vision is Smart's close to the novel and the destruction of the anarchic organicism advocated by the New Apocalpyse and implicit in her allusive structure. Without placing Smart in the context of her 1945 novel, published by Tamibuttu under the Editions Poetry London imprint that bound this group of authors together, we could not reach such a reading. And a reading of the politics of Smart's novel reinvigorates her work a great deal.

Robert Duncan's "An Ark for Lawrence Durrell"

Robert Duncan's short poem "An Ark for Lawrence Durrell" first appeared in his journal *Experimental Review* in the January 1941, number 2, supplement issue. He included it again unrevised in *The Years as Catches* in 1966 but lists the poem as written in 1940. It has received scant critical attention, despite the significant work done on Duncan's oeuvre and its compelling connection to European influences on Duncan's formative work.[19] He recalls in his Introduction to the latter printing that he was at the time "striving to imitate the demi-surrealist rhetorics of contemporary mannerist poets—Charles Henri Ford, George Barker, or Dylan Thomas. In 1940 it was George Barker's *Calamiterror* that most persuaded me. I used to read it aloud, rapt in the intoxication of his verse" (Duncan, Introduction ii). Notably, this timeline demonstrates that Duncan was already significantly engaged with the post-surrealist materials he accessed from Miller through Cooney prior to his contact with Nin in 1941, in contrast to the timelines offered by the biographical works. To this he adds an acknowledgement of Thomas and Barker's influence over his subsequent work as well as their importance to his thoughts on sexuality. Notably, however, the only poem from this period that expressly takes up another poet's works is dedicated to Durrell (despite Duncan's many influences at this time). The poem reveals both the influence of English post-Surrealism on Duncan at this turning point in his poetic career as well as his own understanding of and readings in these works. Furthermore, "An Ark for Lawrence Durrell" shows the importance of anarchist thought to Duncan's poetry of this period in a sense that agrees with that of the personalist poets as well as the anti-authoritarian approach to the Ego in Durrell's works. This is striking for Duncan in 1940. As Andy Weaver has argued, Duncan's "underlying political anarchism often goes unnoticed. Perceptive critics of Duncan's work, including, among others, Norman Finkelstein and Nathaniel Mackey, consistently overlook or give short shrift to the importance of anarchism in Duncan's personal ideology and in his poetry, generally preferring to focus on Duncan's mysticism" (75).[20] Following on the earlier materials presented in this book, I contend Duncan's anarchism informs his mysticism and poetics, and his fascination with Durrell, Miller, Barker, and the other Personalists is both a consequence of his anarchism just as his increasing interest in anarchism is a consequence of his interest in their verse and prose. We do not have a record of Duncan's nuanced readings of the English post-Surrealists or his sense of the relationship between praxis and politics, as we have in his H.D. Book, but by noticing the method of the latter work in its nascent form in his "An Ark for Lawrence Durrell," a revised sense of Duncan's works for this period may be coaxed out.

> If we are to cross the barriers of snow
> into the cave-home of our childhood, dark
> among the darkened lights, telling our beads,
> if we are to cross over the wheel of night
> and dwell among the roots of sorrow—
> let us take with us the fox,
> for he is quicker than our sickness;
> let us take the cock, for he remembers the day
> and leaps for light. And let us take
> the white-haird ass who is gentle
> and bows his head.

> The snake has his own way among us.

The first line of Duncan's poem immediately recalls his several advertisements in *Experimental Review* as well as in other magazines for an edition of Durrell's "Asylum in the Snow" with illustrations and a cover design by Virginia Admiral: "If we are to cross the barriers of snow" (Duncan, "An Ark" 11). In Durrell's work, the snow is akin to Nietzsche's cause creating drive, a psychic barrier between unreason and creativity akin to a check or impasse that stymies the poetic endeavour by attempting to impose a coherence or order on it.[21] To cross this barrier, Duncan turns to the same "deep" or "dark" that emerges again in a fuller form in his "Toward an African Elegy," first published in George Leite's *Circle*. Like the archetypal quest motif as exploration of the unconscious, moving "into the cave-home of our childhood" in his Durrellian Ark is, for Duncan, a way of crossing these barriers (Duncan, "An Ark" 11). Like Durrell's *The Black Book*, which Duncan was also setting and attempting to publish at the same time, the cave of childhood is a return to the womb in a mythic process of self-willed rebirth. Most notable, however, the poem at no point crosses these barriers or attempts to narrate such a quest or journey; it is instead mitigated by the crucial "If" that opens the poem. Durrell's "Asylum in the Snow" culminates in the artist's rebirth, also as in *The Black Book*, from this chaotic turn to the deep amidst organic images of snow, snakes, and sorrow. Duncan, in contrast, gives only the suggestion of what he would make if such an undertaking began. If this process were to be initiated, then "let us take with us the fox," and a variety of other beasts that displace the fragmentary and partial selves uncovered in Durrell's quasi-archetypal short story. The fox, cock, and white-haird ass of Duncan's poem each bring a talent or virtue to the speaker and his companion (implicit in "us") if such a quest begins. The fox outraces sickness, though "quicker" in Duncan's phrasing relies on the double meaning of outpacing as well as outliving sickness. This ambiguity signals increasing uncertainty for the other companions. The cock recalls the "day," which is also the Ego in this "cave-home of our childhood, dark / among darkened lights" that cast the unconscious contents in the common trope of a cave or underground space of self-confrontation. The cock recalls the reformulated Self that reemerges after this struggle. Finally, we have the "white-haird ass" who submits to the process with gentleness but also opens the mystical or religious component of such an inward journey implicit in bowing his head, as if in prayer ("An Ark" 11).

But if there is a lesson to be learned for Duncan's "An Ark for Lawrence Durrell" from Durrell's method in "Asylum in the Snow" (and perhaps from Durrell's "Carol on Corfu," which has similar organic imagery and was published in the same 1938 third issue of *Seven* in which Duncan would have first read the story), it would be the same lesson Duncan himself is keen to teach in *The H.D. Book* about process and engagement. In contrast to the authoritarian structure of institutions through which creative works, education, or poetry flow,[22] the successful work prompts the examination of self: "I was to grow through them in some hidden way. What I would make of *The Man Who Died* or *The Waves* would be what I would make of myself, the course of a life....I sought to find...not...some estimate of their literary worth but...the love of a way of being that they had known" (Duncan, H.D. 39–40). By looking to this process in Duncan's poem, the same way he looks to H.D.'s in "Garden," we find a miniature expression of the process of coming to write that mirrors exactly the process in Durrell's "Asylum." Even in the conditional form (almost a form of apophasis), it is *doing* the process, engaging in it, just as "If I write" is itself writing. The poem is itself the crossing over of "the barriers of snow" through poetic creation, which at the end of Durrell's story leads to the assumption of self-identity and the initiation of the creative process in writing, or for Duncan becomes the poem looking backward on itself in the moment of its own opening. "If we are the cross the barriers of snow" becomes "If we are to write this poem," which has already happened as it is said in the conditional statement. The "if" is its own beginning, its own apodosis resolving its protasis. The kinship in Durrell, to draw from his "Carol on Corfu," would be stylistically much different yet carries the same poetic backward glance at process as a becoming of the self:

> I, per se I, I sing on.
> Let flesh falter, or let bone break
> Break, yet the salt of a poem holds on,
> Even in empty weather
> When beak and feather have done. (Durrell, "Carol" 56)

Though Duncan is more cautious in his articulation, for both poets this act of looking back on the poem even while it is still in the process of becoming is itself a statement of the poem's function. For Durrell (and implicitly in Duncan), this backward glance at its own creation parallels the Ego's own backward glance in constructing itself: the "I am" grown from the "I was." Like Duncan's anecdote about being given books by his teacher, the poem does not lead the reader to a particular "self-development" or to a particular closed meaning—it engages with the reader in a process in which meaning is reader-imminent and based on the reader's own decision to create, just as "What I would make of *The Man Who Died* or *The Waves* would be what I would make of myself, the course of a life" (39). Hence, "telling our beads" during this exploration of self that, like the poem, comes into being only by reflecting back upon itself during the process of being, holds sympathy with a self that is mystical as well as common and in both instances uncertain. Our companions in this process, like the creature companions in Duncan's poem, are like amulets, warding off woes, and they are likewise called into existence through the conditional reflections of "if."

However, the most potent charge of Duncan's short "An Ark for Lawrence Durrell" comes from the two smallest components of the poem: "we" and "the snake." That this journey is shared suggests a number of companions apart from those conditionally named (the fox, the cock, and the ass). Most obvious is Durrell as the addressee, a fellow poet engaged in this process of creation. That, however, is simple since Duncan came to Durrell as a reader, and "if we are to cross the barriers of snow" reflects on Duncan's position as a reader of Durrell's journey through these barriers in the stories, "Zero" and "Asylum in the Snow," that Duncan was working to print in Woodstock. This makes Duncan a companion to Durrell on Durrell's journey, just as he was an independent companion on Lawrence's and Woolf's journeys as described in *The H.D. Book*. While this functions in the poem, with Duncan discovering "what I would make of myself" (H.D. 39), it is only one part of this community called into being through the poem's first subject. While Duncan might also be calling Durrell to join as his companion, more provocatively the poem echoes the call that Duncan felt to accompany Durrell when reading

"Asylum in the Snow." Duncan includes his reading in his community through "we," so that "An Ark for Lawrence Durrell" might provoke more self-discovery (rather than self-development). It calls the reader to accompany Duncan in the process. In this, the "cave-home of our childhood" is pluralized, indicating a shared history and memory even amidst the individual Id or unconscious of the "dark." These are still "we" and "our." The individual, distinct from this, returns in the serpent, a constant companion yet not a part of this "we" who "has his own way among us" (Duncan, "An Ark" 11). Like Durrell's "I, per se I" in which the singular subject is presented hesitantly and with a known incompleteness, Duncan's snake in the final line gestures to the unrecognized companions, such as desire, which pursues its own ends whether they agree with or differ from those of the Ego. "The snake has his own way" indeed, and in its independence, the lie is shown to the whole and to the contained notion of identity, one tied together by the perverse *authority* of the superego. Some companions we may bring with us, but others, even while travelling beside us, follow their own winding route and will.

Duncan's anarchism is clear in his poem, but it also demonstrates the anti-authoritarian spirit he recognized in reading Durrell's "Asylum in the Snow" and very likely his "Carol on Corfu" in Nicholas Moore's and John Goodland's *Seven* (Durrell's poem and story open and close the issue as a whole). The same issue also contains Miller's pacifist "Peace! It's Wonderful!," two surrealist poems by Dylan Thomas, J.F. Hendry's anarcho-pacifist narrative "The Eye in the Triangle," and Dorian Cooke's Apocalyptic prose work "The Priest and the Server" (as well as two pacifist poems), Henry Treece's essay "Dylan Thomas and the Surrealists," and one of the first reviews of Durrell's *The Black Book*. When considering Duncan's offering in his Ark, his invitation to exploration, his own position as a companion to the narrators of these texts in *Seven* must prefigure our accompanying him through his own in *Experimental Review*. That these works would easily function through the same egoic anarchism of the post-surrealist paradigm in which he writes his response seems clear, and in that companionship we must revise our sense of the whole on which we have focused our attention.

Conclusion

This book has argued that a key generation in American and British literature has been elided from critical scrutiny. The generation came of age between the influence of the High Modernists and Auden group on one end of their period and the dispersals of the Second World War on the other. Their literature is book-ended by defining forces, and they resisted both. Their international migrations marked out a network of like-minded figures in Egypt, Greece, France, Britain, the United States, Canada, and China. By returning attention to their networks of mutual support as well as their extensive distribution channels for literary works, it is difficult to avoid recognizing their importance as predecessors to the postwar literary groups that emerged both in sympathy with their vision and against it. Regardless, the history of this personalist group shaped the literary communities to which it belonged in a tightly connected series of relationships. An inescapable component of this study is recuperative, and its success is for the reader to judge; however, this project also gestures more broadly to how anti-authoritarian ideas exist in Modernism already, even if often overlooked or underscrutinized. Allan Antliff, David Kadlec, and Jesse Cohn have made this case prior to me in their respective works, *Anarchist Modernism*, *Mosaic Modernism*, and *Anarchism and the Crisis of Representation*. Nevertheless, it would probably be easier to find their views circulating in art history than in the New Modernist Studies, which remains stubbornly entrenched in literary concerns and generally committed to a Jamesonian sense of Marxist critical theory and progressive conceptualizations. Nonetheless, by being attentive to the flexibility of anti-authoritarian groups to nurture and maintain communications between disparate locations and to express their politics through form less than through direct statement, we may find not only a missing generation but an extended trend across modernist literature and into the development of the postmodern. Such a perspective would challenge our comfortable interpretive paradigms for relating the modern and postmodern, but conceptual frameworks are available through Lewis Call's *Postmodern Anarchism* (2002), Todd May's *The Political Philosophy of Poststructuralist Anarchism* (1994), and Saul Newman's *From Bakunin to Lacan: Anti-Authoritarianism and the Dislocation of Power* (2001). Meaningful analyses have begun in this vein by Antliff ("Anarchy" 56–66), Newman ("Voluntary" 31–49) in Call's special 2010 issue *Post-Anarchism Today* of *Anarchist Developments in Cultural Studies*, and Cohn ("Anarchism" 54–63). The reconsideration of mainstream Modernist Studies offered by these works would be both productive and provocative, and it would certainly lead to recuperative projects extending to either chronological end of this study.

I began this book by arguing against the accepted narrative of Late Modernism and 1930s writing pointing to an anti-authoritarian generation of authors who turned from their peers' predominantly Marxist engagement with the Spanish Civil War and who continued an English-language form of post-Surrealism after the 1936 London International Surrealist Exhibition. I conclude the argument by suggesting a kindred reading for four of their works by authors from the east and west coasts of America, Canada, and Britain (albeit a non-patrial British subject). This could extend to include a revitalized approach to David Gascoyne's very fine body of poetry, which is largely excluded from Modernist Studies; the potential comparison of method between the experimental prose of Durrell's *The Black Book*, Djuna Barnes's *Nightwood*, and Samuel Beckett's *Murphy*; and the further internationalization of this study by expanding study of Albert Cossery's later novels about the Egyptian lower classes or pursuing Hsiao Ch'ien's short fiction and interests in a distinctly Chinese form of anti-authoritarian thought fostered by E.M. Forster and the works of Henrik Ibsen. As with Henry Miller's argument that he could best encourage others to discover how to live their own lives simply by living his own, I must plead a similar argument with my literary choices. My personal interests in Smart and Durrell in particular surely shaped my selections, as well as my one poetic subject,

Duncan. A recuperation of Hendry seems highly viable, not from my selections here, but based on the fine work begun by Leo Mellor. Great interest in George Barker in Late Modernism also seems much needed, as well as correcting the unconscionable exclusion of Dylan Thomas from much contemporary criticism. That Thomas's poetry could prove difficult led to scholarly selections and anthologizations that emphasized his less syntactically complex works; however, that we now deem him more suitable for the high school or composition classroom is more a product of criticism's own work shaping his oeuvre than it is a reflection of the body of work itself. Though their rediscovery is less likely, Alex Comfort's early poetry and in particular his novels will reward attention, almost as surely as Henry Treece's will prove informative even if the larger portion may be no longer aesthetically captivating. There are, however, real kernels of pithy complexity in Treece needing recuperation.

Finally, if this project has achieved even a part of its ends, the reader's disagreements and personal interests will lead to new directions, new reconsiderations, revisions to this work (and corrections of its errors), and an expansion of its scope. I would hope it will make the task of teaching the stereotypical pre- and post-1945 American and British literature surveys more complex and challenging—just as the anarchist vision behind these works make the British-American national literatures distinction increasingly difficult to uphold due to their continual interfertilization, the generational gap that made a mid-century division both a convenience and a certainty also becomes increasingly untenable. With great luck, we may even foster readers with an increasing sense of their own self-exploration in the process of reading, readers more willing to take a knife to the page, to take their own experience of reading into their criticism, and to take the page forward to their own projects.

Notes

Introduction

1 The "core" figures of the "Paris school" would be Miller, Anaïs Nin, Alfred Perlès, and Lawrence Durrell, though many other writers and artists interacted closely with them, resided in the same location, published through them, and supported their works. The "Villa Seurat" group is named for Miller's home in Paris after the publication of *Tropic of Cancer*.

2 The New Apocalypse began with its anthology of the same name in 1939, publishing *The White Horseman* in 1941, and *The Crown and the Sickle* in 1944. They later called themselves New Romantics but maintained the same group and views. Henry Treece and J.F. Hendry were the centre of the group with significant support from Herbert Read and critical perspective from G.S. Fraser as well as much publishing support from Nicholas Moore's *Seven* with John Goodland and John Waller's *Bolero* and later *Kingdom Come* at Worcester College, University of Oxford. Dorian Cooke also had a crucial but uncertain role.

3 *Personal Landscape* was a journal created in Cairo principally for the authors in the Middle East campaign, but it also had a strong philhellenic focus derived from two of its editors' and many of its contributors' escape from Greece to Egypt during the Nazi invasion. The San Francisco Renaissance both prefigured and nurtured the Beats while also enjoying a close rapport with the Black Mountain poets and much of the West Coast poetry scene that grew enormously in the 1960s.

4 Henry Treece and Stefan Schimanski cement "post-Surrealism" in 1943 as their definition of the New Apocalypse ("Towards a Personalist Attitude," 14), although it was already implicit in the Villa Seurat. They define their continuing view as aligned with Herbert Read's vision of anarchism at the same time (15). Treece's anti-statist views continue in his fantasy novels after the war to the mid-1960s.

5 Read is perhaps the most famous British anarchist of his generation as well as a part of High Modernism, an important editor at Routledge in a position akin to Eliot's at Faber & Faber for nurturing young talent, and was perhaps the pre-eminent British art critic after Roger Fry. Oddly, he remains largely overlooked in Modernist Studies despite his stature, broad influence, and cross-media activities.

6 I have discussed this in more detail in *The Henry Miller–Herbert Read Letters: 1935–58* and "Surrealism's Anglo-American Afterlife: The Herbert Read and Henry Miller Network" (36–64).

7 The same language and mode of disagreement is a recurrence from Miller's 1935 rejection of the Surrealists' interests in Trotsky.

8 Ezra Pound's wartime speeches, T.S. Eliot's anti-Semitism, and Wyndham Lewis's writings on Hitler are all commonly cited examples. Alastair Hamilton's *The Appeal of Fascism: A Study of Intellectuals and Fascism 1919–1945* is a good resource for a critical overview, though more recent work has attempted to bring greater nuance to fascist and authoritarian ideas in Modernism (see Paul Morrison's *The Poetics of Fascism: Ezra Pound, T.S. Eliot, Paul de Man* or Leon Surette's *Dreams of a Totalitarian Utopia: Literary Modernism and Politics* among other works).

9 Treece's Celtic Tetralogy (1952–1958) stands out among these. His first novel, *The Dark Island*, was published in 1952 by Victor Gollancz, though his short story collection *I Cannot Go Hunting Tomorrow* first appeared in 1946 when he assumed the position of senior English master at Barton and Humber Grammar School in Barton-upon-Humber, Lincolnshire. He produced a few dozen novels from 1953 until his death in 1966, mostly for young adults and mainly historical with a trace of magic and fantasy. Michael Moorcock contributed introductions that emphasize Treece's anarchism to the Savoy Books reprints of the Celtic Tetralogy in the 1980s, from which *The Golden Strangers* also contains Treece's essay "Notes on Perception and Vision," in which Treece detailed his writing philosophy shortly before his death. The other Savoy volumes with Moorcock's introductions are *The Dark Island*, *The Great Captains*, and *Red Queen, White Queen*. The anarchist content in each presents itself through the bleak impact powerful leaders have on those over whom they exert power and the symbolic destruction of the state. Each ruler dies badly with an irrational thirst for power in the midst of the failure of his ideals—the death of rulers opens and closes *The Great Captains* and *The Green Man*, Treece's retelling of *Hamlet*, as well as several of this other works. The implicit moral for young readers is that rulers and rule are in a bad way by their very nature.

10 Even in a typically nationalist and patriotic volume like *Oasis: The Middle*

East Anthology of Poetry from the Forces, John Cromer could comment to an audience of British patriots and service men, "It is easy to be revolutionary in word and action by destroying the insignia and literary canons of an existing regime. But mere destruction results in impasse unless a constructive pattern is built upon the ruins. And the bases of reconstruction will always be found among the debris, for no system which has lasted for centuries can be altogether bad, and no culture which has developed alongside social progress can be snuffed out like a candle" (xv). Cromer would go on to refer positively to Herbert Read's Preface to Alex Comfort's anarchist journal *Lyra*, which is a strikingly individualist view for him to take. G.S. Fraser's student guide *The Modern Writer and His World* also identifies Comfort expressly as an anarchist (324) as well as his colleague the dramatist and war correspondent Denis Johnston (209–10) who reported on Al Alamein with Fraser and also on Buchenwald.

11 Henry Miller's very productive disagreement with Herbert Read returns to this specific rejection of the stabilization of naming in October 1937, particularly in relation to naming and Surrealism. Durrell's "Asylum in the Snow" repeats the same rejection of stabilization and naming, and the work's migration from the Villa Seurat to publication in England in *Seven*, Robert Duncan's attempted republication in Woodstock, and the San Francisco Renaissance's publication in Berkeley are telling. The insistence on individual self-determination without the predetermination of naming or the surrender of agency to the unconscious in automatism recurs across all of the groups I loosely understand as personalist through their affinities rather than heir adherence to a set code.

1   Late Modernism Inside the Whale

1 Most criticism turns to Marx's statement in *The German Ideology* that "It is not the consciousness of men that determines their being, but, on the contrary, their social being that determines their consciousness" (*Selected* 389), though the same concept is already in *The Communist Manifesto*. Hence, ideology produces consciousness rather than the reverse, and it does so in order to reproduce the existing relations of production or to further develop their logic. Marx, of course, was a complex individual whose thought circulated down through his own unique life experiences in circumstances highly proximate to and inalienably linked to his own embodied experiences, and as a consequence, his thinking changed and redeveloped over time. Related but distinct and differing versions of this concept are articulated by Marx at different stages in his life in his first

thesis in *Theses on Feuerbach*, his rebuttal of anarchism in the fifth and sixth observations in *The Poverty of Philosophy*, and his Afterword to *Capital*. This is the crux of what Marx rejects in Proudhon's vision that "men [can be] both the authors and the actors of their own drama" (*Writings* 485). Many modern readers will encounter these concepts through György Lukács's *History and Class Consciousness*.

2 See Auden's repeated rallying cry for "the struggle" in his 1937 poem "Spain," which is unique in its explicit propaganda function.

3 The Villa Seurat, the New Apocalypse, the activities of anarchist poets, and the Cairo War Poets all remain unmentioned in Spender's collection *The Thirties and After*; nor does Keith Douglas make the list, despite Spender's discussion of war poetry.

4 That *Seven*, the Grey Walls Press, most of the New Apocalypse anthologies, the New Romantics anthologies, Alex Comfort's various periodicals, and most English surrealist material from the late 1930s and 1940s were created through one small press should also be noted, especially since the two printers, Moore and Wrey Gardiner, were close to the Villa Seurat and identified with English Surrealism while also continuing to publish Durrell and Miller for decades. The exceptions are volumes published through Herbert Read at Routledge.

5 The Poetry London imprint later drew largely on the network created around the Villa Seurat. Notable authors and books include Elizabeth Smart's *By Grand Central Station I Sat Down and Wept*, Durrell's *Cefalû*, Miller's *The Cosmological Eye* and *Sunday After the War*, Vladimir Nabokov's *The Real Life of Sebastian Knight*, Keith Douglas's *Alamein to Zem Zem*, and Cleanth Brooks's *Modern Poetry and the Tradition*. Notably, Durrell introduced Elizabeth Smart to his longstanding friend George Barker, who was also David Gascoyne's flatmate. The ensuing affair is recounted in Smart's *By Grand Central Station I Sat Down and Wept* and Barker's *The Dead Seagull*.

6 Tambimuttu's rebuttal is uncharacteristically harsh and points to the commonalities between London and Cairo, without either being a centre (Tambimuttu, "Dear Fraser" 219).

7 It is also worth noting that biographies of Thomas and his published letters overlook or misdate materials that demonstrate this influence, such as Fitzgibbon's *Selected Letters of Dylan Thomas* (210) and Ferris's *Dylan Thomas: The Biography* (167).

8 Francis Scarfe's summary from 1942 parallels Hynes's twenty-five years later: "In 1936 Roger Roughton founded the only successful Surrealist review that has appeared in England, 'Contemporary Poetry and Prose'.

Produced at his own expense, it ran for eighteen months....In about the same year appeared David Gascoyne's 'Short Survey of Surealism', a rather scrappy book, but one which attracted some attention, partly because of the extraordinary anecdotes it contained" (Scarfe 147). This view, of course, overlooks the international activities of the English Surrealists as well as subsequent English periodicals.

9   For instance, Scarfe argues, "But Surrealism rapidly advanced to its academic stage in Britain, and was not really absorbed" (148). In contrast to Scarfe's position, even in the comparatively mild mannered *Poetry Quarterly* published through Grey Walls Press by Wrey Gardiner, we find more than a decade later, after the end of the Second World War, an editorial that can claim unabashedly, "Poetry is the language in which the unconscious aspirations of the minds of the peoples realize themselves, become evident and concrete" (Gardiner, "Editorial" 3). The language of Surrealism certainly lived on abundantly, and unless an anarchist press specializing in international poetry can be deemed "academic," Scarfe's contention must be reconsidered.

10 Notably, the 1939 edition differs significantly from Nin's subsequent and more widely available reprints. The Obelisk Press ceased during the Nazi invasion and its owner, Jack Kahane, committed suicide rather than face the war. A facsimile edition was published in 2008, which has made this work available once again to scholars.

11 Even Francis Scarfe was demonstrably aware of the politics of the New Apocalypse, and hence his own dismissal and that followed by Hynes, had clear motives. In analyzing Hendry's poetry, he remarks, "This poem is an allegorical presentation of the anarchist conception of an organic society. Hendry points to the trees and flowers and sees in their lives an example of organic pattern which is not followed in human societies" (Scarfe 161).

12 Allan Antliff has given much attention to Herbert Read's influence over "organic form" at this point in time ("Open" 6–20).

13 See Mellor's *Reading the Ruins* for the most nuanced re-articulation of the proposition from Hynes that in war-torn London, Surrealism became a visible feature of the everyday (Hynes 227).

14 Charles M. Tung contends that in quietism we find a distinctly modernist problem: "if we think of modernism's investigations of temporality and detemporalization as an engagement with and a resistance to the disquieting time of the twentieth century, then postmodernism's plots of undoing do not merely express the disappearance of the truly temporal present.

They also present the necessity of a continuing desire for that present" (396).

15 When Treece came to collect his works in *How I See Apocalypse* in 1946, he tellingly makes his first literary reference on the first page to Henry Miller, defining his own interests in admiration of, though difference from, Miller (in relation to faith not politics, where the two are in agreement) (Treece, *How* vii). Moreover, he notes that his later analysis of Miller derives from a specifically political context: "writers whose works may most appropriately be assessed from a Romantic and Anarchic standpoint" (viii).

16 Hendry's poetry and series of elegies in Alex Comfort's *New Road* are symptomatic of his stated preference for the organic and rural over the mechanical and urban. "Elegy no. 9" opens and closes its five stanzas with "To you the chill rain cleansing as sieves of the river, / ... / and still is the column of green in the turbulent tree" (64). Likewise, his "From an Elegy" focuses on a "secret city," but it is wrapped in myth and organic materials as "a wave," "a city, you may say, or rivers," and "a city whose walls of water, / Adrift on an ocean's breath," which leads the narrators of the poem to witness bird and people "Shattering the crown's magnificence / In a cloud-burst of anarchy" (64–65).

17 Treece links Hendry's style to his politics when he sets Nicholas Moore in contrast to Hendry, noting that both share the Apocalypse's anarchism yet produce very different works stylistically. For Treece, Hendry "is a writer of tortured and tortuous imagery, whose lines are twisted and broken with meopoeia....His words are frequently difficult to hear or read, some lines being harrowing in the extreme because of this difficulty" (Treece, *How* 176). His example is the same as Mellor's, "Picasso: for Guernica," but this politicized vision of Hendry by his contemporaries and collaborators would substantially revise Mellor's argument.

18 Published in the United States as *The Modern Novel in Britain and the United States* (1964).

19 This is perhaps nowhere more painful than in E.P. Thompson's "Inside *Which* Whale," where he argues, "The premise is found in the phrase—'Progress and reaction have both turned out to be swindles'—so reminiscent of Auden's dismissal of a 'low, dishonest decade'" (81). Thompson's rejection of Miller's politics is also explicit when he states "the fiddling of Henry Miller is close to the exchange of ironic points of light between the Just" (80) and can only offer for his view a false binary: "the democratic elements in the Communist tradition were submerged by the authoritarian" (85), which neglects the topic

of anarchism in the subject matter and falsely equates democracy with liberty. Jerald Zaslove summarizes the improverished thinking tidily, "E.P. Thompson's silence about [Herbert Read] is in fact exemplary of the narrow sectarianism of the British modernist tradition that saw culture subsumed into the laborist traditions which were in turn historically placed as a struggle between Morris and Marx" (21).

20 These sentiments remain remarkably consistent across Miller's life. His published May 10, 1945 letter to Stefan Schimanski at the end of the Second World War states, "Whatever programme for world peace, world order, world justice, is arrived at at the San Francisco Conference, or any other conference of diplomats and war lords, means little to me. These are not, and never were, the men to bring about peace and order. Whatever is accomplished in this direction must be accomplished through the creative efforts of the individuals who compose the various countries of the world" (Miller, "Golden" 293). In the same piece, he relies heavily on the New Apocalypse's notion of the object-machine and anti-utopianism as outlined in Chapter 3 of this book, ideals for the New Apocalypse inspired by Miller himself (296).

21 For instance, Durrell's Justine and Kerouac's On the Road are both 1957 novels arising from the fecundity of the 1930s and 1940s milieu under discussion.

22 Mellor also notes that the poem is "difficult to place initially" (27). His close reading of the formal work of the poem is admirable (26–30), though it sidelines the poem's politics.

23 Robert Fraser's very fine biography of Barker, The Chameleon Poet: A Life of George Barker, takes relatively little interest in Barker's interactions with Miller or with the Villa Seurat figures as a whole. A far more British Barker is depicted, and even his major works on foreign topics, such as "Elegy on Spain" receive only a cursory mention (206). The influences on Barker play a secondary role to Barker's influences.

24 Demonstrating the deep interpretive bias of the period, Scarfe would describe Barker by arguing, "The most important thing about this book [Sequence of Ten Sonnets] is the fact that, at that date, a young poet could be so self-contained as to ignore the stifling but necessary influences of the Eliot and Auden generations" (119). The same avoidance of Auden's strong influence is what made Barker a hero to other poets of the period.

25 Although Fraser does not link Barker to the Villa Seurat group until 1939, he and Durrell were already good friends in 1932 (MacNiven, Lawrence Durrell 82), and Durrell met up with Barker on the same return visits to England after 1935 during which he met with Thomas.

2 Narrative Itinerary

1 Dylan Thomas recalls hiding the book in his stove, and John Waller (remarkably) recounts accessing Miller's works through the English Ministry of Information Middle East reference library in Athens and Cairo in 1945, including Miller's *Colossus of Maroussi*, which Fraser had read in Cairo not long after its American publication. This subversion of government resources to promote the anarchist post-surrealist vision recalls the co-opting of the American Country Club of Paris's magazine by the Villa Seurat to create *The Booster* and *Delta*. In the interstices of state power, they blossom by subversion and redirection rather than violent revolution.

2 Derek Stanford's description of this moment for Gascoyne is clear in its politics: "While the Left Wing poets of the 'thirties were trying to preach Marx in verse to people (but little interested in Marx and modern verse); while Laura Riding continued to publish her 'strictly private' hieroglyphic ruminations; while William Empson and Ronald Bottrall were explaining their psychoses in terms of erudition, David Gascoyne was writing in a style whose syntax dispensed with the need for analysis; a style, for the most part, as sensuous and immediate as that of the great English Romantics" (*Freedom* 41).

3 Though it is often not recognized, Wilde's "The Soul of Man under Socialism" draws significantly from the anarchist Peter Kropotkin. See Woodcock's *The Paradox of Oscar Wilde* for a full treatment.

4 Perlès also self-identifies as an anarchist in his own later works (Perlès, *Round Trip*, 115–19).

5 Porteus was also published by Durrell in Cairo during the Second World War in *Personal Landscape*.

6 Several other authors use the term in the same way, as an indication of a form of Personalism that they regard as contrary to the collectivist or nationalist orientation during the war (Raine 15; Fraser, "Apocalypse" 6).

7 Stanford notices, in 1947, the same tendency in Gascoyne's works "to journey from the thought of revolution to the goal of Christian quietism. In some ways the poetry of Gascoyne affords a symbiosis of these ideas; of revolution and mysticism. At least, his idea of revolution has little in common with the Marxist creed which the poets of Socialist Realism held" (*Freedom* 59).

8 Stanford notices Perlès's self-identification as well and links him with "these four libertarian *francs-tireurs*"—Miller, Wrey Gardiner, Perlès, and Paul Goodman—and contends "he professes anarchism" (Stanford, "Independent" 62, 64).

9   Durrell's tendency to be politically obscure has led to much critical
     disagreement. For instance, Durrell's "No Clue to Living" appeared in
     a politically charged series on the artist and politics edited by Stephen
     Spender, and he wrote it after his years in Yugoslavia and the cementing
     of his anti-Marxist beliefs. Yet, Durrell's rejection of "that ineradicable
     predisposition to legislate for the man next door" demonstrates his
     desire to emphasize the "limitations of Time, on whose slippery surface
     neither kings nor empires nor dictators could find more than a precar-
     ious and temporary purchase" ("No Clue" 23). Doomed kings, empires,
     and dictators make a striking combination for an author who was a royal
     subject, servant of empire, and recent resident in Péron's Argentina and
     Tito's Yugoslavia, especially if those like Richard Pine wish to regard
     him as a conservative, reactionary royalist. It is difficult to recognize
     the Durrell who wrote "No Clue to Living" as the same man. His *Revolt
     of Aphrodite* ends with the burning of all forms of contractual obligation,
     literally, which is presented as a positive event.
10   Apart from his covert intelligence work, Cooke later directed the Yugoslav
     section of the BBC and actively translated Czech and Slovak literature,
     even during the war while on intelligence-gathering operations in the
     Balkans.
11   He also recounts Durrell's arrival as a refugee in Egypt in *Autumn Gleanings*
     (78–79).
12   Howarth's "Deannarchist" is a joke on Deanna Durbin, the Canadian film
     and song performer. It is difficult to place Howarth's position because of
     the humour, and this is very likely the point. He first mocks the careful
     construction of a mass media object of desire, recognizing in her the
     constructed starlet designed to focus male desire into socially controlled
     paths. He then shifts to her own private self as distinct from this social
     construct, and ends by noting,

> The title to these notes accuses Deanna of anarchism. The term
> anarchist is often applied to the Marx Brothers, but when it is, that
> is the loose sense of the word. I give the word its strict political
> meaning when I apply it to Deanna Durbin. For she never intends
> to destroy, as the Marx Brothers do or did. She is a putter-right, but
> she puts the world right by methods individualist, instantaneous,
> domestic, in fact Utopian. (n. pag.)

     Howarth closes by casting this component of Deanna Durbin as the
     proper form of resistance against Hitler and his appeals to obedience
     and authority through the mass media.
13   Howarth is best known as a critic, but he also co-edited and

co-translated with Ibrahim Shukrallah, *Images from the Arab World* (London: Pilot Press, 1944).

14 James Brigham recounts from an October 18, 1974 interview with Waller, Sir John Waller recalls how he first published, and later first met Lawrence Durrell. During his final year at Oxford, Sir John edited Kingdom Come....

> At this time, Nicholas Moore was editing *Seven*, another review, and when it collapsed for want of funds, Waller received "stacks of stuff"...Among this material was Lawrence Durrell's "In Arcadia," which duly appeared in the 4th issue of *Kingdom Come*.

> When Waller enlisted after coming down from Oxford, he was posted first to the Middle East and Cairo. The only civilian he knew there was Herbert Howarth, who had a teaching post at Fuad University. During his first leave, Waller stayed with the Howarths and found that Lawrence and Nancy Durrell (and, I presume Penelope Berengaria) were also staying in the house. Waller happened to be carrying about the back issues of *Kingdom Come*. Coincidentally, Durrell had no copy of "In Arcadia," so he copied the poem from the 4th issue of the magazine. (n. pag.)

15 Fraser is now best known as a critic writing primers on Ezra Pound and Lawrence Durrell as well as several surveys of twentieth-century poetry for the university student population. He was a professor at the University of Leicester and a close friend to William Empson.

16 Stanford, writing of Durrell, gives very close attention to Durrell's discussion of his concept of the "Heraldic Universe," an idea first articulated when Durrell acted as an interlocutor in Henry Miller and Herbert Read's correspondence about Surrealism, communism, and anarchism. Stanford quotes directly from the version of Durrell's essay on the Heraldic Universe that appeared only in the journal *Personal Landscape* in Egypt and in no other publication (Stanford, *Freedom* 124–25). This demonstrates the New Apocalypse's access to these rare materials in a short print run produced in Cairo during the war.

17 Again, I must note that the dating of his letters and interactions with Miller and Durrell is often inaccurate.

18 Fraser would later write *Lawrence Durrell: A Study* in 1968.

19 Stanford notes Wrey Gardiner was "influenced by the writing of Henry Miller and passages from the works of each reveal...proximities of thought....If both these writers are seen to share a theory of the world and of writing as flux, their conception of the status of the individual is an even closer affair" (Stanford, *Freedom* 197–98). George Woodcock

unifies Gardiner, Miller, and Moore as well. Gardiner published Denise Levertov's first poetry, and the two remained friends and correspondents long after her marriage and move to America. Gardiner's anarchism also subtly recontextualizes Levertov's later political break with Robert Duncan.

20 Tony del Renzio's wife, Ithell Colquhoun, would also translate George Henein's anarchist poetry for Circle after it was forwarded from Egypt, almost certainly by Lawrence Durrell, who had dispatched Albert Cossery's novel Men God Forgot for Circle at the same time.

21 As noted, Derek Stanford had wartime access to the Egyptian periodical Personal Landscape, and Durrell was in correspondence with Alex Comfort.

22 A fragment of Comfort and Durrell's correspondences between London and Egypt survives in the Comfort Papers housed in University College London.

23 In November 1944, the police raided Freedom Press and the homes of several people involved with it. This led to the arrest of four editors of War Commentary. Woodcock was the secretary of the Freedom Defense Committee with Herbert Read as chairman. His choice of publisher was clearly political.

24 The critical literature debates the extent of Miller's contact with Goldman, ranging from Erica Jong's suggestion that Miller invented it (66) to Miller's statements in many works that he met and wrote to her. However, Orend is the first to clarify the matter by establishing the meeting, most likely in Los Angeles (53) and her extensive influence over Miller (54). Orend's work is also the most explicit exploration of Miller's readings in and influences from Goldman, Peter Kropotkin, and Max Stirner as well as his contact with the anarchist groups in Berkeley (66) and lifelong ties to anarchism.

25 Tolley's two books, 1975 and 2007, are almost identical, and a slight variant of the latter appeared in 2004. Tolley's views are useful as a history but are quite partisan in interpretation.

26 Although Liddell was both a poet and novelist, for which his Unreal City stands out the most, he is mainly remembered now for writing the first biography of the Alexandrian Greek poet C.P. Cavafy.

27 Spencer was co-editor of Oxford Poetry with Stephen Spender (1930) and John Goodland (1931; Goodland later became the driving force behind Nicholas Moore's journal Seven and published the final issue of Durrell and Miller's Delta). Spencer was involved in several translation projects of Greek poets after the Second World War, which involved Greek surrealist and post-surrealist influences.

28 Durrell describes these English and Greek writers in Cairo and

Alexandria in "Airgraph on Refugee Poets in Africa," *Poetry London* 2, no. 10 (1944): 212–15. Also see Theodore Stephanides, *Autumn Gleanings: Corfu Memoirs and Poems*, 78–85.

29 *Bolero* became *Kingdom Come*, and both student poetry magazines at Worcester College and Wadham College, Oxford, included a wide range of authors from Britain and Europe. It was finally taken over by Henry Treece under the banner of the New Apocalypse. Waller would continue publishing with Durrell after the war in *Greek Horizons*, Derek Patmore's single-issue journal produced in 1946, to which Waller contributed poetry and Durrell "The Telephone," which became "The Little Summer of Saint Demetrius" in *Reflections on a Marine Venus*. All three had known each other in Egypt, where Patmore was a war correspondent. Patmore's wife was close friends with Ezra Pound—she was "Vail de Lencour" in his pseudonym and wrote "Ezra Pound in England" (Patmore 69–81). Also see Derek Patmore's *Private History: An Autobiography*, which details his life in Egypt during the Second World War.

30 As Jacquemond notes, "The francophone writers were far from being exclusively francophone. Thus, the surrealist Art and Freedom group... organized by Georges Henein and the painter Ramses Yunan, produced its review *al-Tatawwur* (1940) in Arabic rather than French, published the first Arabic translations of Éluard and Rimbaud....Of them all, the career of Albert Cossery (born 1913) is the most specifically Egyptian....Charlot has suggested that what struck Miller and Camus the most in Cossery's work may have been...his use of an absurdist aesthetic and his anarchist or nihilist philosophy" (116). Andrea Flores's work is the most effective recognition of the Art and Freedom group's anarchism, though she has related it principally to the visual arts (Flores 98).

31 As Lee Bartlett describes it, "The most important literary journal to appear in the Bay Area during the period was *Circle*, edited by George Leite and Bern Porter, published in Berkeley....Its focus was literary, though it was both pacifist and anarchist as well; its credo 'When a technique becomes a school, death of creation is the result. Eclecticism is the only approach to Art in which there is no death. *Circle* is completely eclectic'" (98). Michael Davidson also identifies the journal, along with *Ark*, as anarchist (26, 39).

32 Anaïs Nin ensured that Lawrence R. Maxwell Books, of Christopher Street in New York, where she was once employed, also sold Circle Editions.

33 Miller was the European editor for the journal. Derek Savage, a major anarchist figure in London, replaced him in this role when he returned to America.

34 See G.S. Fraser's *A Stranger and Afraid: The Autobiography of an Intellectual*; Derek Stanford's *Inside the Forties: Literary Memoirs, 1937–1957*; and Joanna Hodgkin's recent memoir of her mother *Amateurs in Eden: The Story of a Bohemian Marriage*.

35 Roland Penrose also contributed an introduction to the manifesto with "From Egypt" (15) and a reproduction of Picasso's *Guernica* further cements the anarchist connections.

36 Even Herbert Read's *Surrealism*, which was drawn from the 1936 London International Surrealist Exhibition, expressly endorsed communism despite Read's own then as yet undeclared anarchism.

37 See Williams's "Base and Superstructure in Marxist Cultural Theory," 31–49.

38 The established view is that Henein's *Art and Liberté* group was Trotskyist (just as critics misrepresented Herbert Read), but their network and rejection of Marxism make the anarchist stream in their work clear. For the predominant view, as well as the contention "there is no such thing as a genuine 'Surrealist movement' in the Arab world," see Krainick (343). Flores powerfully and persuasively refutes this misprision (98).

39 Fraser would later write of Henderson warmly: "One fine poet of war, who survived, and who is unjustly neglected, is the Scottish poet Hamish Henderson. His *Elegies for the Dead of Cyrenaica* suffered, perhaps, like Keith Douglas's *Collected Poems*, from coming out a few years after the war was over. They are vigorous…, with a technique of juxtaposition and association, that owes something to Pound….A Scottish Nationalist, and a Marxist, a firm believer that the deep and healthy roots of all culture are in the common people" (Fraser, "English" 294).

40 Derek Stanford would later read these "Ideas about Poems" as an anarchist expression of ideals (*Freedom* 124–25).

41 I cannot, however, claim even to be the first critic to notice this component of the *Personal Landscape* poets, only the first to have worked extensively on the group who has noticed it, and the first to note its connections to other movements and figures. Although he does not develop the idea, Adam Piette has already noted in 2007,

> the *Personal Landscape* journal [was] founded by Lawrence Durrell, Robin Fedden, and Bernard Spencer. Their stance was apolitical, anarchist-individualist, standing back from the war effort to examine the deep histories of precisely "personal" experiences in wartime….The *Landscape* group were contemptuous of the war poet anthologies and looked askance at the whole idea of war poetry as a genre. Lawrence Durrell wrote to John Waller with typical disdain: "I think this war-poet stuff is bogus and vulgar really…the only kind of work

worth while is work that wears no uniform but its own merits."

> The contradiction between the radical democracy of the ABCA Army and the individualism of the Personal Landscapers went more than skin-deep, however. In the gulf between the war as private catastrophe and as collective experience lies the principal set of differences structuring the war poetry of the 1940s. (121–22)

Hartwig Isernhagen has noted similar concepts (76–77, 82), as does Jonathan Bolton ("*Personal*" 64) and Gordon Bowker when he comments on "a literary anarchist like Durrell" (230).

42 These brief aesthetic manifestos continue across the journal's print run as a feature for each issue.

43 This is contrary to Melba Cuddy-Keane's argument with Adam Hammond and Alexandra Peat for Miller's and Durrell's emphasis on an Eliotic impersonal Modernism in conflict with Anaïs Nin's personal emphasis (160–61). They are quite right to note this conflict in Nin's diaries, but Nin's need to gender the difference of her work from that of her milieu does not reflect a tie to Eliot's notion of impersonality. Both Durrell and Miller also resisted Eliot's strong influence—Durrell in particular who had Eliot as his editor at Faber & Faber (Gifford, "Real" 15–16)."

44 This chronology can be retraced in Treece and Read's unpublished correspondence held at the McPherson Library, University of Victoria.

45 "Comforter, Where, Where is Your Comforting?" and Smart's other poems from the same period are overlooked in her *Collected Poems*, introduction by David Gascoyne (London: Paladin, 1992).

46 This network of authors published extensively through James Meary Tambimuttu's *Poetry London* and Editions Poetry London. Rosemary Sullivan also speculates convincingly that Miller had helped Smart in her first attempts to publish *By Grand Central Station I Sat Down and Wept* through the experimental Colt Press in San Francisco (189).

47 The challenge of working across various autobiographies and biographies (distinct from yet exemplified in Miller) is that each work considers its own subject the centre of the various actions. For instance, in Miller's interactions with George Leite in California, Robert Ferguson casts Leite as merely a cult-fan of Miller's (284–85) who was only a taxi driver. Robert Duncan and Henry Treece do not figure in the biography at all, though they certainly figure in Miller's letters, in which Leite is certainly far more than a "fan." Likewise, Deidre Bair casts Anaïs Nin as the primary if not exclusive point of contact between Duncan and Miller (and by proxy the Villa Seurat as a whole) (257, 260, 264), but this is also troubled by Miller's own contact with James Cooney, who

first introduced Duncan to Miller's, Durrell's, and Nin's works (and who introduced Nin and Duncan to each other). Miller and Cooney were mutually advertising in each other's magazines (Phoenix and The Booster) from 1937 on, and Miller was already introducing Cooney to Durrell's The Black Book while it still only existed in typescript in 1937. Miller had sent Cooney an excerpt from The Black Book as well "Asylum in the Snow" by April 13, 1938, and in the same letter, he placed Cooney in direct contact with Durrell in Greece as well as John Goodland in England (co-editor of Seven with Nicholas Moore). Miller sent Cooney Dylan Thomas's works only six days later, and Thomas's letter of support for Cooney's advertisements for selling Tropic of Cancer followed on May 4, 1938. On May 11, 1938, Miller also reveals he had already sent poetry from David Gascoyne and his own "Open Letter to Surrealists Everywhere" (Miller, SUNY-B letters to Phoenix). When Duncan would begin publishing all three of them in 1940—Miller, Durrell, and Nin— Miller would receive his direct praise and Durrell his greatest support and promotion, while Nin received little of either. Jack Johnson's diaries of the same period show him and Duncan reading and dreaming about Durrell, meeting intimately with Nin, and say little of Miller. Only the amalgamation of all these materials can provide a coherent sense of the group dynamic.

48 This vision culminates forcefully in Ernst Kaiser's "The Development from Surrealism" in the ninth issue of Circle (74–81) and is itself a development from Kenneth Rexroth's understanding of the English post-Surrealists, evidenced in this blunt assessment: "British Surrealism [distinct from the post-surrealist New Apocalypse] never fell into the idle silliness of male hair dressers and parfumistes [sic], like its American counterpart, but it never took on. Since it had already died at its source—the best French Surrealists had long since become Stalinists— the British, closer to France than the Americas, realized that Breton's little remnant were as isolated, as furious, and as meaningless, as the political bedfellows, the Troptskyists" (Rexroth, Introduction xiv).

49 Miller reports other points of contact with Egypt through Durrell. To his friend Wallace Fowlie, the James B. Duke French Professor at Duke Univeristy, he writes, "Just received the first number of Valeurs from Alexandria….Camus, I understand from Durrell, has written something excellent" (Miller, Letters of Henry 93).

50 Duncan's communications and friendship with Russell also show the breadth of his contacts. When George Barker visited with Anaïs Nin, it was with Russell accompanying her, and behind both lie contacts

initiated through Duncan and Durrell, and in particular Durrell who had put Elizabeth Smart in contact with Barker and had made both aware of Nin. This meeting is recorded in Barker's letters to Smart, and Smart sided with Durrell in favour of Nin (Fraser, *Night* 180).

51 The poem is "Toward an African Elegy." In the end, the correspondence did not appear with the poem when it was published in *Circle*.

52 Richard Pine has advanced the argument that Durrell knew other writers but never associated with them (57–58). As the preceding pages have demonstrated, such an argument cannot hold. Pine's main contention is that through Durrell lived with Spencer, he was part of no group in Egypt around *Personal Landscape* (57), though he cites no evidence in this respect. This leads him to then suggest that the other poets were sent to Egypt in order to be safe from wartime dangers in London or elsewhere (58), which is absurd and based on an opinion piece in the *Times Literary Supplement* that gives no direct information on the authors involved, which leads him to finally quote G.S. Fraser as asserting that Durrell was part of no group when, in fact, Fraser states that Durrell didn't become engaged in the squabbles of London literary life. Durrell was, demonstrably, a part of several literary networks for which the evidence of his active engagement is extensive.

53 The same issue contains Durrell's *tour de force* poem sequence "The Sonnet of Hamlet" as well as new works from Gascoyne, Howarth, Tambimuttu, Dorian Cooke, Nicholas Moore, Dylan Thomas, and Anne Ridler. The same network of authors recur across the Apocalypse materials as well. Smart's work in *Delta* does not appear in her *The Collected Poems* in 1992.

54 Some have suggested that this placed the Anarchist Circle in conflict with the unnamed "Miller" group, but the great friendships between the two prove this wrong. It is more likely a product of contemporary reactionary attempts to sow dissent or more recent disagreements between the so-called "lifestyle" anarchists and "social" anarchists articulated by Murray Bookchin (12–13).

55 Robert Bertholf describes Duncan's "understanding of anarchist think-ing...[as] acquired in the 1940s" (2), but it was already established by the late 1930s and figures in his interpretations of Miller's works in his various comments on the pages of *Experimental Review* beginning in 1940. Lisa Jarnot notes the solidification of his ideas in 1941 (78).

56 Miller also recounts to Wallace Fowlie how Leite "is printing only good books. Began with the Egyptian's book (*Men God Forgot*), followed by Durrell's *Black Book*" (Miller, *Letters of Henry* 109) and that Leite "is always on the edge of bankruptcy. Durrell's book hasn't come out either, and I

remember reading proofs on it when the baby was being born" (Miller, *Letters of Henry* 122).

57 The poem is an intriguing combination of an imagist focus on objects, which typically does not accord well with most of the critical and anarchist views in this group of authors, as well as an echo of Durrell's focus on organic objects in the same manner. For both poets, these found objects relate to a missing subject that plays an interpretive or meaning-ascribing role, hence leaving the poet or reader to assemble meaning without an authoritative guide.

58 Miller is even Fowlie's point of contact to discover his works had been accepted by Stefan Schimanski for *Transformation* (Miller, *Letters* 41, 92).

59 The volume also opens with Durrell's "This Unimportant Morning" (1), demonstrating Moore's esteem of his work as well as the certainly intentional choice of the works juxtaposed against his in the collection.

60 Miller, after World War II, was also actively publishing through anarchist small presses such as the Delphic Press, which would have made his appeal to *Circle* and Rexroth clear.

61 The character Marlowe writes a book on the subject, and across the novel as a whole Durrell repeatedly alludes to Miguel de Molinos, the author of *Guida Spirituale* and chief reviver of quietism. For both Durrell and Miller, quietism is a continual reference and source for allusion at this time.

62 Ch'ien went on to translate Henrik Ibsen into Mandarin Chinese as well as James Joyce's *Ulysses*, which was only released in 1994.

3 Authority's Apocalypse

1 For instance, see Richard Pine's *Lawrence Durrell: The Mindscape* (393) or Herbrechter's discussions of reactionary politics throughout *Lawrence Durrell, Postmodernism and the Ethics of Alterity* (263). The former appears as a form of personal identification with the subject matter and the latter a result of a notion of the postmodern influenced by Jameson.

2 Treece also expresses many of these opinions in 1943 through "Considerations on Revolt" in Alex Comfort's anthology *New Road 1943* through Wrey Gardiner's Grey Walls Press (140–48). The text was published adjacent to Orwell's "Looking Back on the Spanish War."

3 Alternatively, Christian and Muslim forms of anarchism subsume all authority under the authority of God. This is an important distinction when approaching Leo Tolstoy or Hakim Bay, as well as the New Apocalypse poet Derek Savage.

4 Durrell also uses "Ego and Id," "Ego," and "Ego and Id" as titles to each of the "books" or sections of *The Black Book*, a work much admired by Duncan at this time, in which there is no superego included. The superego, when mentioned, is perverse and resisted.

5 Note as well J.F. Hendry's clearly Lawrentian use of "blood" in his prose writings about the critical vision of the New Apocalypse: "Freedom is an illusion, yes; but not 'the bourgeois' illusion. The bourgeois throughout Europe surrendered it because they did not believe in ideals or illusions. They did not know they affected the blood" (Hendry, "Art" 146).

6 For an alternative view, see Gay Louise Balliet's *Henry Miller and Surrealist Metaphor: "Riding the Ovarian Trolley"* (58–64).

4 Rereading and Recasting

1 In *Tropic of Cancer*, the strongest image of this machine appears in the scene in which Miller, Van Norden, and an unnamed prostitute futilely attempt copulation: "a machine whose cogs have slipped" (Miller, *Tropic of Cancer* 144).

2 Even Andrew Barrow, who is very sympathetic to O'Connor, notes that he would "clumsily review" the book, perhaps because he had only read it in typescript more than a year before (n. pag.).

3 Barrow reports that the surrealist poet Phillip O'Connor read the novel in the same typescript while visiting Gascoyne in Paris, apparently in the midst of a mild spree (n. pag.).

4 Thomas is also famously mercurial, often praising and damning the same figure at the same time in letters to different people. This occurs in his various assessments of Miller, Durrell, Treece, Read, and Eliot, among others. In this instance, his letters show he was in the midst of reading *The Black Book* in its complete form for the first time in February of 1939 but would write only a handful of weeks later to John Davenport that the book was dated since its 1938 release though highly impressive on a first reading (Thomas, *Collected Letters* 355, 378).

5 This can only be seen in the first edition and the contemporary excerpts. The publications from 1959 onward do not bear these section titles.

6 Joanna Hodgkin poignantly discusses Nancy Durrell's first abortion when she and her husband lived on Corfu:

> the staff of the nursing home had wanted him to examine the fetus.... He could have kicked it "for all the jitters it gave me."...Three years later, in "A Small Scripture," a poem dedicated to Nancy, he wrote:
> *A bleeding egg was the pain of testament,*

Murder of self within murder to reach the Self... (Hodgkin 177–78)
The yolk and egg of the self as both progeny and one's own being is
indeed sensitive.

7   Durrell's use of Groddeck is well known (Sobhy 26–39) as is his use of
Gnosticism (Carley 284–304), and his creative reconstruction of both as
fodder for his fictional fabulations is also established (Gifford, "Noses"
2–4; Gifford and Osadetz 1–8; Gifford and Stevens 173–93).

8   Durrell also has an indirect connection to Crowley at this time. His good
friend John Gawsworth was editing a collection on supernatural fiction,
for which he included Durrell's surrealist short story "The Cherries,"
while at the same time working with Frederick Carter of Cecil Court,
who was in close contact with Crowley. Durrell went on to title his first
post-World War II novel *Cefalû* before retitling it *The Dark Labyrinth*. The
location Cefalu is certainly not the same as the novel, but Crowley's commune in Cefalu would go a long way to reconceiving the novel's quasi-
mystical transformations. Moreover, Miller may have met Crowley in
1933 through Conrad Moricand, who was a mutual friend of Durrell and
Miller, though it is ambiguous and may simply have been his interest in
Crowley. Durrell's letters to Miller link Graham Howe, whom they both
wrote about, to kindred concepts as Crowley (*Durrell–Miller* 115). Durrell's
personal library, held by SIU Carbondale, includes Crowley's translation
of Eliphas Levi's *The Key of the Mysteries* in a 1959 printing, though much of
Durrell's pre-1939 library was lost.

9   I should stress that Durrell picked up and discarded many such ideas
routinely, as did Miller. The point is not that they were (or were not)
members of Crowley's occult Thelemic Magical Fraternity but rather the
creative appeal of such notions for fiction.

10 Some critics, such as Richard Pine (*Mindscape* 393–94) have made much
of Durrell's comments on being a royalist, but this only occurs by virtue
of ignoring their context and irony.

11 Fifteen of Crowley's works are held in Duncan's library at SUNY Buffalo.
He also discusses Crowley in *The H.D. Book* (142–43).

12 The same wry critique appears in his 1937 contemporaneous novel,
published under the pseudonym Charles Norden, *Panic Spring*: "'Is poetry
still Communism?' asked Walsh.... 'You see,' said Marlowe, with a hint
of apology in his tones, 'everything is built on a foundation of nihilism
and nimiety. Hence the whine of the young. Communism, like a gigantic
Procrustes, is just beginning to take a hand. America, with her cinema,
her hot jazz and her dreadful idiot-mind has virtually conquered the
world...Oh, it's fantastic'" (Durrell, *Panic* 30).

13 This rejection of the city recurs across Durrell's works, beginning in 1937 with *Panic Spring*, continuing through *The Alexandria Quartet*, and finally in the destructive corpse of the city in *The Avignon Quintet*, which is also parallel to the New Apocalypse.

14 The nocturnally flatulent Cicely Bumtrinket from Thomas Dekker's 1599 comic play *The Shoemaker's Holiday* is alluded to in Durrell's *Panic Spring* (17); Thomas Lodge's 1595 satirical prose work *Momus* appears in his "Hamlet, Prince of China" (43); and the Welsh writer James Howell's 1642 book *Instructions for Forrainne Travell* is alluded to repeatedly in Durrell's "Prospero's Isle: To Caliban" (130–39).

15 Anne Ridler also identifies the political component of Durrell's discussion of Hamlet by noting, in her discussion of her own politics in the war, "The Lustre Jug," how "Of course, we knew that the bloodshed must come. As Lawrence Durrell put it to me in a letter, 'Hamlet prowls about the Maginot Line unable to stab the kneeling King; but the stage is going to be littered with corpses before the end'" (200).

16 As Podnieks notes, across 1939 "Smart is still corresponding with Durrell…[and] in the diary she kept for a brief period from April to June 1940…Smart places Durrell's name and address first in an unalphabetized address list" ("'OO—I have'" 51). The address was Durrell's then current home in Athens after departing from Corfu prior to his move to Kalamata later that year, thence fleeing to Egypt. She records reading Miller's *Tropic of Cancer* and Nin's *Winter of Artifice* (all three, including *The Black Book*, from the Obelisk Press) at around the same time. Podnieks's claim that Smart's novel and diaries, *Necessary Secrets*, owe a debt to Durrell and Nin is indisputable, and in fact is more significant and extensive that Podnieks details since she does not consider the actual texts in relation to each other, only critical responses.

17 Smart's first person is remarkably flexible here, refusing the stabilizing organization and stabilization of the Ego: "So I say now, for the record of my own self, and to remember when I may be other than I am now:… Remember also that I said, Though this is all there is, though it is the one and vulnerable, mortal to all attack, a poverty-stricken word against the highly-financed world, yet it is not meager, it is enough" (Smart, *By Grand* 65).

18 Setting Smart's work, in this context, next to Auden's *The Age of Anxiety* marks their common concerns yet antithetical perspectives and practices.

19 For instance, Lisa Jarnot mentions the poem in relation to a list of contents (62, 71), and it is otherwise almost entirely overlooked in the criticism. Even in the admirable collection by Stephen Collis and Graham

Lyons, *Reading Duncan Reading*, which considers Duncan's work in relation to his readings of his precursors and contemporaries, no mention appears of Durrell, Miller, or any of the authors considered in this study.

20 Weaver also states, Duncan's "personal support of anarchism is generally well known by his readers...[as] far back as 1945," though this date may be safely set back by at least five years (74).

21 For instance, Durrell denies the stabilizing force of naming: "When you are afraid of something, or want to hate it, you give it a name out of the alphabet. Then you can let it into the house and it will not hurt you. It is covered in a name, and you do not see it properly, you only see the little black letters" ("Asylum" 261). In the same sense that resists the imposed coherence of the superego and instrumental reason, and that emphasizes poetic process, the narrator calls the reader with "Come. Enter into the creative activity in which you do not need your understandings. Do not mistake truth for the possessive process any longer—ratiocination, knowledge" ("Zero" 252).

22 Duncan notes that his teacher "had, after all, to project an authority over us. She was paid to carry out the intentions of an education system that was devoted not to the discovery of self but to self-improvement" (H.D. 39).

Works Cited

Aldington, Richard, and Lawrence Durrell. *Literary Lifelines: The Richard Aldington–Lawrence Durrell Correspondence*. Eds. Ian S. MacNiven and Harry T. Moore. New York: Viking Press, 1981. Print.

Allen, Walter. *Tradition and Dream: The English and American Novel from the Twenties to Our Time*. London: Phoenix House, 1964. Print.

Antliff, Allan. *Anarchist Modernism: Art, Politics, and the First American Avant-Garde*. Chicago: Chicago UP, 2001. Print.

———. *Anarchy and Art: From the Paris Commune to the Fall of the Berlin Wall*. Vancouver: Arsenal Pulp Press, 1998. Print.

———. "Anarchy, Power, and Poststructuralism." *SubStance* 36.2 (2007): 56–66. Print.

———. "Donald Judd's 'First Element': An Anarchist Genealogy." *The Writings of Donald Judd*. Marfa, TX: Chinati Foundation, 2009: 173–92. Print.

———. "Open Form and the Abstract Imperative: Herbert Read and Contemporary Anarchist Art." *Anarchist Studies* 16.1 (2008): 6–20. Print.

Bair, Deirdre. *Anaïs Nin: A Biography*. London: Bloomsbury Publishing, 1995. Print.

Balliet, Gay Louise. *Henry Miller and Surrealist Metaphor: "Riding the Ovarian Trolley."* New York: Peter Lang, 1996. Print.

Barker, George. *Calamiterror*. London: Faber & Faber, 1947. Print.

———. "Elegy on Spain." *Collected Poems 1930–1955*. New York: Criterion Books, 1957. 98–103. Print.

Barrow, Andrew. *Quentin and Philip: A Double Portrait*. London: Pan Macmillan, 2011. Web.

Bartlett, Lee. *William Everson: The Life of Brother Antonius*. New York: New Directions, 1988. Print.

Bergonzi, Bernard. *Wartime and Aftermath: English Literature and its Background 1939–1960*. Oxford: Oxford UP, 1993. Print.

Bertholf, Robert J. "Decision at the Apogee: Robert Duncan's Anarchist Critique of Denise Levertov." *Robert Duncan and Denise Levertov: The Poetry of Politics, the Politics of Poetry*. Eds. Albert Gelpi and Robert J. Bertholf. Stanford: Stanford UP, 2006. 1–17. Print.

Bloshteyn, Maria R. *The Making of a Counter-Culture Icon: Henry Miller's Dostoevsky*. Toronto: U of Toronto P, 2007. Print.

Bolton, Jonathan. "*Personal Landscape* and the Poetry of the 1940s." *Deus Loci: The Lawrence Durrell Journal* NS 4 (1995–1996): 62–72. Print.

———. *Personal Landscapes: British Poets in Egypt during the Second World War*. New York: St. Martin's Press, 1997. Print.

Bookchin, Murray. *Social Anarchism or Lifestyle Anarchism: An Unbridgeable Chasm*. Edinburgh: AK Press, 1995. Print.

Bowen, Roger. *Many Histories Deep: The Personal Landscape Poets in Egypt*. Madison, NJ: Fairleigh Dickinson UP, 1995. Print.

Bowker, Gordon. *Through the Dark Labyrinth: A Biography of Lawrence Durrell*. New York: St. Martin's Press, 1997. Print.

Brady, Mildred Edie. "The New Cult of Sex and Anarchy." *Harper's Magazine* 194 (April 1947): 312–22. Print.

Brigham, James. Notebook 3.1. Brigham Fonds. McPherson Library, University of Victoria. 1974. N. pag. MS.

Brock, Peter. *Against the Draft: Essays on Conscientious Objection from the Radical Reformation to the Second World War*. Toronto: U of Toronto P, 2006. Print.

Brown, Sharon Lee. "*The Black Book*: The Search for Method." *Modern Fiction Studies* 13.3 (1967): 319–28. Print.

Bush, Clive. *The Century's Midnight: Dissenting European and American Writers of the Second World War*. New York: Peter Lang, 2009. Print.

Call, Lewis. *Postmodern Anarchism*. Lexington: Lexington Books, 2002. Print.

———. "Postmodern Anarchism in the Novels of Ursula K. Le Guin." *SubStance* 36.2 (2007): 87–105. Print.

Carley, James P. "Lawrence Durrell's Avignon Quincunx and Gnostic Heresy." *Deus Loci: The Lawrence Durrell Quarterly* 5.1 (1981): 284–304. Print.

Carlisle, Olga Andreyev. *Voices in the Snow: Encounters with Russian Writers*. New York: Random House, 1962. Print.

Caudwell, Christopher. *Illusion and Reality: A Study of the Sources of Poetry*. Oxford: Bodley Head, 1938. Print.

———. *Studies in a Dying Culture*. London: Bodley Head, 1938. Westport, CT: Greenwood Press, 1973. Print.

"A Change of Landscape." *Personal Landscape* 2.4 (1945): 2. Print.

Charques, R.D. "Apocalyptics and Others: Writes With Manifestoes." *Times Literary Supplement* 7 August 1943: 381. Print.

Childs, Peter. *The Twentieth Century in Poetry: A Critical Survey*. London: Routledge, 1999. Print.

Chomsky, Noam. "Notes on Anarchism." *Chomsky on Anarchism*. Ed. Barry Pateman. Oakland, CA: AK Press, 2005. 118–32. Print.

Cianci, Giovanni, and Jason Harding. Introduction. *T.S. Eliot and the Concept of Tradition*. Eds. Giovanni Cianci and Jason Harding. Cambridge: Cambridge UP, 2007. 1–9. Print.

Cohn, Jesse. *Anarchism and the Crisis of Representation: Hermeneutics, Aesthetics, Politics*. Selinsgrove, PA: Susquehanna UP, 2006. Print.

———. "Anarchism, Representation, and Culture." *Culture + the State: Alternative Interventions*. Vol. 4. Eds. James Gifford and Gabrielle Zezulka-Mailloux. Edmonton, AB: CRC Humanities Studio, 2003. 54–63. Print.

———. "What is Anarchist Literary Theory?" *Anarchist Studies* 15.2 (2007): 115–31. Print.

———. "What is Postanarchism Post?" *Postmodern Culture* 13.1 (2002): n. pag. Web.

Collis, Stephen, and Graham Lyons eds. *Reading Duncan Reading: Robert Duncan and the Poetics of Derivation*. Iowa City: U of Iowa P, 2012. Print.

Comfort, Alex. "Art and Social Responsibility." *NOW* NS 2 (1943): 39–51. Print.

———. "Art [II] and Social Responsibility." *Against Power and Death*. Ed. David Goodway. London: Freedom Press, 1994. 52–78. Print.

———. "October, 1944." *NOW* NS 4 (1944): 44–48. Print.

Comfort, Alex, and John Bayliss. *New Road 1943: New Directions in European Art and Letters*. London: Grey Walls Press, 1943. Print.

Cossery, Albert. *The House of Certain Death*. Trans. Erik de Mauny. London: Hutchinson International, 1947. New York: New Directions, 1949. Print.

———. "The Human Sound of the Street." *Orientations* (September 1943): 6–10. Print.

———. Letter to Lawrence Durrell. Nanterre: Université Paris Ouest La Defense. N.d. MS.

———. *Men God Forgot*. Trans. Harold Edwards. Berkeley: Circle Editions, 1946. Intro. Henry Miller. San Francisco: City Lights Books, 1963. Print.

———. "The Postman Gets His Own Back." *Middle East Anthology*. Eds. John Waller and Erik de Mauny. London: Lindsay Drummond, 1946. 58–73. Print.

Cromer, John. "Poetry To-day." *Oasis: The Middle East Anthology of Poetry from the Forces*. Eds. Almendra [Denis Saunders], Victor Selwyn, and David Burk. Cairo: Salamander Productions, 1943. Print.

Cuddy-Keane, Melba, Adam Hammond, and Alexandra Peat. *Modernism: Keywords*. Oxford: John Wiley & Sons, 2014. Print.

Cunningham, Valentine. *British Writers of the Thirties*. Oxford: Oxford UP, 1988. Print.

Davidson, Michael. *The San Francisco Renaissance: Poetics and Community at Mid-Century*. New York: Cambridge UP, 1989. Print.

Deleuze, Gilles, and Félix Guattari. *Anti-Oedipus: Capitalism and Schizophrenia*. Minneapolis: U of Minnesota P, 1983. Print.

Dewey, Anne. "Poetic Authority and the Public Sphere of Politics in the Activist 1960s: The Duncan-Levertov Debate." *Robert Duncan and Denise Levertov: The Poetry of Politics, The Politics of Poetry*. Eds. Albert Gelpi and Robert Bertholf. Palo Alto: Stanford UP, 2006. 109–25. Print.

Dirlik, Arif. *Anarchism in the Chinese Revolution*. Berkeley: U of California P, 1991. Print.

———. "Vision and Revolution: Anarchism in Chinese Revolutionary Thought on the Eve of the 1911 Revolution." *Modern China* 12.2 (1986): 123–65. Print.

Douglas, Keith. "On A Return From Egypt." *Collected Poems*. Eds. John Waller, G.S. Fraser, and J.C. Hall. New York: Chilmark Press, 1966. 130. Print.

Duncan, Robert. "An Ark for Lawrence Durrell." *Experimental Review* 2 (1941): n. pag. *The Years as Catches*. Berkeley: Oyez, 1966. 11. Print.

———. *The H.D. Book*. Berkeley: U of California P, 2011. Print.

———. "Homosexual in Society." *A Selected Prose*. New York: New Directions, 1995. 38–50. Print.

———. Introduction. *The Years as Catches*. Berkeley: Oyez, 1966. i–xi. Print.

———. Letter to Sanders Russell, undated. Robert Duncan Fonds. SUNY Buffalo. Buffalo, NY. N. pag. MS.

———. Letter to John Crowe Ransom, undated. Robert Duncan Papers. Washington University Libraries. St. Louis, MO. N. pag. TS.

———. "Toward an African Elegy." *Circle* 10 (1948): 94–96. Print.

———. *The Truth and Life of Myth: An Essay in Essential Autobiography*. Fremont, MI: Sumac Press, 1968. Print.

———. "The Years as Catches." *Circle* 7–8 (1946): 1–4. Print.

Duncan, Robert, and Denise Levertoff. *The Letters of Robert Duncan and Denise Levertoff*. Eds. Robert J. Bertholf and Albert Gelpi. Stanford: Stanford UP, 2004. Print.

Duncan, Robert, and H.D. *A Great Admiration: H.D./Robert Duncan Correspondence*. Ed. Robert J. Bertholf. Berkeley: Lapis Press, 1991. Print.

Durrell, Lawrence. *The Alexandria Quartet*. London: Faber & Faber, 1962. Print.

———. "Asylum in the Snow." *Seven* 3 (1938): 43–84. *Spirit of Place: Letters and Essays on Travel*. Ed. Alan G. Thomas. London: Faber & Faber, 1969. 258–72. Print.

————. *Balthazar*. London: Faber & Faber, 1958. Print.

————. "Bernard Spencer." *The London Magazine* 3.10 (1964): 42–47. Print.

————. *The Black Book*. 1938. Faber & Faber, 1973. Print.

————. "The Black Book (Coda to Nancy)." *The Booster* 2.8 (October 1937): 19–23. Print.

————. "Carol on Corfu." *Seven* 3 (1938): 2. *Collected Poems: 1931–74*. Ed. James A. Brigham. London: Faber & Faber, 1980. 56–57. Print.

————. "Coptic Poem." *New Poetry*. Ed. Nicholas Moore. London: Fortune Press, 1945. 7. Print.

————. "Editor's Note." *Personal Landscape* 1.2 (1942): 7. Print.

————. "Elegy on the Closing of the French Brothels." *NOW* 8 (1947): 30–32. Print.

————. "From the Elephant's Back," *Poetry London-New York* 2 (1982): 1–9. Print.

————. "Hamlet, Prince of China." *Delta* 2.3 (1938): 38–45. Print.

————. "Ideas about Poems [I]." *Personal Landscape* 1.1 (1942): 3. Print.

————. "Ideas about Poems [II]." *Personal Landscape* 1.2 (1942): 2. Print.

————. *Justine*. 1957. London: Faber & Faber, 2000. Print.

————. *Key to Modern Poetry*. London: Peter Nevill, 1952. Print.

————. "The Kneller Tape." *The World of Lawrence Durrell*. Ed. Harry T. Moore. Carbondale: Southern Illinois UP, 1962. ix–xix. "Persuading the World to Tap the Source of Laughter in Itself." *Lawrence Durrell: Conversations*. Ed. Earl Ingersoll. Madison, NJ: Fairleigh Dickinson UP, 1998. 70–75. Print.

————. [Charles Norden]. "Landmark Gone." *Orientations* (March 1942): 29–31. *Middle East Anthology of Prose and Verse*. Eds. John Waller and Erik de Mauny. London: Lindsay Drummond, 1946. 19–21. Print.

————. "A Letter From The Land of the Gods." *The Right Review* 9 (1939): n. pag. Print.

————. *Monsieur, or The Prince of Darkness*. London: Faber & Faber, 1974. Print.

————. "No Clue to Living." *The Writer's Dilemma: Essays First Published in The Times Literary Supplement Under the Heading 'Limits of Control.'* Ed. Stephen Spender. London: Oxford UP, 1961. 17–24. Print.

————. "The Other Eliot." *The Atlantic Monthly* 215.5 (May 1965): 60–64. Print.

————. *Panic Spring: A Romance*. Ed. James Gifford. London: Faber & Faber, 1937. Victoria, BC: ELS Editions, 2008. Print.

————. *Pied Piper of Lovers*. Ed. James Gifford. London: Cassells, 1935. Victoria, BC: ELS Editions, 2008. Print.

————. "The Prince and Hamlet: A Diagnosis." *The New English Weekly* 10.14 (1937): 271–73. Print.

————. "Prospero's Isle ('to Caliban')." *T'ien Hsia Monthly* 9.2 (1939): 129–39. Print.

———. "Shades of Dylan Thomas." *Encounter* 9.6 (1957): 56–59. Print.

———. *Spirit of Place: Letters and Essays on Travel.* Ed. Alan G. Thomas. London: Faber & Faber, 1969. Print.

———. "Studies in Genius VIII—Henry Miller." *Horizon* (20 July 1949): 45–61. Print.

———. "This Unimportant Morning." *New Poetry.* Ed. Nicholas Moore. London: Fortune Press, 1945. 1. Print.

———. "To Argos." *Personal Landscape* 1.1 (1942): 11. Print.

Durrell, Lawrence, and Henry Miller. *The Durrell–Miller Letters, 1935–80.* Ed. Ian MacNiven. London: Faber & Faber, 1985. Print.

Ellis, R.J. "'They…took their time over the coming': The Postwar British/ Beat, 1957–1965." *The Transnational Beat Generation.* Eds. Nancy M. Grace and Jennie Skerl. New York: Palgrave Macmillan, 2012. 145–63. Print.

Fausset, Hugh I'Anson. "The 'New Apocalypse': Image and Myth." *Times Literary Supplement* 26 July 1941: 361. Print.

———. "Where Poetry Stands: Disharmony of Our Time." *Times Literary Supplement* 6 September 1941: 450. Print.

Fedden, Robin. "Camp on the Red Sea." *Personal Landscape* 1.1 (1942): 9. Print.

———. "Personal Landscape." *Personal Landscape* 1.1 (1942): 8. Print.

Ferguson, Robert. *Henry Miller: A Life.* New York: W.W. Norton & Co., 1991. Print.

Ferris, Paul. *Dylan Thomas: The Biography.* 1977. 2nd ed. Washington: Counterpoint, 2000. Print.

Fitting, Peter. "Readers and Responsibility: A Reply to Ken Roemer." *Utopian Studies* 2.1/2 (1991): 24–29. Print.

Fitzgibbon, Constantine. *The Life of Dylan Thomas.* London: J.M. Dent, 1965. Print.

Fitzgibbon, Constantine, ed. *Selected Letters of Dylan Thomas.* London: J.M. Dent, 1967. Print.

Flores, Andrea. "The Myth of the False: Ramses Younan's Post-Structuralism *avant la lettre.*" *The Arab Studies Journal* 8/9.2/1 (Fall 2000/Spring 2001): 97–110. Print.

Ford, Mark. "The Analyst is Always Right." *London Review of Books* 33.22 (17 November 2011): 23–25. Print.

Fowlie, Wallace. Introduction. *Letters of Henry Miller and Wallace Fowlie 1943–72.* Intro. Wallace Fowlie. New York: Grove Press, 1975. 3–18. Print.

Foucault, Michel. "The Subject and Power." *Critical Inquiry* 8 (1982): 777–95. Print.

Fraser, G.S. "Apocalypse in Poetry." *The White Horseman.* London: Routledge, 1941. 3–31. Print.

———. "English Poetry 1930–1960." The Twentieth Century. Ed. Bernard
Bergonzi. History of Literature in the English Language. Vol. 7. London: Barrie &
Jenkins Ltd., 1970. 277–309. Print.

———. "Inside Story." Transformation. Eds. Henry Treece and Stefan
Schimanski. London: Victor Gollancz, 1944. 190–99. Print.

———. Lawrence Durrell: A Study. 1968. London: Faber & Faber, 1973. Print.

———. "A Letter to Henry Treece." Transformation Four. Eds. Stefan Schimanski
and Henry Treece. London: Lindsay Drummond, 1945. 164–70. Print.

———. The Modern Writer and His World. London: Andre Deutsch, 1964. London:
Penguin, 1970. Print.

———. "Recent Verse: London and Cairo." Poetry London 2.10 (1944): 215–19.
Print.

———. A Stranger and Afraid: Autobiography of an Intellectual. Manchester: Carcanet
New Press, 1983. Print.

Fraser, Robert. The Chameleon Poet: A Life of George Barker. London: Random House,
2002. Print.

———. Night Thoughts: The Surreal Life of the Poet David Gascoyne. Oxford: Oxford UP,
2012. Print.

Fryer, Jonathan. Dylan: The Nine Lives of Dylan Thomas. London: Kyle Cathie, 1993.
Print.

Furth, Charlotte. "Intellectual Change: From the Reform movement to the
May Fourth Movement, 1895–1920." An Intellectual History of Modern China. Eds.
Merle Goldman and Leo Ou-Fan Lee. Cambridge: Cambridge UP, 2002.
13–96. Print.

Gardiner, Wrey. "Editorial." Poetry Quarterly 8.4 (1946–47): 195–96. Print.

———. "Editorial." Poetry Quarterly 8.1 (1946): 3. Print.

Gascoyne, David. "Farewell Chorus." Poetry of the Thirties. Ed. Robin Skelton.
1964. Harmondsworth: Penguin, 1968. 283–87. Print.

———. "Fellow Bondsmen." Deus Loci: The Lawrence Durrell Journal NS 1 (1992):
4–7. Print.

———. "Henry Miller." Selected Prose: 1934–1996. Ed. Roger Scott. London:
Enitharmon Press, 1998. 287–89. Print.

———. Paris Journal 1937–1939. Pref. Lawrence Durrell. London: Enitharmon
Press, 1978. Print.

———. A Short Survey of Surrealism. London: Routledge, 1935. Print.

———. "Snow in Europe." Poems 1937–1942. London: Poetry London Editions,
1943. 49. Print.

———. "The Uncertain Battle." Poems of This War by Younger Poets. Eds. Patricia
Ledward and Colin Strang. Intro. Edmund Blunden. Cambridge:
Cambridge UP, 1942. 7. Print.

Gere, Cathy. *Knossos and the Prophets of Modernism.* Chicago: U of Chicago P, 2009. Print.

Gibbons, Thomas. "'Allotropic States' and 'Fiddle-bow': D.H. Lawrence's Occult Sources." *Notes and Queries* 35.3 (1988): 338–41. Print.

Gifford, James. "Anarchist Transformations of English Surrealism: The Villa Seurat Network." *JML: Journal of Modern Literature* 33.4 (Summer 2010): 57–71. Print.

———. "'Convinced of the dead certainty of death': Henry Miller's *Tropic of Capricorn* and the Nexus of Fear and Violence." *Nexus: The International Henry Miller Journal* 2 (2004): 106–18. Print.

———. "Durrell's *Delta* and Dylan Thomas' 'Prologue to an Adventure.'" *In-between: Studies in Literary Criticism* 13.1 (2004): 19–23. Print.

———. "Durrell's *Revolt of Aphrodite*: Nietzschean Influences." *Mosaic: A Journal For the Interdisciplinary Study of Literature* 36.2 (2003): 111–27. Print.

———. "Noses in *The Alexandria Quartet.*" *Notes on Contemporary Literature* 34.1 (2004): 2–4. Print.

———. Preface. *Panic Spring: A Romance.* Lawrence Durrell. Victoria, BC: ELS Editions, 2008. vii–xiv. Print.

———. "Real and Unreal Cities: The Modernist Origins of Durrell's Alexandria." *Durrell and the City: Reconstructing the Urban Landscape.* Ed. Donald P. Kaczvinsky. Madison, NJ: Fairleigh Dickinson UP, 2011. 13–29. Print.

———. "Self-Authenticity as Social Resistance: Reading Empiric Approaches to Social Identity, Self-Esteem, and Fear in Durrell's *Monsieur.*" *Culture + the State: Alternative Interventions.* Vol. 4. Eds. James Gifford and Gabrielle Zezulka-Mailloux. Edmonton, AB: CRC Humanities Studio, 2004. 212–24. Print.

———. "Surrealism's Anglo-American Afterlife: The Herbert Read and Henry Miller Network." *Nexus: The International Henry Miller Journal* 5 (2008): 36–64. Print.

Gifford, James, and Michael Stevens. "A Variant of Lawrence Durrell's *Livia; or, Buried Alive* and the Composition of *Monsieur; or, the Prince of Darkness.*" *Lawrence Durrell at the Crossroads of Arts and Sciences.* Eds. Corinne Alexandre-Garner, Isabelle Keller-Privat, and Murielle Philippe. Paris: Presses Universitaires de Paris Ouest, 2010. 173–93. Print.

Gifford, James, and Stephen Osadetz. "Gnosticism in Lawrence Durrell's *Monsieur*: New Textual Evidence for Source Materials." *Agora: An Online Graduate Journal* 3.1 (2004): 1–8. Web.

Goldman, Jane. *Modernism, 1910–1945: Image to Apocalypse.* London: Palgrave Macmillan, 2004. Print.

Marxism
    in *The Black Book*, 221–22
    criticism of in *New Roads*, 88
    Durrell's attitude towards, 164,
        165–66
    Egyptian Surrealists' critique of,
        100–02
    Gascoyne's views of, 20–21
    and individuality, 13–14
    Miller's rejection of, 11
    and misrepresentation of
        anarchism, 154–57
    Orwell and, 27
    and social being, 241n1
Mass-Observation, 9, 170
Mellor, Anthony, 19–24, 42, 45–46,
    244n17
Men God Forgot (Cossery), 98, 99–100,
    103, 120, 136
Miller, David, 150–51
Miller, Henry
    anarchistic view of, xiii, xv,
        10–11, 24–25, 31–32, 33, 34,
        35, 62–63, 91, 113, 208–10,
        245n20
    anti-authoritarian view of, 76,
        84–85, 167
    and Berdyaev, 142
    and *The Black Book*, 127, 128, 210,
        211, 213, 214, 217, 252n47
    and *Black Spring*, 9, 12, 33
    in California, 118, 128, 131, 139
    and *Circle*, 119–20, 127, 136
    and *The Colossus of Maroussi*, 206–10
    criticism of, 24–25, 27, 30, 34,
        41–42
    and Crowley, 257n8
    and desublimation of desire, 184
    friendship with Durrell, 66, 67,
        71, 79, 80–81, 113, 128, 138

    and Goldman, 62, 91, 249n24
    and *Hamlet*, 105, 110, 135, 200
    and Heraldic Universe, 105, 165
    impact of Lawrence on, 186,
        187–88
    and Leite, 127, 252n47, 254n56
    importance of death in work of,
        195–98
    influence of, 84–85, 140–43
    and London International
        Surrealist Exhibition, xii, xv,
        10–11, 77, 84, 105, 164
    Moore's book on, 75–76, 93,
        187
    moves during WWII, 71, 96
    and *Murder the Murderer*, 113–14,
        119, 135
    Orwell's view of, 31–36, 68, 141
    politics of, 11, 14, 31–36, 68
    praise for Cossery, 100, 120
    promoting Patchen, 129, 131
    published by journals, 31, 70, 73,
        75, 79, 85, 89, 90–91, 92, 93,
        127, 129, 135
    published by small presses,
        255n60
    and quietism, 32, 34, 68, 141, 179,
        209–10
    and Read, 13–14, 15, 77, 164
    rereading of *The Colossus of Maroussi*,
        206–10
    as sexual liberator, 91
    and *Sexus*, 10–11
    and Smart, 118, 126, 131, 224, 226,
        252n46
    stylistic connection to Kerouac,
        134
    as Surrealist, xii, 9, 12, 15, 63, 85
    and Thomas, 63, 79, 80–81, 140,
        253n47

and Duncan, 98, 129, 130,
    252n47
and personal emphasis of
    writing, 252n43
published in California, 129, 135
published in journals, 69, 75, 85,
    250n32
and Rank, 194
and war departure, 71
and Winter of Artifice, 9
Norman, Mrs., 128
NOW (magazine), 74, 89–91, 92, 139

Oasis (journal), 89
Obelisk Press, 9, 61, 75, 243n10
O'Connor, Phillip, 211, 256n2, 256n3
Orend, Karl, 91
Orientations (journal), 99
Orwell, George
    and Down and Out in Paris and London,
        33–34
    and Durrell, 33, 68–69
    and Inside the Whale, 26–27, 30–31,
        34, 35–36, 41, 58
    in Late Modernism, 41–42
    review of The Booster, 67–68
    view of Miller's politics, 31–36,
        68, 141
Oxford Poetry (journal), 72

pacifism, 74–75, 90, 111, 207–10
Papadimitriou, Elie, 117
Patchen, Kenneth, 89, 128, 129, 131
Patmore, Derek, 250n29
Peake, Mervyn, 94, 162
Perlès, Alfred, 67, 69, 71, 75, 246n8
Personalism
    anarchism of, xii–xv, xvii, 132–33,
        170–79
    attached to "quietist" label, 32

core tenets of, 132–33, 163–70
Durrell's ideas on, 165
excluded from Late Modernism, 41,
    42
identifies as post-Surrealist, xii,
    xv–xvi
ignored by literary critics, ix–x,
    xvi–xvii, 38, 43, 52
members of, xi
and Miller, 35, 76
and open form/incoherence,
    202–04
as part of Personal Landscape vision,
    116, 117–18
published in Transformation, 78
Rexroth's view of, 142–43
role of embodiment in, 189–201
and self-realization, 48–50
and social realism, 47
and syntax problem, 108
viewed without political social
    context, 39–40
view of death in, 195–98
view of selfhood, 180–89
and womb analogy, 198–201
See also Egyptian anarcho-
    Surrealists; English post-
    Surrealists in Egypt; New
    Apocalypse movement;
    San Francisco Renaissance;
    Shanghai-based individualists;
    Villa Seurat
Personal Landscape (journal), 74, 103–04,
    105, 116–18, 137, 239n3, 251n41
The Phoenix (journal), 35, 69, 73, 90,
    127
Pierre, D.B.C., 213
Poems of this War by Younger Poets, 75
poetry, autochthonous, 132
Poetry Folios (journal), 89, 131, 135

Other Titles from The University of Alberta Press

Landscapes of War and Memory
The Two World Wars in Canadian Literature and the Arts,
1977–2007
SHERRILL GRACE
600 pages | 30 B&W photographs, notes, bibliography, index
978–1–77212–000–4 | $49.95 (T) paper
War & Cultural Memory/Literature, Visual Arts & Film

From the Elephant's Back
Collected Essays & Travel Writings
LAWRENCE DURRELL
Edited and with an Introduction by JAMES GIFFORD
PETER BALDWIN, Foreword
300 pages | Preface, notes, bibliography, index
978–1–77212–051–6 | $39.95 (T) paper
978–1–77212–059–2 | $31.99 (T) EPUB
978–1–77212–060–8 | $31.99 (T) Amazon Kindle
978–1–77212–061–5 | $31.99 (T) PDF
Literary Essays/Cultural Studies/Travel Writing

"Collecting Stamps Would Have Been More Fun"
Canadian Publishing and the Correspondence of Sinclair Ross,
1933–1986
JORDAN STOUCK & DAVID STOUCK, Editors
344 pages | B&W photographs, appendix, biographical
chronology, index
978–0–88864–521–0 | $34.95 (T) paper
978–0–88864–755–9 | $27.99 (T) PDF
Letters/Canadian Literature